# BLUEGRASS WINNERS

## A COOKBOOK.

*The Garden Club of Lexington, Inc.*
*Lexington, Kentucky*

Member of The Garden Club of America

Copies of
# Bluegrass Winners
may be obtained from:
The Garden Club of Lexington, Inc.
P.O. Box 22091
Lexington, Kentucky 40522

COPYRIGHT © 1985
THE GARDEN CLUB OF LEXINGTON, INC.
LEXINGTON, KENTUCKY

Fourth Printing, June 1988
Library of Congress Catalog Card Number: 85-60214
ISBN 0-9614442-0-7

Design: Cindy Baker, Art Dept., Inc.
Farm Descriptions: Ed Bowen, The Blood-Horse

PRINTED IN U.S.A.
S.C. TOOF & COMPANY
MEMPHIS, TENNESSEE

# INTRODUCTION

Horse farm photographs and recipes might seem an incongruous combination, but not in a cookbook published in Lexington, Kentucky, the heart of the Bluegrass.

There is an intimate relationship between horse farms and entertainment that has made the hospitality of central Kentucky famous throughout the world. Meals and parties are apt to be times when horsemen strike deals, trade information, or syndicate stallions. In the fraternity of horsemen, conversation is never lacking because of the common and all-consuming interest of its members.

Each farm has its own style of entertaining whether a quiet dinner or an eagerly awaited event such as a Derby breakfast or sales extravaganza.

One of the early horsemen and purveyors of hospitality in Lexington was Henry Clay, the Great Compromiser and Sage of the West. At his home, Ashland, he entertained the foremost statesmen of his time. The house stood on some 600 acres of land where Henry Clay raised fine Thoroughbred horses, including three Kentucky Derby winners: Day Star in 1878, Riley in 1890, and Alan-a-Dale in 1902; as well as Survivor, the first winner of the Preakness Stakes. Many champions today trace their bloodlines back to his stock. On the last page of the 1899 sale catalogue of brood mares at Ashland Stud Farm is the following quotation: "To show well, to brag little, to crow gently if in luck; and to pay up, own up, and shut up when beaten are the virtues of a sporting man."

L'Enfant, the landscape engineer who designed Washington, D.C., planned the landscaping at Ashland. It was said that he used every tree and bush indigenous to Kentucky in his scheme. These beautiful old trees surround the 90' x 180' formal Ashland Garden maintained by the Garden Club of Lexington.

When the expenses of the garden outstripped the resources of the Garden Club, its members appealed to the horse farms who generously contributed to the publication of this book. The proceeds from its sale will be used for the maintenance of Ashland Garden and other beautification projects in the Bluegrass area.

The recipes have been collected from the farms, from friends, and from local caterers.

Here are the best—Bluegrass Winners all!

# TABLE OF CONTENTS

# HORSE FARMS

# HORSE FARMS

# HORSE FARMS
# OF THE
# BLUEGRASS

# ASHLAND GARDEN

## A PARTY IN THE GARDEN

*Pecan-Cheese Wafers*
*Fresh Shrimp Dip with Crackers*
*Raw Vegetables with Spinach Dip Beau Monde*
*Watercress Sandwiches*
*Sliced Chicken Sandwiches*
*Chicken Liver and Mushroom Pâté with Melba Toast*

In its glory days, Ashland was the home of the distinguished Kentucky statesman Henry Clay. There he entertained the great of his day among them Martin Van Buren, the Marquis de LaFayette, Daniel Webster, and Abraham Lincoln; and there he bred and raised Thoroughbred horses on some 600 acres of land.

Since 1948 the Italianate villa house and approximately 20 acres of land have been maintained by the Henry Clay Memorial Foundation and have been open to the public.

The garden at Ashland dates from 1950, when The Garden Club of Lexington was asked by the Foundation to undertake its creation. The Club chose Henry Fletcher Kenney of Cincinnati to draw up a ten-year plan for the garden and for planting the estate. Work was begun in 1951, with large sections of the parterre garden completed in each of the next few years. A dipping pool and birdbath, as well as benches and a 100-year-old bronze figure of a child by Raingo were added later.

The garden is maintained by the members of The Garden Club of Lexington who not only did most of the work in executing the original plan, but still meet each Wednesday of the growing season and continue their labor to preserve the beauty of the garden.

11

## POOL PARTY

*Fresh Tomatoes with Shakertown Chicken Salad*
*Pimiento Cheese Finger Sandwiches*
*Deviled Eggs*
*Potato Chips*
*Pecan Balls with Butterscotch or Grand Chocolate Sauce*

The heart of Airdrie Farm includes nearly 700 acres of land which were part of a 5,000-acre Land Grant acquired by Robert Alexander in 1791. Alexander purchased the land from Hugh Mercer and named the farm "Woodburn," a name still used by Alexander descendants today. Under Robert Alexander's son, R. A. Alexander, the farm became the forerunner for most modern Thoroughbred breeding operations: with an emphasis on breeding horses for the market rather than retaining them exclusively for private use.

Airdrie House was built in 1904 by Mr. and Mrs. William E. Simms and was named for the Alexanders' ancestral home in Scotland. The present owners are Mr. and Mrs. Brereton C. Jones; Mrs. Jones being the sixth generation descending from the Alexanders to live on this land.

Mr. Jones is a major commercial breeder and stallion syndicator and has added more than 2,000 acres to the original Airdrie Farm.

Mrs. Jones is restoring the gardens of the residence which were designed by Jens Jensen of Denmark in 1916.

## LUNCHEON BRIDGE

*Layered Chicken and Cranberry Salad*
*Marinated Green Beans with Herbed French Dressing*
*Cheese Soufflé Sandwiches*
*Lemon Angel Pie*

The land known as Almahurst Farm was settled in 1778 by James Knight. The land remained in the Knight family for four generations—181 years.

Henry Knight, the fourth generation, became one of the nation's leading horsemen and bred champion Standardbreds and Thoroughbreds. The Knight family bred the Kentucky Derby winner, Exterminator, and the great Hambletonian winner, Greyhound. It was Henry Knight who gave the farm the name "Almahurst" after his wife, Alma Horine. Mr. Knight was an entrepreneur as well as a horseman, and his night at the annual Saratoga Thoroughbred yearling sales became an annual highlight of the August season there.

In 1963, P. J. Baugh purchased the farm. His respect for its history has been responsible for much of the restoration at Almahurst. Mr. Baugh has produced many world champions, among them the successful sire, Falcon Almahurst, and the World Champion pacing filly, Sherry Almahurst, as well as the winner of the Kentucky Futurity, Arnie Almahurst.

The stallion barn houses such great stallions as Ralph Hanover, winner of the Triple Crown of Pacing and $1,711,000 in a single season as a three-year-old, and the World Champion, Trim The Tree. These stallions, along with the exquisite broodmare band, continue to place Almahurst Farm among great breeding farms of the world.

## INFORMAL DINNER

*Shrimp Stew over Rice*
*Mixed Green Salad*
*French Bread*
*Champagne Sherbet on Pound Cake with Whipped Cream*

E. V. Benjamin, master of Big Sink Farm, is a native of New Orleans and Pass Christian, Mississippi, where he and his forebears have been prominent residents for generations.

During a visit to Central Kentucky in 1958, Mr. Benjamin became enthralled with the Bluegrass area and decided to make it his home. Within a two-year period he bought a house and ninety-two acres of land on the Big Sink Pike near Versailles, Kentucky, settled his affairs in Louisiana, and brought his wife, son, and daughter-in-law to Kentucky. Although Mr. Benjamin was familiar with horses, such a move was unprecedented.

His first horse was an old mare named Stare which had been left on the farm by her former owner. She produced a filly, Loving Eyes, which became a champion in Puerto Rico.

Mr. Benjamin bought several mares from his friend, Bull Hancock of Claiborne Farm, and increased his land holdings to 325 acres. He has become a prominent commercial breeder and has raised many good stakes winners.

## COUNTRY SUPPER

*Southern Fried Chicken    Country Ham*
*Fresh Black-eyed Peas*
*Green Beans with Toasted Sesame Seeds*
*Sliced Fresh Tomatoes with Sliced Red and White Onions*
*Jalepeño Corn Bread*
*Peach Cobbler with Whipped Cream*
*Lemonade Mint Tea*
*Coffee*
*Tattinger Champagne*

Nelson Bunker Hunt's well-known interests in petroleum, mining, and agricultural enterprises are worldwide; but his favorite pursuit of breeding and racing Thoroughbred horses led to the development of Bluegrass Farm, encompassing 5,000 acres of Kentucky land. This land, in several Kentucky counties, houses more than 300 mares and their offspring.

Horses bred and raced by Mr. Hunt have won major races in Europe and Canada, as well as the United States. The great mare Dahlia won two runnings of the King George VI and Queen Elizabeth Stakes at Ascot, for which Her Majesty Queen Elizabeth II personally presented trophies. Other races won by Hunt horses include the English Derby, French Derby, Canadian International, and the Washington, D. C., International.

The house on the main division of Bluegrass Farm on the Versailles Road was built in 1857 by William Jones for his mother-in-law, Mrs. Mary Cloud. The house features articulated chimney stacks and projecting bay windows and thus is described as of romantic style rather than Greek Revival. Owners of years past have variously named the house Cloud House, Clover Land, and Trevilla.

# BROWNWOOD FARM

## COOKOUT

*Mexican Fiesta Dip*
*Shish Kabob*
*Herb Rice*
*Spinach Salad*
*French Bread Parmesan*
*Rich Fresh Peach Ice Cream*
*Frosted Brownies*

Prior to 1957 Barbara Hunter and her mother lived on a southern Georgia plantation which was adjacent to the Headley Thoroughbred training track.

After two Hunter-owned fillies went on to become stakes winners, the ladies came to Central Kentucky, the center of the horse world, to set up a breeding and racing operation. They began purchasing parcels of land which would comprise the more than 500 acres of Brownwood Farm. Miss Hunter, having just graduated from the University of Maryland, became farm manager.

Under her management Brownwood Farm has developed into a modern breeding operation. Now there are more than 100 horses on the farm which produces more than its fair share of stakes winners. Two-thirds of the horses are Thoroughbreds; the other one-third being Quarter horses which Miss Hunter trains and shows.

The land of Brownwood Farm still yields arrowheads and stone axes dating to early Indian tribes, and the old sugar maples bear the scars of long-ago tappings.

An eighteenth century log cabin serves as the front hall of the main residence.

# BUCKRAM OAK FARM

## LUNCHEON

*Shakertown Tomato-Celery Soup*
*Cheese Soufflé*
*Asparagus Vinaigrette*
*Bran Rolls*
*Very Lemony Meringue Pie*

In the late autumn of 1978, Mahmoud Fustok acquired Buckram Oak Farm, 400 acres strategically located in the heart of the Bluegrass. Work was immediately begun, transforming the former cattle farm into a spectacular and efficient brood mare operation. The farm is the current home of approximately fifty brood mares and their offspring. It is also the American base for Mr. Fustok's international Thoroughbred activities which include racing and breeding operations in the United States, France and England.

The central focus of the farm are the five spacious twenty-stall barns. The interiors feature red oak stalls with polished stainless steel hardware, while the exteriors include slate roofs with traditional steepled cupolas and side dormers. The farm's other distinctive features include two 130-foot bridges faced with Kentucky River marble, spanning a five-acre lake, surrounded by grounds meticulously landscaped with over 5,000 trees, shrubs and foundation plantings. Thousands of narcissus have been planted around the lake and on the one-acre island within.

The farm appears to be an achievement of Mr. Fustok's goal to provide nice surroundings for his horses while retaining the character of the Bluegrass area.

# CALUMET FARM

## COCKTAILS AFTER THE RACES

*Fresh Fruits and Assorted Cheeses*
*Artichoke Dip*
*Crispy Cheese Wafers*
*Country Ham and Biscuits*
*Marinated Shrimp*
*Olive-filled Cheese Balls*
*Miniature Quiche Lorraine*
*Guacamole*

Calumet Farm is the undisputed jewel of the Bluegrass. In the 1940's and 1950's its racing stable dominated the American turf. After a decline of several decades, the runners in the devil's red and blue silks have returned the name of Calumet to the winners' rolls of some of America's great stakes races.

The handsome white barns with their gray slate roofs, red trim, and stately cupolas again are producing race horses in the tradition of some 150 stakes winners bred by Calumet. Eight winners of the Kentucky Derby were bred at the farm, a record unmatched by any other breeder, and all eight won the Run for the Roses in the farm's silks. Citation and Whirlaway, perhaps the most famous of Calumet horses, also won the Preakness and Belmont to complete the Triple Crown. They are honored in the handsome farm cemetery and in the extraordinary Calumet trophy collection now housed in the Kentucky Horse Park.

The Calumet Thoroughbred breeding operation was begun by Warren Wright, Sr., whose father raised Standardbreds there before him. Mrs. Wright continued the farm after Mr. Wright's death. She later married Admiral Gene Markey, novelist and film producer. Upon her death, J. T. Lundy became president of the farm.

The resurgence of Calumet was led by Alydar, which won the Bluegrass Stakes and has become one of America's top stallions.

# CASTLETON FARM

## BLACK TIE DINNER

*Hot Cheese Puffs*
*Egg and Caviar on Toast Rounds*
*Shrimp Cocktail*
*Rack of Lamb Rosemary*
*Noisette Potatoes*
*Kentucky Lemon Asparagus*
*Belgian Endive with Creamy Dressing*
*Hot Rolls*
*Lemon Mousse with Fresh Raspberry Sauce*

Castleton Farm's immaculate stone fences and well-clipped paddocks siding the Iron Works Pike offer one of the loveliest scenes in the Bluegrass. The farm was purchased in 1945 and is currently owned by Mr. and Mrs. Frederick L. Van Lennep.

Since 1812 when Castleton Farm was established by David Castleman and his bride, Mary Breckinridge, Castleton has been home to three breeds of horses.

Thoroughbreds roamed the fields at the turn of the century when the farm was owned by James R. Keene, the Silver Fox of Wall Street. Saddlebreds appeared in the late 19th century and again from 1945—1970 when the Dodge Stables produced such champions as the five-gaited Wing Commander.

Today Castleton Farm is one of the most prominent Standardbred farms in the world, and its 2,000 acres are home to some 800 horses. Speedy Scot, Yankee Lass, and Race Time are among the distinguished competitors raised there.

The house was built in the 1840's in the Greek Revival style. Various Indian burial mounds have been discovered on the farm which also boasts "Breckinridge Spring", which has never run dry.

# CLAIBORNE FARM

## BRUNCH

*Hominy Ring with Turkey Hash*
*Smoked Sausage*
*Broiled Tomatoes*
*Apple Fritters*
*Hot Biscuits and Preserves*
*Coffee*

Claiborne Farm was founded in 1910 by Arthur B. Hancock upon land inherited by his wife, the former Nancy Clay. In 1915, he established a branch of his Virginia Ellerslie Farm at Claiborne, moving most of the operation to Kentucky. Since that time, Claiborne has been a leader in the world's blood-stock industry.

Hancock was succeeded by his son, A. B. (Bull) Hancock, Jr., who built upon the founder's reputation for acquiring outstanding stallions. Blenheim II, Sir Gallahad III, Princequillo, Nasrullah, Bold Ruler and Round Table were among the international stallions which stood at Claiborne.

Bull Hancock died in 1972, and his son, Seth, took over the management of Claiborne on behalf of the family. Under his guidance, the tradition of breeding champions and standing great stallions has continued. Currently at stud at Claiborne are Secretariat, Triple Crown winner of 1973; Nijinsky II; Spectacular Bid; Sir Ivor; Mr. Prospector; Cox's Ridge; Conquistador Cielo; Danzig; and Damascus.

## KENTUCKY CATFISH DINNER

*Beer Cheese with Celery*
*Fried Banana Peppers*
*Fresh Kentucky Catfish*
*Fried Onion Rings*
*Shakertown Coleslaw*
*Hushpuppies*
*Coconut Cream Pie*

This 1200 acres on the Bryan Station Road in Lexington has the "new look" for horse farms. Under development since 1976, the buildings are of modern construction and are uniquely designed to insure maximum lighting and ventilation, thus insuring the safety, comfort and good health of the horses. The recently completed training facilities at Crescent are among the finest in the United States and the first to employ the European style grass gallops.

The brood mare band at Crescent includes the dams of five Champions and the dams of three equine "Millionaires". In 1983 a yearling colt bred by Crescent topped the Keeneland summer Sale for a world record $10.2 million.

In addition to the Thoroughbred operation, Donald and Linda Johnson breed and show champion Saddlebred horses, proving that a love of horses encompasses all breeds.

## DERBY PICNIC IN THE PARK

*Individual Baskets filled with Fried Chicken*
*Country Ham and Beaten Biscuits*
*Watercress Sandwiches     Cucumber Sandwiches*
*Cream Cheese and Olive-Nut Sandwiches*
*Fresh Green Pea Salad*
*Fresh Whole Strawberries with Powdered Sugar*
*Splits of Champagne*
*Almond Macaroons*

Crestview Farm, near Keeneland Racetrack, was purchased in 1977 by Mr. and Mrs. Richard Broadbent. The 42 acres of land is used as a nursery for Thoroughbred barren and maiden mares.

Due to the increase in the horse population in central Kentucky and the complexities caused by this fast moving industry, the tedia of obtaining race results and pedigree information has increased significantly. Accordingly, in 1961 Mr. and Mrs. Broadbent began to collect the data on Thoroughbreds that evolved into the Bloodstock Research and Statistical Bureau. They started with one comptroller and, moonlighting on a friend's computer, created a memory bank. With this racing information they produced records and expectancy data on more than a million Thoroughbred race horses from 1880 until today. The company now occupies one floor of an office building and has 46 employees.

Mr. Broadbent consults with a number of clients on matings and purchases of yearlings, brood mares and stallion shares. In addition, subscribers may tap into his computer by phone from any place in the world to obtain a variety of data.

# DOMINO STUD

## THANKSGIVING DINNER

*Pecan-Cheese Wafers     Pineapple Fritters*
*Roast Turkey with Stuffing*
*Giblet Gravy*
*Kentucky Country Ham     Scalloped Oysters*
*Creamed Potatoes*
*Broccoli Ring filled with Sautéed Mushrooms*
*Avocado and Grapefruit on Bibb Lettuce with Dressing*
*Rolls     Relish Tray     Cranberry Sauce*
*Pumpkin Pie     Mincemeat Pie*

Now owned by Lexington entrepreneur, W. B. Terry, Domino Stud lies on land that was once part of the historic Dixiana Farm developed by the late Charles T. Fisher. (Mr. Fisher's daughter, Miss Mary Fisher, still operates the remainder of Dixiana Farm as a thriving breeding farm.) Mr. Terry's son, Timothy E. N. Terry, is President of Domino Stud.

Domino Stud occupies some 380 acres of land and is a growing force in the stallion business. Sires at Domino Stud include Grey Dawn, a former French champion, which is one of the major stallions in the United States. Recent additions to the stallion roster include Sunny's Halo, a Canadian-bred, which won the Kentucky Derby in 1983 and stood his first year at stud in 1984.

Mr. Terry's son, Patrick Terry, is the president and owner of THE THOROUGHBRED RECORD, one of the prominent trade publications serving racing.

The house at Domino Stud is a modified Greek revival structure which has been remodeled several times since it was built in 1830. The bricks were made from the clay of the farm; and the ash floors, from planks taken from home-grown trees. Originally a small four-room house with a lean-to kitchen, the house now comprises 23,000 square feet with the additions Mr. Terry added in conformity with the era in which it was built.

35

# ELMENDORF FARM

## COCKTAILS

*Thin-sliced Beef Tenderloin on Miniature Onion Buns*
*Henry Bain Sauce        Mustard Sauce*
*Chicken Salad Piled High on Silver Platter*
*Surrounded with Fresh Fruits and Crackers*
*Kentucky Country Ham on Tiny Biscuits*
*Bluegrass Creamed Oysters in Toast Cups*
*Fresh Vegetable Platter with Dip*
*Bacon-wrapped Crackers*
*Assorted Cheeses*
*Lemon Bars        Chocolate Mint Squares*

Few structures so typify the aura of the Bluegrass as do the elegant columns of Elmendorf Farm. The columns and lion sculptures beside them are lingering reminders of the mansion, Green Hills, the home of James Ben Ali Haggin, who purchased Elmendorf Farm in 1897. The farm was increased to some 10,000 acres by the copper baron and for a time embraced the land now occupied by many well-known Thoroughbred operations such as Spendthrift Farm, Greentree Stud, and Gainesway Farm. In a sense Elmendorf was the heart of the Bluegrass.

Although the farm now occupies only some 550 acres, the land and the name continue to be synonymous with quality horses. In the 1950's Elmendorf was purchased by Maxwell Gluck, a former Ambassador to Ceylon. Mr. Gluck has bred and raced more than 100 stakes winners in the intervening years including a leading brood mare sire, Prince John; champion filly Talking Pictures; Millionaire Super Moment; and classic winner Big Spruce. Mr. Gluck three times has been America's leading breeder and twice leading owner in earnings won.

Mr. Gluck's contributions to the sport include a $3-million challenge grant to fund the Maxwell Gluck Equine Research Center, a project begun at the University of Kentucky in 1983.

# FOREST RETREAT FARM

## POST DERBY LUNCH

*Assorted Cheeses*
*Beef Stick with Mustard Sauce*
*Assorted Crackers and Breads*
*Kentucky Cured Country Ham*
*Turkey and Dressing*
*Green Beans*
*Corn Pudding*
*Biscuits*
*Cranberry Sauce      Relish Tray*
*Assorted Pastries*

Dr. Eslie Asbury's and his family's Forest Retreat Farm was owned years ago by Kentucky's tenth governor, Thomas Metcalf. Governor Metcalf named the 1,200-acre farm "Forest Retreat" after it had been so described by his friend, Henry Clay.

In addition to having maintained a successful Thoroughbred operation which has produced winners of the Kentucky Derby and Kentucky Oaks, Dr. Asbury has been dedicated to preserving the natural history of the farm. He has maintained a policy of ensuring that at least one example of every tree species native to Kentucky is maintained thereon. Forest Retreat's many trees and living fences provide windbreaks and constitute a shelter for wildlife.

While conservation is of paramount importance, preservation is not forgotten at Forest Retreat. A cabin believed to have been the only dwelling built in the state by Daniel Boone is one of five sites on the farm listed on the National Register of Historic Places. The others include the Federal-style house built by Governor Metcalf in 1814; the pre-Civil War Forest Retreat Tavern, now used as the farm office; a stone barn built without mortar; and the family graveyard wherein are buried family members, slaves, and the farm's two foundation mares.

## CHRISTMAS EVE

*Peanut Bars*
*Raw Vegetables with Chutney Dip*
*Mushroom Bisque in Mugs*
*Chicken Breasts with Grapes on Country Ham Slices*
*Risotto*
*Spinach Ring filled with Buttered Baby Beets*
*Bibb Lettuce with Mustard Sauce*
*Herb Butter      French Bread*
*Chocolate Torte*
*Demi-tasse*
*After Dinner Mints*

In the tradition of such famous Kentucky breeders of John E. Madden and Henry H. Knight, John R. Gaines, a third-generation horseman, is a breeder of both champion trotters and champion runners at Gainesway Farm.

The original Gainesway was established by Thomas P. Gaines in Chenango County, New York, in 1891, as a Standardbred nursery and Grand Circuit racing stable. His son, Clarence F. Gaines, expanded the operation to Fayette County, Kentucky, in 1944.

Gainesway trotters have won every major stakes race in America including the Hambletonian and the Kentucky Futurity. Classical Way, the world's fastest trotting mare, was bred and raced by Gainesway Farm.

John Gaines created Gainesway's Thoroughbred division in 1964 with the acquisition of three horses: champion Bold Bidder; champion Oil Royalty; and Brood Mare of the Year Cosmah, the granddam of Kentucky Derby winner Cannonade. From this foundation Gainesway is today one of the premier breeding farms of the world, standing 40 stallions including Vaguely Noble, Lyphard, and Blushing Groom.

In 1984 the Stallion Complex at Gainesway received an Honor Award from the American Institute of Architects for design excellence.

## SUMMER SALES PARTY FOR 1500

*Country Ham and Biscuits     Smoked Turkey*
*Cold Rice Salad*
*Broccoli Salad Vinaigrette*
*Scalloped Pineapple*
*Assorted Breads*
*Ice Cream*
*Chocolate Kahlua Cake*

Tom Gentry was born and reared in the horse business. His father, Olin Gentry, managed one of the major farms in the Bluegrass for over sixty years where he raised five Kentucky Derby winners: Bubbling Over, Burgoo King, Brokers Tip, Chateaugay, and Proud Clarion.

Tom Gentry's white-fenced farm occupies 550 acres of land on the Harp Innis Pike. The residence is a renovated farmhouse containing beams from the oldest Catholic Church in Kentucky and is furnished with Kentucky antiques.

Mr. Gentry is a flamboyant promoter and salesman. A Gentry yearling held the world auction record of $1.6 million for a time. His sales consignment has included the brilliant filly Terlingua and the major winner Marfa. The 1966 Kentucky Derby winner, Kauai King, was purchased by Michael Ford on Gentry's advice.

Tom and Kathy Gentry's pre-Keeneland-sales party has become a social highlight of the year, involving elephant rides, helicopter rides, and surprise guest entertainers such as Bob Hope and Burt Bachrach.

## AFTER THE RACES

*Chicken Tetrazzini Glencrest*
*Layered Vegetable Salad*
*Buttered Beaten Biscuits with Sliced Ham*
*Chess Tarts*
*Hummers*

Two of Kentucky's famed products, horses and bourbon, combine in the history of Glencrest Farm, which is owned by John W. Greathouse and his sons. In 1854 Captain James Stone built a distillery on the banks of the Elkhorn Creek on property which is now part of the 1,300-acre Glencrest Farm. By 1869 he was the most prominent distiller in Scott County. Along with the distillery he constructed a large brick storage house. Today the warehouse is still utilized but in a different fashion. Stalls were built on the lower level for horses, while the upper levels are used for straw and hay storage.

The Greek Revival house on Glencrest Farm was built in the 1830's by Merritt Williams. It is a fine rendition of the Greek Temple style of Greek Revival architecture.

Mr. Greathouse, a past president of the Kentucky Thoroughbred Breeders' Association, is a prominent central Kentucky horseman. Among the champions bred and raised at Glencrest Farm are: the 1960 Kentucky Derby winner Venetian Way; the champion filly Lady Pitt; and important stakes winner Wavering Monarch. As one generation succeeds another the proud tradition of land and horses is cherished and maintained.

## BLUE BLAST BUFFET

*Chicken Kiev*
*Fresh Kentucky Asparagus Hollandaise*
*Daly Dozen Tomatoes*
*Spinach Salad*
*Cheese Bread*
*Chocolate Eclairs*

Hamburg Place is a link to the charm of the past, but it bespeaks none of the sadness of magic lost which such a place sometimes engenders. It is a place of memories, of grand times, but the success and grandness continue.

The farm was developed by the late John E. Madden, who named the farm for Hamburg, one of the best horses he raced. Five Kentucky Derby winners were bred there.

In the early part of the century, Hamburg Place was a benign fiefdom with Madden providing living quarters, a school house, and other necessities for families of employees. There are still grooms today employed at farms and tracks who remember growing up at Hamburg Place.

Preston and Anita Madden, the present owners, are well known socially, and in many minds epitomize the glamor of the Sport of Kings. Nevertheless, they are also professional in their approach to breeding, selling, and racing. As a young man, Mr. Madden purchased T. V. Lark who defeated Kelso in the Laurel International and who went on to top the stallion rankings.

Hamburg Place now encompasses 2,000 acres of land and is home to 100 horses. The proud tradition continues.

## AFTER TENNIS

*Gazpacho*
*Shrimp and Cheddar Pie*
*Strawberries White House*
*Iced Tea*

Before the purchase of Hardboot Farm in 1968, the land was an unimproved cattle and tobacco farm in northern Fayette County. Now it is a small family-operated Thoroughbred farm on 102 acres with approximately 35 horses. Generally the colts are sold as yearlings at the Keeneland Sales and the fillies retained for racing and later brought back to the brood mare band.

Mrs. Patricia Headley Green, the farm's owner, is a daughter of the late Hal Price Headley, master horseman, founder of Keeneland Race Track and Sales, and one of the original "hardboots" (hence the farm's name). Mr. Headley is represented by sixteen children and grandchildren in the Thoroughbred business in central Kentucky. Seven own farms, five manage farms for others, and one is a trainer.

Three mares owned by Mrs. Green are direct descendants of a mare given her by her father in the early fifties.

The recently built main residence was constructed with stone, walnut and poplar paneling, and ash flooring salvaged from "Beaumont" where Mrs. Green was born and "Old Sunnyside," her father's birthplace.

## AROUND THE KITCHEN TABLE
## SUMMER SALE:

*Crudités with Dill Dip*
*Pimiento Cheese and Assorted Crackers*
*Banana-Nut Bread*
*Fresh Fruit in Season*

## AND LATER:
*Smoked Turkey on Whole Wheat*
*Pepper Jelly on Cream Cheese with Rye Crackers*
*Cooked Vegetables in Celery Seed Marinade*
*Toasted Dill Bread*

Hedgewood Farm has been owned and operated by Asbury father-son partnerships for four generations. Begun with five brood mares and 100 acres of land, the farm now has 450 acres of land and cares for 110 Thoroughbreds during the peak of the breeding season.

Charles Asbury, the first to own Thoroughbreds, was one of the founding members of the Breeders' Sales Company which initiated what are now known as the Keeneland Sales.

His son, Thomas Asbury, was brought into the business in 1942 when at 15 years of age he received a Thoroughbred mare through a 4-H project sponsored by Greentree Farm manager, Major Louis A. Beard. He bred her to Bull Lea, standing that year for a stud fee of $250.

Carson Asbury, now in partnership with his father, continues their tradition as market breeders with a fine eye for conformation. In all, Hedgewood Farm has bred 22 stakes winners. Stone Manor heads the list, winning the Ohio Derby (Gr. II), and the Sheridan Stakes (Gr. II) for a total of $246,000 in 1980.

# HURRICANE HALL STUD

## CHRISTMAS NIGHT

*Hot Tomato Bouillon*
*Pâté      Cheese Mold*
*Cold Filet of Beef      Cold Sliced Turkey*
*Homemade Mayonnaise*
*Thin Sliced Bread for Sandwiches*
*Fresh Vegetable Tray with Dill Dip*
*Peanut Butter and Jelly Sandwiches and Popcorn for the Children*
*Egg Nog      White Wine      Champagne*
*Brownies      White Chocolate Cake      Coconut Cake*

Hurricane Hall, described by architectural historian Clay Lancaster in his **Antebellum Houses of the Bluegrass** as "The most engaging residence in Fayette county of which a part predates 1800," was begun in 1794 by Samuel Loughead. In 1801 his Virginia-like Federal brick structure (now the central block) was bought by Roger Quarles, who in 1806 added a typically Kentucky Federal wing. In 1840 a Greek Revival wing was added by his grandson.

In 1962 Hurricane Hall was bought by Mr. and Mrs. Stanley D. Petter, Jr., who have carefully restored the old house, paying great attention to authenticity. The scenic wallpaper in the parlor, hand blocked in the 1770's, was hung in 1817 and remains there today. A fine complement of original outbuildings still stands, including a stone spring house, a stone and brick smokehouse "large enough to hang 100 hogs," and a brick schoolhouse, now adapted for use as a guest house.

As Mr. Petter is active in the commercial breeding and sale of bloodstock, both for himself and as agent, Hurricane Hall Stud houses about 60 Thoroughbreds at all times. The Petter family's sporting interests are also reflected in the hunters, Hackney horses, greyhounds, and foxhounds, which are in evidence.

# HURSTLAND FARM

## SUNDAY LUNCH

*Crème de Volaille*
*Fresh Buttered Asparagus*
*Parsleyed New Potatoes*
*Bibb Lettuce and Grapefruit Salad with French Dressing*
*Hot Rolls*
*Schaum Torte*

Hurstland Farm's yearling barn occupies a site historic in American racing and breeding annals. Two great champions of the last century, American Eclipse and Boston, stood at stud there for Col. E. M. Blackburn. These horses represented an era long forgotten in Thoroughbred racing when the sport was conducted in heats. A contest might consist of four-mile heats, and the winner of two out of three heats in a day was the winner of the overall contest.

Hurstland today is owned by brothers, Charles and Alfred Nuckols, who with various members of their families operate a successful commercial breeding operation. Hurstland's name has been prominent among consignors at the Keeneland sales for many years; and horses the brothers have raised range from the sprint champions Decathlon and White Skies, to European champions Habitat and Broadway Dancer, to the rugged champion mare, Typecast, which for a time held the record ($725,000) for a horse in training sold at auction.

Four generations of the Nuckols family have operated the farm. Dr. Alfred Hurst traded an original land grant in Versailles, Kentucky, for the present farm in Midway so he could commute from his teaching position at the medical college in Cincinnati. One of the three eighteenth-century houses on the farm was the childhood home of Luke Pryor Blackburn, a governor of Kentucky.

# JONABELL FARM

## LUNCH BEFORE THE BLUEGRASS STAKES

*Corn Fritters*
*Egg and Mushroom Casserole*
*Sausage on Biscuits*
*Fresh Asparagus Hollandaise*
*Watermelon Basket filled with Fresh Fruits*
*Honey Fruit Salad Dressing*
*Orange Rolls*
*Mazarene Tarts*
*Tiny Lemon and Pecan Tarts*

Exemplifying the combination of Thoroughbred business-man and sportsman is John A. Bell III, who with his family operates Jonabell Farm and the Cromwell Bloodstock Agency. Mr. Bell has always given generously of his time on behalf of the sport of Thoroughbred racing. He has testified in Congress on behalf of racing, has chaired and served on countless committees seeking redress or improvement for racing's problems, and was a member of the Kentucky State Racing Commission. He has long been an officer of the Thoroughbred Owners and Breeders Association and is a member of The Jockey Club.

The present Jonabell Farm was purchased in 1954. It includes some 750 acres of land and is home to more than 200 horses. Fitting nicely with the modern stallion complex is a National Trust House built by Andrew Bowman in 1820, and a hand-chipped stone water tower built by the flamboyant Ed Corrigan, the railroad magnate who once owned Hawthorne Race Track in Chicago as well as several tracks in California.

Robert Sterling Clark's Never Say Die, which won England's historic Derby in 1954, was raised at Jonabell Farm. To date the farm has bred or raised 6 champions among its 51 stakes winners.

Closing the old Kentucky Association track in Lexington after more than a century of operation placed the sport of Thoroughbred racing in Lexington at a crossroads. The year was 1933—a time when America's fortunes were wavering and its sporting traditions were on shaky footing.

To the rescue came a band of Bluegrass horsemen, holdovers in many ways from an era when being a farmer often meant knowledge of land, of business, of blooded horses, and of tobacco—all under one hat brim.

Hal Price Headley was just such a package-in-one: a breeder, buyer, and seller of race horses; lord of the manor; and shrewd businessman. Under Headley's direction, a prospectus was circulated urging the formation of a new track, one which proposed "the shadow of a dream in that it envisions a creation the like of which has not been seen in America…In order to accomplish these ends, we shall first ask the aid of sportsmen in building the track. Later, we shall ask them to race their horses and to lend their own presence at the meetings…"

In short, what Headley and his peers were developing was the foundation which would become Keeneland—that half-century of tradition which Kentuckians today view with pride as a combination of beauty, sport, tradition, and world-class auctions.

The group purchased a portion of the James R. Keene farm on which was situated a training track and stone stable with a club room above. This building is the nucleus of the present Keeneland Club House.

Keeneland was opened in 1936, a country track foliated in the spring with fresh greenery among dogwood blossoms and luminated in the fall by native hues. The whole is exemplified by staunch stone construction. If it were idealistic in 1936, it is an anachronism today, but it has worked.

Today, Keeneland races are a tradition for a month in the spring and a month in the fall. Kentucky Derby contenders flock to the track in April. In October the horses return to the track, the crowds are augmented by visitors in town for football games, and the tradition continues.

In July the select yearling sale attracts the elite of the breed, which brings forth the elite of buyers: Middle Eastern sheiks, European entrepreneurs, Japanese industrialists, and stolid American businessmen bid into the millions for the privilege of buying a promise—only that—in the sleek form of a yearling Thoroughbred. The record price of a dream is $10.2 million.

Under the direction of Mr. Headley, later his son-in-law, Louis Lee Haggin II, and currently James E. Bassett III, the high-minded ideals upon which Keeneland was founded have been sustained. Queen Elizabeth II presented a trophy at Keeneland in the fall of 1984. As a patron of the best traditions in Thoroughbred racing, she experienced the best tradition of the Bluegrass.

# KENTUCKY HORSE PARK

 Horses, history, and hospitality await you at the beautiful Kentucky Horse Park. Located in the heart of the famous Bluegrass region which is world-renowned for majestic horse farms, white-fenced countryside, and million-dollar horses, the Kentucky Horse Park shares the spirit and excitement of the horse world. Dedicated to all breeds of horses, the Park was created to honor the timeless bond of man and horse, their inseparable history, and the persistent intrigue.

As a symbol of the strength and courage of all horses, the statue of the immortal Man O' War overlooks the entrance to the Park. The surrounding memorial recalls the saga of the legendary "Big Red" and marks his final resting place.

The visitor is able to view the film "Thou Shalt Fly Without Wings", tour the International Museum of the Horse where the Calumet Farm trophies are exhibited, take a Walking Farm Tour to perceive the sights, sounds, and smells of a horse farm, ride in a carriage or tram, and meet over 30 breeds of horses in the Parade of Breeds.

The Kentucky Horse Park was opened by the Commonwealth of Kentucky to the public in 1978 and dedicated to man's relationship with the horse. Befittingly, the history of the land on which the Park is situated dates back over 200 years.

In 1777 Patrick Henry, then Governor of Virginia, granted 9,000 acres of land in the Kentucky Territory to his brother-in-law, William Christian, as a reward for his services in the military. In 1786, Christian's daughter, Elizabeth Dickerson, inherited this tract and sold all but 1,000 acres.

In 1826 the land was purchased by Dr. William H. Richardson, one of the first physicians to teach at the newly formed medical school at Transylvania University. The farm, which he named Caneland, became known for its beautiful English gardens, the first greenhouse in Kentucky, and the first Thoroughbred horses to be raised on this land.

A later owner, S. J. Salyer, built the residence in 1866. This house is now used for offices at the Park.

In 1890 John D. Creighton purchased the farm and renamed it Ashland-Wilkes Farm. He built a training track in 1897 which is still used today.

Later, the farm was known as Senorita Stud Farm, and in 1906 it was bought at public auction by Lamon V. Harkness who incorporated it into his Walnut Hall Farm, which would eventually encompass almost 2,000 acres of the original Christian land holding.

The farm was divided in half by the heirs of Mr. Harkness, and in 1972 Mrs. Sherman Jenney sold her property to the Commonwealth of Kentucky.

If you are ever in Kentucky, come to the Kentucky Horse Park! Come discover the splendor of the Bluegrass and the magic of the horse!

# LANE'S END FARM

## GAME DINNER

*Squash Soup*
*Doves in Wine*
*Herb Rice*
*Carrot Soufflé*
*Fabulous Fudge Nut Pudding*

Some 1,500 acres of land at the end of a lane between Midway and Versailles, Kentucky, have been home since 1980 to Mr. and Mrs. William S. Farish III. Mr. Farish, a Texas businessman, was well established as a breeder and owner in Houston prior to moving the bulk of his breeding operation to Kentucky.

Their one-and-a-half-story house, originally known as Pleasant Lawn, was built in the 1820's. It resembles two houses built back-to-back connected by recessed porticos with columns (21 in all) and arches. Mr. and Mrs. Farish were hosts at Lane's End Farm to Her Majesty Queen Elizabeth II on her visit to the United States in the Fall of 1984.

Over 200 horses are housed on the farm. The broodmare barns have unusual herringbone-patterned brick floors, interiors of solid oak, and a specially designed ventilation system. New buildings have been constructed to compliment the design of the existing structures.

Roads and fencing were planned to match the contour of the land, both for aesthetics and safety. There are approximately 30 miles of fencing with no corners in paddocks or fields.

## DINNER

*Sausage-stuffed Mushrooms*
*Cheese Wafers*
*Charcoal-grilled Lamb Chops*
*Wild Rice*
*Creamed Pearl Onions*
*Buttered Snow Peas or French Green Beans Almondine*
*Popovers*
*Lemon Ice       Molasses Cookies*
*Demi-tasse*

Centerpiece of racing in Europe is the Epsom Derby, a race which bespeaks the traditions of the sport in its country of origin. Naturally, sporting folk being as they are, the race grew out of a gathering of convivial friends among the gentry of the English countryside in the 18th century. Among the first American Thoroughbreds to win the storied race was Sir Ivor, a handsome colt bred by Mrs. Alice Chandler, who owns Mill Ridge Farm with her children and her husband, Dr. John Chandler.

Mrs. Chandler is a daughter of the late Hal Price Headley, whose Beaumont and La Belle Farms used to spread over vast areas of Lexington.

Mill Ridge has two divisions, one purchased in Fayette County in 1962, the other in Jessamine County in 1974. Two of Mrs. Chandler's sons, Reynolds and Headley, are closely involved in the operation of the farms, while another son, Mike, is a trainer. Her daughter, Patricia, is married to Jim Houston who manages Stonechurch Farm in Lexington. Dr. Chandler is a veterinarian from South Africa.

The Fayette portion of the 800-acre complex earlier was known as Elmwood and was owned by A. H. Shropshire who raised Shorthorn cattle. In those times the land was graced by avenues of elm and walnut trees. Today, more than 200 horses roam its fields.

## SPRING DINNER

*Mushrooms stuffed with Crabmeat*
*Leg of Lamb with Mint Sauce*
*Parsleyed New Potatoes*
*Fresh Buttered Spring Peas*
*Kentucky Limestone Lettuce with French Dressing*
*Rolls*
*Amaretto Mousse*

Since their entrance onto the Thoroughbred scene in Lexington in 1975, it is obvious that Mr. and Mrs. Franklin Groves intend that their Thoroughbred enterprises be first-class. They had exhibited champion show horses from their Minnesota base, where Mr. Groves heads a large construction firm, and they understood the importance of good bloodlines in producing champions.

At the Keeneland July sale in 1975, Mr. Groves paid a then record price for a Thoroughbred yearling. He later purchased Queen Sucree, the dam of the Kentucky Derby winner Cannonade, followed by champion Desert Vixen.

This fine bloodstock is housed like the champions they are in barns with copper cupolas on the 1,250-acre North Ridge Farm. Three hundred horses graze the paddocked fields bound on the road's edge by meticulously restored rock walls.

In 1983 Mr. and Mrs. Groves opened one of the most attractive stallion complexes seen anywhere in the world. The 24-stall North Ridge stallion unit is U-shaped and incorporates ideas of design and animal management noted by Mr. Groves in Ireland and France. The roadway to the complex is lined by pin oaks and sugar maples which are some of the more than 5,000 trees that have been planted to beautify the farm.

## KENTUCKY SUPPER

*Baked Chicken-in-a-Bag*
*Fresh Sautéed Garden Vegetables*
*Sliced Tomatoes*
*Hot Biscuits*
*Overbrook Vanilla Ice Cream*
*Ice Cream Wafers*

Changing fast are the old-fashioned farms with their dirt-floored barns, wire fence rows, and pot-holed roads. They are to the newly developing equine nurseries what Currier and Ives prints are to today's landscape.

In 1972, Mr. and Mrs. William T. Young purchased and restored an eighteenth-century mill cottage overlooking East Hickman Creek on the Delong Road. Daniel Boone is said to have spent his lonely and discontented winter of 1770 at the spring nearby. Additional land was later added to create Overbrook Farm.

In accordance with their sensitivity toward the rolling land, architectural design, and Kentucky history, Mr. and Mrs. Young have focused on each detail of the work done on the farm. Fields have been plowed, fences raised, and roads laid. Brick tenant houses of Federal design and a barn have been built.

In 1984 a 20-stall brick foaling barn, designed along the lines of the early cottage, was erected.

Continuing in excellence, Mr. Young has assembled an impressive group of mares, including a European champion, the dam of a Preakness winner, and a spectacular racing daughter of Secretariat.

While architectural styles differ, construction, luxury, and scientific innovations have become the norm on Bluegrass horse farms.

**69**

# PAYSON STUD

## SUNDAY NIGHT SUPPER POOLSIDE

*Cold Zucchini Soup with Sour Cream*
*Cold Meat Platter*
*Beef Tenderloin, Smoked Turkey, Beef Tongue*
*Horseradish Mayonnaise*
*New Potato Salad*
*Sliced Tomatoes Vinaigrette*
*French Bread Parmesan*
*Chocolate Dessert Cups with Coffee Ice Cream*

Payson Stud occupies land which in earlier times was part of Elmendorf Farm, Duntreath Farm, and Greentree Stud. The brick manor house owned by Mr. and Mrs. Charles Shipman Payson is attributed to Lexington builder John McMurtry. It was built around 1850 for Thomas Hughes and was originally named "Fairlawn". The house was purchased by the Payne Whitney family in the 1920's from Ellen Davis and her son. Miss Davis was the Negro mistress of John Thomas Hughes, a wealthy bachelor who willed her the home.

The Paysons' brick manor house is considered one of the purest examples of the neoclassical style of the mid-19th century. The imposing Greek Revival building has a portico supported by four Corinthian columns. An adjacent cottage is a miniature of the main house.

Another building on the farm includes an authentic Travelers Room. To protect themselves from highwaymen, farm owners devised the rooms which had access only by ladder. Once the visitor was safe and warm, the ladder was taken away until morning.

Since 1981 Charles and Virginia Kraft Payson have expanded the barn and foaling facilities and have extensively landscaped the farm, planting more than 1,000 trees.

## PASTA SUPPER

*Marinated Shrimp*
*Homemade Pasta with Red Sauce, White Sauce, and Pesto Sauce*
*Italian Bread*
*Watercress and Romaine with French Dressing*
*Peach Ice with Fresh Sliced Peaches*
*Almond Cookies*

DuPont is a name long associated with Thoroughbred racing and breeding. William duPont III, the developer and owner of Pillar Stud, is the most recent duPont to enter the sport, and the first to make his Thoroughbred operation truly international. Mr. duPont races his horses in the United States, England, Australia, Italy, France, and South Africa. He also has breeding farms in Kentucky, Australia, and France.

Mr. duPont was enormously influenced by two people whose lives were centered around racing and breeding: his father, William, Jr., who owned Foxcatcher farm in Pennsylvania and his aunt, Marion duPont Scott, who owned Montpelier Stud in Virginia. Rather than pursue his career in the east, Mr. duPont came to Kentucky knowing it to be the center of the horse world and in 1975 began purchasing the land that comprises Pillar Stud. The name "Pillar" was chosen from the duPont coat of arms which is a shield with a single standing pillar.

In Kentucky he has acquired three farms, some seventy mares, and ten stallions. He has stallions in France and Australia and is acquiring more breeding stock world wide.

To date Pillar Stud encompasses 2,500 acres of land and is producing yearlings for Mr. duPont's racing stable and the commercial market here and abroad.

# THE RED MILE

From that Autumn day in September 1875 when a horse named Odd Fellow won the first mile heat ever contested over the famous red clay surface in 2:44¼ until the present time, The Red Mile has presented the very finest in the sport of harness racing. More official two-minute miles have been recorded at The Red Mile than on any other race track in the world.

Giant strides have been made by the Standardbred breeding and racing industries in the past 100 years. The Red Mile has been an integral part of that growth.

"See you in Lexington," has been a statement of fact, not a question, for over one hundred years. The greatest horses have been meeting each Autumn in Kentucky's Bluegrass to decide national championships and establish world records. Names of the legends of trotting and pacing elevate the history of The Red Mile—Dan Patch, Greyhound, Billy Direct, Bret Hanover, and Niatross.

Dan Patch, a pacer, held the track record for 33 years. In 1980 Niatross, driven by Clint Galbraith, established the present pacing record of 1:49¹/₅. The great trotter, Greyhound, driven by Sep Palin, established a track record which stood for 31 years. Today that record is held by Arndon who trotted in 1:54 in 1982, driven by Delvin Miller.

The Red Mile is the home of the Kentucky Futurity, which was begun in 1893, making it the oldest classic race in harness racing. It can safely be stated that this classic has been won by more great horses, great breeders, great owners, and great drivers than any other harness race.

The most distinguishing landmark at The Red Mile is an octagonal building originally designed as a floral exhibition hall. In 1879 the Agricultural and Mechanical Fair Association, then owners of the race track, commissioned Lexington architect, John McMurtry, to design such a building. In later years it was known as the "Berry Barn" for the great trainer, Tom Berry, who stabled there. In 1971 it was designated the Standardbred Stable of Memories.

Tattersalls, the largest Standardbred/Saddlebred sales organization in the world is located at The Red Mile, occupying a facility containing an 1100-seat pavilion and 350 permanent stalls. During World Wars I and II horses were purchased through Tattersalls for the United States and Allied troops. In 1982 a world record price for a Standardbred yearling was set at the Fall sales.

Each year as the late afternoon October shadows settle in on the old circuit, the heats of the Kentucky Futurity are staged, evoking memories of an America which exists only in storybooks but is still a way of life in the Bluegrass.

## LARGE BUFFET DINNER

*Roquefort Wafers      Country Ham Canapés*
*Lobster Cream on Toast Rounds*
*Chicken Curry with Saffron Rice*
*Condiments:*
*Shredded Coconut, Chutney, Chopped Eggs,*
*Crisp Bacon, Green Onions, Raisins, Peanuts*
*Fresh Green Salad*
*Pleasant Hill Molded Fruit Salad*
*Rolls*
*Chocolate Mousse*

Runnymede Farm in the latter 1800's was owned by Col. Ezekiel F. Clay, who with his brother-in-law, Col. Catesby Woodford, bred some of the storied horses of an era when post Civil War America was blossoming as a sporting nation. Hanover, the great stallion which won 20 of 27 races as a three year old, was bred at Runnymede, as was Ben Brush, while the partners also owned Miss Woodford, the first horse in America to earn $100,000 as a racer.

Today's scion of the Runnymede tradition is grandson, Catesby Woodford Clay. Recent prominent Runnymede-breds include stakes winners and sires Royal Ski, Terrible Tiger, Angle Light (only three-year-old to defeat Secretariat) and Full Extent (English Stakes winner of the historic Gimcrack Stakes) as well as champion Kentucky-bred handicap mare Plankton.

The house at Runnymede was built in the 1830's. Gracing its walls are a number of portraits of former Runnymede champions painted by Henry Stull, a prominent American sporting artist of the 19th century.

A stone barn on the farm dating from 1803 was originally built as Cooper's Run Baptist Church.

# SPENDTHRIFT FARM

## POST DERBY BREAKFAST

*Turkey Hash with Corn Cakes      Country Ham*
*Lamb Fries with Cream Gravy*
*Egg and Mushroom Casserole*
*Fresh Asparagus      Grits      Corn Pudding*
*Corn Muffins      Biscuits*
*Assorted Fresh Fruits*
*Lemon, Strawberry, Chocolate and Pecan Finger Pies*

When Leslie Combs II started Spendthrift Farm in 1937 with 127 acres of land, he was the fourth generation of his family in the Thoroughbred business. Today his son, Brownell Combs II, is President of a Thoroughbred operation encompassing approximately 2,350 acres of land and two training facilities, one in Kentucky and the other in Florida.

Over the years Leslie Combs has been a master at raising and selling Thoroughbreds and perfected the art of stallion syndication starting with Nashua who was syndicated in 1955 for $1 million. Currently 46 stallions stand at Spendthrift Farm including Seattle Slew and Affirmed, both Triple Crown winners. Spendthrift stallions have sired such champions as Majestic Prince, Alydar, and Affirmed.

Spendthrift Farm was named for the Belmont Stakes winner Spendthrift, sire of champions and great-grand sire of Man O' War.

The residence, built about 1804 has been enlarged and modernized and provides a magnificent backdrop for the famed Derby breakfast and other glittering social events which have made the name "Spendthrift" synonymous with southern hospitality.

# STONER CREEK FARM

## TAILGATE PARTY

*Green Onion Soup*
*Thin-sliced Beef Tenderloin*
*with*
*Shakertown Horseradish Sauce*
*Vegetarian Sandwich Spread*
*Tossed Salad with Marinated Olives and Dill*
*Scotch Shortbread*
*Fresh Pineapple and Strawberries*
*with*
*Sour Cream Dip*

Three Triple Crown winners in various branches of racing have been raised at Stoner Creek Stud. In the 1940's when the farm was owned by the late Mr. and Mrs. John D. Hertz (Mr. Hertz founded the Hertz Rent-A-Car Company), the home stallion, Reigh Count, sired the Thoroughbred Triple Crown winner Count Fleet. The latter went home to stud there and became a leading stallion, continuing a three-generation line of Kentucky Derby winners: Reigh Count in 1928; Count Fleet in 1943; and Count Turf in 1951.

The farm was acquired in 1964 by Norman Woolworth and Mr. and Mrs. David R. Johnston and was converted into a leading Standardbred farm. The tradition of Triple Crown winners was continued when Bonefish (a trotter) and Most Happy Fella (a pacer) swept triples in their respective divisions. Major Standardbred stallions came in to take the place of the Thoroughbred Count Fleet, among them Nevele Pride and Meadow Skipper.

Stoner Creek, presently covering 1,000 acres, is on land rumored to have been the site of one of the earliest stills in Bourbon County. In another era the land has been known as Hinton Farm and Brooks Farm.

# SYCAMORE FARM

## FALL BLACK TIE DINNER

*Crab Parmesan Canapés*
*Pâté de Fois Gras*
*Clear Mushroom Broth*
*Breast of Duck on Wild Rice with Orange Sauce*
*French Green Beans Almondine*
*Rolls*
*Mixed Green Salad*
*Camembert and Bel Paese Cheeses*
*Bent Biscuits        Crackers*
*Tangerine Ice and Burnt Almond Ice Cream Bombe*
*Small Coconut Cakes*
*Demi-tasse*

It has been said that Sycamore Farm, located just over the Fayette County line on Shannon Run Road in Woodford County, is like an enchanted island: so still, so idyllic, and remote. This is because of the location, the age of the house and trees, and the "natural" landscaping.

Sycamore Farm was once part of a 6,000-acre Land Grant, and the 1,500 acres that comprise the farm were bought just after the Revolutionary War and named "Sycamore Park". The residence was built in 1828.

Sycamore Farm has been the home of Mr. and Mrs. Louis Lee Haggin II since 1940 when Mr. Haggin purchased the farm to breed Thoroughbreds for his racing stable. For many years Mr. Haggin was President of the Keeneland Association which oversees the Keeneland Race Track and the Keeneland Sales Company.

In the early 1940's Innocenti and Webel, landscape architects from New York, designed the lovely vistas, small formal gardens, statuary, and stone walls which make the gardens at Sycamore Farm so unique.

The same firm designed the landscaping at Keeneland Race Track. Mrs. Haggin is deeply interested in and directs new designs and plantings both at Sycamore Farm and at Keeneland.

# WATERFORD FARM

## SUMMER LUNCHEON

*Gazpacho*
*Whole Cold Poached Salmon with Cucumber Sauce*
*Kentucky Bibb Lettuce with Marinated Hearts of Palm*
*and Tomato Wedges*
*Ice Box Rolls*
*Strawberry Ice*
*Pecan Cookies Supreme*
*Mint Tea*

Dr. and Mrs. Robert Smiser West's Waterford Farm in Woodford County, near the town of Midway, Kentucky, lies on a portion of the Hancock Taylor survey of 1774. It was among the first lands surveyed in Kentucky and formerly was buffalo hunting grounds for Indians. Lee's Big Spring originates on the farm and supplies water for it and Midway.

The land has been in the same family for five generations, more than 100 years, and involves 650 acres, home to Thoroughbred horses. Among the distinguished boarding mares at Waterford in recent years is Bert and Diana Firestone's lovely Genuine Risk, who in 1980 became only the second filly to win the Kentucky Derby. In partnership with trainer MacKenzie Miller, Dr. and Mrs. West bred De La Rose, who in 1981 became the champion three year old filly racing on the turf.

Part of the original farm was named "Calumet" in 1882 when an ancestor of Mrs. West lived on an adjacent 300 acres. The word "Calumet" is Indian for "Pipe of Peace," and in the 1930's was used for another well-known Central Kentucky horse farm. The Wests' property is named after Waterford, Ireland.

The main house on the farm is a mile from the entrance and was built about 1850, when three now-huge cypress trees in the front yard were supposedly brought as seedlings by barge up the Mississippi, Ohio, and Kentucky Rivers.

# C. V. WHITNEY FARM

## DERBY EVE DINNER IN THE ATRIUM

*Mint Juleps*
*Thin Slices of Old Kentucky Ham in Buttered Beaten Biscuits*
*Chicken Finger Pies*
*Crab Bisque with Cheese Straws*
*Filet of Beef    Sauce Maison*
*Parsleyed Potato Balls    Fresh Wild Greens*
*Corn Puffs*
*Bibb Lettuce Salad*
*Brie Cheese and Crackers*
*Strawberry Fluff with Sherry Sauce*
*Demi-tasse*

C. V. Whitney has bred more stakes winning horses than any other American Thoroughbred breeder. More importantly, he has bred or raced six champions: Equipoise, First Flight, Top Flight, Counterpoint, Silver Spoon, and Bug Brush.

Prior to his inheriting the farm in 1930, Regret, the first filly to win the Kentucky Derby, Whiskbroom II, and Broomstick were part of the dominance of Whitney bred and raced horses.

In addition to the Whitney Stakes at Saratoga Race Track, races at tracks nationwide have been named for Whitney horses including the Regret Stakes, the Equipoise Mile Handicap, and the Top Flight Handicap.

For years Mr. Whitney accompanied his father, Harry Payne Whitney, when he visited the farm, arriving on his private railroad car with a coterie of friends. The car would be parked on the railroad siding that ran through the farm.

In 1958 C. V. Whitney and his wife, Mary Lou, remodeled the historic residence, Maple Hill, creating a lovely home which is the setting for their many magnificent parties for friends, celebrities, and royalty.

In 1965 Mr. Whitney sold all but 565 acres of his farm to John R. Gaines of Gainesway Farm, retaining his best mares to supply his small but highly successful racing stable.

## COUNTRY SOIRÉE

*Mushroom Broth*
*Rare Filet of Beef*
*Asparagus Vinaigrette*
*Baked Corn Pudding*
*Shrimp-filled Avocado Half on Bibb Lettuce*
*Remoulade Sauce*
*White Chocolate Soufflé*
*with*
*Grand Marnier Sauce*

As Kentucky is the center of the horse world and Wimbledon, England, is the center of the tennis world, so Wimbledon Farm in Lexington is the center of its owner's two consuming interests.

Hilary Boone, Jr., bought the first part of his farm in 1970 as an investment, a hobby, and a weekend retreat. His first interest being tennis, he built two courts and named his farm. When he started riding with the nearby Iroquois Hunt, he remodeled the one existing barn for his Hunters. Along the way, he indulged his third interest, historic renovation, by restoring two farm houses: one built originally in 1795; and the other, in 1805.

Soon the focus of his life changed and in quick succession Mr. Boone added five more pieces of land; retired from his insurance business; built barns, fences and roads; acquired mares, stallions, and boarding stock; and was solidly in the Thoroughbred horse business.

Presently Mr. Boone and his son manage a top market breeding operation including syndicated stallions, brood mares, and yearlings. American champion Spectacular Bid and English Derby winner Golden Fleece were raised on the 1,015-acre farm.

## HOT ARTICHOKE CHEESE SQUARES

1/3 cup onion, chopped
1 clove garlic, mashed
  (optional)
2 tablespoons bacon fat
4 eggs, beaten until frothy
1 (14-ounce) can artichoke
  hearts, drained and
  chopped
1/4 cup dry bread crumbs

1/2 pound Swiss cheese,
  shredded
2 tablespoons minced
  parsley
1/2 teaspoon salt
Pepper to taste
1/4 teaspoon oregano
1/8 teaspoon Tabasco
  sauce

Sauté onion and garlic in fat. Combine with remaining ingredients. Bake in a greased 7"x 11" baking dish at 325° for 25 to 30 minutes. Cut into 1 1/2" squares to serve.

## HOT ARTICHOKE SPREAD

1 (14-ounce) can artichoke
  hearts, drained and
  chopped
3/4 to 1 cup Hellmann's
  mayonnaise

1 cup grated Parmesan
  cheese
1/2 teaspoon garlic salt
Dash of lemon juice

Combine all ingredients, mixing well. Spoon into a lightly greased 3-cup casserole. Bake at 350° for 25 minutes. Serve with assorted crackers. Makes about 2 1/2 cups.

## ASPARAGUS ROLL-UPS

*…this Kentucky favorite can be served hot or cold*

1 (15-ounce) can small green
asparagus spears, drained
18 slices white bread
(approximately), with crusts
removed
2 tablespoons French dressing
1/8 teaspoon salt
1/8 teaspoon freshly ground
pepper

1/2 cup highly seasoned
mayonnaise
1/2 teaspoon anchovy
paste (optional), mixed
into mayonnaise
1 stick butter, melted (for
hot sandwiches only)

Spread each slice of bread with mayonnaise. Place one asparagus spear on bread; sprinkle each with salt and pepper and a few drops of French dressing. Roll up the bread from corner to corner or jelly roll style. Secure with a toothpick (when ready to serve, remove toothpick). To serve as a hot appetizer, brush each roll-up with melted butter and broil until lightly browned.

## BACON-WRAPPED CRACKERS

Waverly Wafers                    Thin sliced bacon

Wrap a Waverly cracker with a thin slice of bacon. Bake in a 250° oven for 50 minutes. Serve immediately or store in an airtight tin.

## CHICKEN FINGER PIES

2 eggs, separated
1 cup butter
2 tablespoons heavy cream

2 cups flour
1 teaspoon sugar
Dash salt

Sift dry ingredients together. Cut in butter and add egg yolks and cream. Form into dough and roll very thin. Cut with 2" cookie cutter. Place filling in center; cover with another circle of dough, pressing edges together. Brush with egg whites. Bake at 375° until browned. Makes 10 to 12.

*Chicken Filling*
1 large chicken breast or
   3 medium halves

2 tablespoons heavy
   cream
Salt and cayenne pepper
   to taste

Boil chicken in highly-seasoned water until tender. Cool and break into pieces. Moisten with cream.

## CHEESE SOUFFLÉ SANDWICHES

2 small loaves Pepperidge
   Farm thin sandwich bread
2 1/2 sticks margarine or butter
3 (5-ounce) jars Old English
   cheese spread
3/4 teaspoon Tabasco sauce

1 1/4 teaspoons
   Worcestershire sauce
3/4 teaspoon Beau Monde
   seasoning
1 1/4 teaspoons dillweed
3 teaspoons grated onion

Place bread in stacks of 3 slices each; trim crusts from bread. Combine remaining ingredients in bowl; blend until smooth with an electric beater. *Do not beat* until fluffy! Spread mixture between slices and on top of each stack of bread, as you would a sandwich. Cut each stack into fourths; ice sides. Do *not* ice bottoms. Place on a cookie sheet; refrigerate until ready to bake. Bake at 400° until brown.

*Note:* To freeze, place cookie sheet in freezer. When frozen, package in foil. Defrost before baking.

## HOT CHEESE PUFFS

¹/₄ cup soft bread crumbs
1 cup grated Cheddar cheese
1 egg, separated

¹/₄ teaspoon prepared
  mustard
Salt and cayenne to taste

Combine bread crumbs, cheese, egg yolk and seasonings. Beat egg white until stiff; fold into mixture. Shape mixture into balls the size of large marbles, using fingers or butter paddles; roll balls in sieved, dry bread crumbs. Put a few balls in a frying basket; plunge into deep, hot (380°) fat until balls are a delicate golden color. Drain and serve on a hot plate.

## MINIATURE QUICHE LORRAINE

*Pastry*
Using any pie dough recipe, line a 15"x 10" baking pan. Bake at 425° for 10 minutes until lightly browned.

*Filling*
4 eggs, well beaten
2 cups half-and-half
Dash of cayenne pepper
Dash of nutmeg

7 ounces chopped natural
  swiss cheese
15 strips cooked,
  well-drained bacon,
  chopped

Mix all ingredients together and pour into lightly browned crust. Bake at 325° for 30 minutes or until filling appears to set. Cut into 1" squares; serve hot or at room temperature.

*This recipe from Calumet Farm chef, Richard Paul*

## HOT CRABMEAT CANAPÉS

1 part crabmeat                    1 part Parmesan cheese
1 part mayonnaise

Mix all ingredients together; spread on thin toast rounds or triangles or stuff large mushroom caps. Place under broiler until hot and bubbly.

## CRAB AND CHEDDAR CANAPÉ

1 (6-ounce) can crabmeat          Dash of Worcestershire
  (good quality)                    sauce
8 ounces sharp Cheddar            ½ teaspoon dry mustard
  cheese, diced small (not        Cayenne pepper to taste
  grated)                         1 loaf sliced sandwich
3 to 4 tablespoons mayonnaise       bread

Flake crabmeat and toss with fork to lighten; add remaining ingredients and mix well. Season to taste. Cut round of bread with a biscuit or cookie cutter; spread mixture on top of each. Bake at 350° for approximately 12 minutes. Makes 3 dozen

Note: Mixture may be used to stuff mushrooms or to fill pastry shells.

## COUNTRY HAM CANAPÉS

2 cups finely-ground country     Mayonnaise
  ham                            24 very thin slices of fresh
1 cup finely-grated sharp          bread
  Cheddar cheese

Combine ham and cheese; add just enough mayonnaise to bind together. Using a biscuit cutter, cut a circle from each bread slice; flatten with hand. Press circles of bread into buttered miniature muffin tins to form cups. Bake at 375° for 10 minutes until lightly browned. Fill toast cups with ham-cheese mixture. Bake at 325° for 15 minutes until cheese is melted. Serve hot.

## OLIVE-PECAN ROLL-UPS

10 ounces Cracker Barrel
  sharp Cheddar cheese,
  grated
3/4 cup chopped green olives
  stuffed with pimiento
3/4 cup chopped pecans
2 tablespoons mayonnaise

1 1/2 cups all-purpose flour
3/4 teaspoon salt
1/2 teaspoon paprika
1/2 cup (1 stick) butter,
  softened
1/2 cup sour cream

Combine grated cheese, olives, pecans and mayonnaise, mixing well; set aside. Sift flour, salt and paprika together. Cream butter; add flour and sour cream, blending thoroughly. Chill dough until firm. Divide dough into two balls. Roll out each on a wooden board until large enough to cut an 8"x 14" rectangle; divide into two 4"x 14" strips. Spread olive-pecan filling down the center of each; fold the long sides toward the center and pinch the edges. Place roll-ups on a baking sheet, seam side down; bake at 375° for 25 minutes or until brown. Allow to cool slightly; cut into slices to serve.

## SPINACH-OLIVE PUFFS

1 (10-ounce) package frozen
  chopped spinach, thawed
1/2 cup chopped ripe olives,
  drained
3/4 cup grated Parmesan
  cheese

3/4 cup Hellmann's
  mayonnaise
36 small rounds of toasted
  bread or Melba toast
  rounds

Squeeze the spinach until dry; add remaining ingredients, mixing thoroughly. Spread thickly on toast rounds; broil 6 to 8 inches under broiler for 3 minutes or until hot and puffy. Makes 3 dozen.

## OLIVE-FILLED CHEESE BALLS

4 ounces Cheddar cheese, grated
2 tablespoons butter, softened
1/2 cup flour

Dash of red pepper
25 medium-size green olives, drained

Beat cheese and butter together well; add flour and red pepper. Enclose each olive with dough and place on an ungreased sheet pan. Bake, uncovered, at 400° for 12 to 15 minutes.

*This recipe from Calumet Farm chef, Richard Paul*

## MUSHROOM CANAPÉS

*Filling*
8 ounces fresh mushrooms, finely chopped
3 tablespoons finely chopped shallots
4 tablespoons butter or margarine

2 tablespoons flour
1/2 teaspoon salt
3/4 to 1 cup half-and-half
1 tablespoon dried parsley
2 to 3 tablespoons grated Parmesan cheese

Sauté mushrooms and shallots in butter or margarine over low heat until most of liquid has evaporated. Remove from heat and add flour and salt, stirring thoroughly. Add half-and-half and parsley; simmer until thickened. Cool.

*Toast cups*
24 slices very thin bread

Softened butter

Cut a 2" circle from each slice of bread; flatten with hand, pressing down firmly. Carefully place in a buttered miniature muffin pan, shaping bread rounds into cups. Bake at 375° for about 10 minutes until light brown. Fill toast cups with filling, sprinkle with Parmesan cheese and bake at 350° about 10 to 12 minutes until hot.

# APPETIZERS

## MUSHROOM SQUARES

1 (4-ounce) can mushroom
   stems and pieces, drained
   and chopped
2 slices crisply-cooked bacon,
   crumbled
2 tablespoons shredded Swiss
   cheese
2 tablespoons mayonnaise or
   salad dressing

1 tablespoon dried parsley
   flakes
1/8 teaspoon dried
   rosemary leaves,
   crumbled
Few grains salt
6 slices white bread
Soft butter

Mix first 7 ingredients. Heat oven to 400°. Trim crusts from bread, butter lightly and cut each into four squares. Place squares, buttered-side down, on a cookie sheet. Spoon a small amount of mushroom mixture onto each square. Bake for 5 minutes and serve hot. Makes 24 canapés.

## BLUEGRASS CREAMED OYSTERS

4 cups small oysters
4 tablespoons butter
4 tablespoons flour
1 cup milk
1 cup cream
2 tablespoons grated onion
3 tablespoons chopped chives

2 teaspoons
   Worcestershire sauce
1 teaspoon salt
1 teaspoon freshly ground
   pepper

Drain oysters and reserve liquor. Melt butter in a large heavy pan; blend in flour and cook 2 minutes. Gradually stir in milk, cream and oyster liquor; continue to stir until thickened. Set sauce aside. In a heavy skillet, heat oysters for 2 minutes until edges curl. Add oysters, onion, chives and seasonings to sauce. Serve from a chafing dish into individual toast cups or patty shells.

## CORN FRITTERS

2 eggs
1 cup milk
2 cups flour
2 cups fresh cut corn or
    canned corn, drained
1 tablespoon sugar

1 1/2 teaspoons salt
2 teaspoons baking
    powder
1/2 teaspoon paprika
2 tablespoons shortening,
    melted

Beat eggs and milk; add remaining ingredients, mixing thoroughly. Drop by spoonsful into hot deep fat (365°) until browned. Drain on paper towels.

## PINEAPPLE FRITTERS

1 cup sifted flour
1/4 teaspoon salt
1 tablespoon sugar
1 teaspoon baking powder
1 egg, beaten
1/4 cup milk

1 tablespoon melted
    Crisco
1 cup drained crushed
    pineapple
Confectioners sugar

Sift flour, salt, sugar and baking powder together. Combine egg, milk, melted Crisco and pineapple; mix well. Stir into dry ingredients, mixing just enough to moisten. Drop by teaspoonsful into deep hot Crisco (365°). Fry 3 to 5 minutes until brown and cooked in center. Sprinkle with confectioners sugar.

## ZUCCHINI TRIANGLES

1 pound unpeeled zucchini,
    thinly sliced or grated
1 cup biscuit mix
1 cup chopped onion
3 ounces grated Parmesan
    cheese
1 tablespoon minced parsley

1/2 teaspoon seasoned salt
1/2 teaspoon salt
1/2 teaspoon oregano
Dash of pepper
1 clove garlic, minced
1/2 cup vegetable oil
4 eggs, slightly beaten

Combine all ingredients, mixing well. Place in a greased 13"x 9"x 2" pan; bake at 350° for 30 minutes. Cool in pan; cut in triangles. Freezes well.

## BENEDICTINE SPREAD

1 medium-sized cucumber,
  peeled and seeded
1 (8-ounce) package cream
  cheese, softened

¹/₂ medium-sized onion,
  finely ground
Dash of salt
Dash of red pepper
Green food coloring

Grind cucumber pulp; place on cheesecloth and squeeze out the juice. Combine pulp with cream cheese, onion and seasonings, mixing thoroughly. Add a very small amount of food coloring--just enough to make the spread a pale green. The spread may be used to make sandwiches and canapés.

## BEER CHEESE

*...an Old Kentucky favorite*

2 (10-ounce) sticks Cracker
  Barrel extra sharp Cheddar
  cheese
2 cloves garlic

1 (7-ounce) bottle beer
¹/₈ teaspoon salt
Tabasco sauce to taste

Grate cheese and garlic in a food processor; add remaining ingredients, mixing until thoroughly blended. The mixture will be soft but will harden in the refrigerator. It is better if made ahead of time. Serve with crackers, celery sticks or radish roses.

## OLIVE-NUT SPREAD

1 (8-ounce) package cream
  cheese, softened
¹/₂ cup mayonnaise
¹/₂ cup chopped pecans

1 cup chopped salad
  olives
2 tablespoons olive juice
Dash of pepper

Combine ingredients and mix well. Put in a container, cover and refrigerate. Allow at least 24 hours for mixture to thicken. It will last for weeks, if you can keep it that long!

## LOBSTER CREAM

$^{1}/_{2}$ pound lobster meat,
  cooked
6 tablespoons butter, softened
6 tablespoons heavy cream
$^{1}/_{2}$ teaspoon lemon rind,
  finely grated

Dash of Tabasco sauce
Salt to taste
White pepper to taste
$^{1}/_{4}$ cup heavy cream,
  whipped

In a food processor, grind lobster meat to a paste; gradually work in butter and cream. Add seasonings and blend for a few seconds. Stir in whipped cream. Pack mixture into a well-oiled mold and chill until firm. To unmold, set the mold briefly in hot water, then invert onto a chilled plate. Serve with rounds of lightly buttered toast.

*Rounds of Toast*
Cut 2" circles from very thin bread (if you are careful, you can get 2 circles from each slice of bread). Place on a cookie sheet and broil one side until lightly browned. Brush other side with melted butter and broil until browned. Allow to cool and serve with lobster cream.

## PIMIENTO CHEESE

1 (4-ounce) jar chopped
  pimiento, drained
1 cup homemade mayonnaise
1 tablespoon fresh lemon
  juice
1 teaspoon Spice Islands hot
  dry mustard
$^{1}/_{4}$ teaspoon Spice Islands
  cayenne pepper

$^{1}/_{2}$ teaspoon
  Worcestershire sauce
1 to 2 cloves garlic,
  crushed
8 ounces Colby cheese,
  grated
8 ounces Cheddar cheese,
  grated

Mix well with a rotary beater, adding cheese last. Continue beating until smooth. Store in tightly sealed crocks in refrigerator. Makes 4 cups.

## BLUE CHEESE MOUSSE

*First layer*

1 envelope unflavored gelatin
¹/₄ cup Curacao liqueur

³/₄ cup boiling chicken
   stock
¹/₄ cup finely slivered
   orange rind

Soften gelatin in liqueur, then dissolve in chicken stock. Add orange rind slivers and cool until syrupy. Pour into mold; chill for 30 minutes or until set.

*Second layer*

4 egg yolks, beaten
¹/₂ cup cream
1 envelope unflavored gelatin
¹/₂ cup orange juice

¹/₂ pound Danish blue
   cheese
3 egg whites, stiffly beaten
³/₄ cup cream, whipped

Combine yolks and cream in the top of a double boiler and cook until thick and light in color. Soften gelatin in orange juice and dissolve in the hot mixture. Remove the custard from the heat and cool, stirring occasionally. Force the blue cheese through a sieve and fold into custard; fold in egg whites, then whipped cream. Pour mixture over first layer in mold; chill for at least 3 hours. Serves 12. The mousse may be served as an appetizer, with crackers. If made in a ring mold, it may be served with fresh fruit in the center as a salad.

## HOT CHEESE

1 medium onion grated
1 (4-ounce) jar pimientos and
   juice
1¹/₂ pounds New York sharp
   Cheddar cheese, grated

1 pint mayonnaise
1 to 2 tablespoons
   Tabasco sauce
1 teaspoon garlic powder

Put onion and pimientos with juice in an electric blender; purée. Combine cheese, mayonnaise, Tabasco sauce and garlic powder; add puréed mixture and beat with an electric mixer until fluffy. Store in a refrigerator in sealed containers. This is good with bread sticks. Makes 3 pints.

## CHICKEN LIVER AND MUSHROOM PÂTÉ

½ pound chicken livers
½ cup butter
1 medium-size onion,
 chopped
1 clove garlic, chopped
¾ cup chopped fresh
 mushrooms (⅛ pound)

1 tablespoon Madeira
 (optional)
Salt and pepper
Pinch of nutmeg
Clarified butter (optional)

Trim white gristle from livers. Heat 6 tablespoons butter in a skillet and cook livers quickly (about 2 minutes on each side) until brown but still pink in the middle. Remove from the pan and place in the electric blender or food mill. Add onion and garlic to the skillet; cook gently until soft. Add the mushrooms and cook 4 to 5 minutes longer; add this mixture to the livers. Melt the remaining butter in the skillet; stir in the Madeira, if used, and scrape the brown bits off the bottom of the pan. Add to the blender or food mill; blend until smooth. Season with salt, pepper and nutmeg to taste; pack into a crock. Cover with a thin layer of clarified butter to keep beyond 2 days. Chilling for 24 to 48 hours improves flavor. About 1¼ cups.

## PÂTÉ

1 pound chicken livers, fresh
 or frozen
1 small onion, peeled and
 sliced
¾ cup chicken stock
1½ sticks butter, softened
1 tablespoon brandy, cognac
 or sherry

1 tablespoon
 Worcestershire sauce
1 teaspoon salt
½ teaspoon paprika
½ teaspoon curry powder
¼ teaspoon pepper
¼ teaspoon nutmeg
⅛ teaspoon ground
 cloves

Simmer livers and onion in chicken stock for 10 minutes, turning them once. Drain well. In a blender or food processor, purée the warm (not hot) livers with the butter, brandy and seasonings. Pack in a small greased mold or bowl; chill. Unmold and serve cold with toast rounds.

# APPETIZERS

## VEGETARIAN SANDWICH SPREAD

1 bunch celery hearts, finely chopped
1 green pepper, finely chopped
½ large onion, finely chopped
1 small tomato, seeded and finely chopped
5 to 6 slices bacon, crisply cooked and crumbled
Homemade mayonnaise

Combine the first 5 ingredients with enough mayonnaise to bind them together. This mixture may be used in the middle of a tomato aspic ring or as a sandwich spread or as a dip (with the addition of more mayonnaise).

## CAVIAR PIE

6 eggs, hard-cooked
½ cup (1 stick) butter, softened
2 small white onions, chopped
2 (4-ounce) jars caviar
1 cup sour cream
Parsley, chopped

Sieve eggs and mix with butter. Spread mixture into a glass serving dish or pie plate, covering the bottom and sides. Chill thoroughly. Add alternate layers of onions and caviar; carefully spread sour cream over caviar. Sprinkle parsley around edge of pie. Serve with assorted crackers or party rye bread.

## GUACAMOLE

1½ avocados
Juice of 1 lemon
2 cloves garlic, pressed
½ teaspoon salt
½ teaspoon chili powder
1 tablespoon minced onion
1 tomato, skinned
2 tablespoons plain yogurt
1 tablespoon Hellmann's mayonnaise

Place all ingredients in food processor and mix well. Chill. Serve with tortilla chips.

*This recipe from Calumet Farm chef, Richard Paul*

## MEXICAN FIESTA DIP

On a large round serving tray or platter, layer in order:

*1st layer*—1 (16-ounce) can refried beans mixed with 1 package dry taco mix

*2nd layer*—Homemade Guacamole (see below)

*3rd layer*—1 (8-ounce) carton sour cream

*4th layer*—3/4 cup chopped tomato mixed with 1/3 cup chopped green onions

*5th layer*—6 ounces sharp Cheddar cheese, grated

*6th layer*—A mixture of 1/3 cup chopped ripe olives and 1/3 cup chopped green olives

*Guacamole*

1 (3-ounce) package cream cheese
1 tablespoon sauterne
2 medium-to-large avocados, mashed

1/4 teaspoon garlic salt
1 teaspoon curry powder
Salt, paprika and Tabasco sauce to taste

Mix ingredients thoroughly. Bury avocado pit in Guacamole to prevent darkening. Serve with toasted tortilla chips. Serves 12.

## DILL DIP

1 pint mayonnaise
1 pint sour cream
3 tablespoons grated onion
3 tablespoons parsley

1 tablespoon dill weed
1 tablespoon Beau Monde Seasoning
Lemon juice to taste

Combine ingredients and mix until well blended. Chill and serve with any or all of following:

Cauliflower florets
Broccoli florets
Carrot sticks
Celery sticks
Fresh green beans, parboiled

Cherry tomatoes
Radishes
Zucchini strips
Artichoke hearts
Cold salmon

## CURRY DIP FOR FRESH FRUITS AND VEGETABLES

1 cup Hellmann's mayonnaise
1 tablespoon horseradish
1 tablespoon tarragon vinegar
1 teaspoon curry powder
1 tablespoon grated onion

Combine all ingredients. Chill and serve.

## SOUR CREAM DIP FOR FRESH FRUIT

2 cups sour cream
1/2 cup plus 2 tablespoons
   brown sugar
2 tablespoons dark rum
4 teaspoons Grand
   Marnier

Combine ingredients, blending thoroughly. Serve chilled with cut-up fresh fruit on toothpicks or in individual dessert dishes topped with 2 tablespoons sauce on each.

## SPINACH DIP BEAU MONDE

2 (10-ounce) packages
   chopped spinach, cooked
   and well drained
2 cups sour cream
1 cup mayonnaise
1 cup fresh minced parsley
1 cup chopped green
   onion tops
1 teaspoon Beau Monde
   seasoning
1 teaspoon dill weed
Salt and pepper to taste

Blend all together and chill. Best made the day before. Serve with assorted crackers.

## CHUTNEY DIP

1 (9-ounce) bottle chutney,
  chopped
1 cup sour cream

¹/₂ to 1 teaspoon curry
  powder
4 strips crisply-cooked
  bacon, crumbled

Mix chutney and sour cream; add curry powder to taste. Sprinkle crumbled bacon on top and serve cold with crackers or chips.

## FRESH SHRIMP DIP

1 (8-ounce) package cream
  cheese, softened
Juice of 1 lemon
¹/₂ cup mayonnaise
¹/₄ cup catsup
¹/₂ cup chopped celery
¹/₄ cup minced onion

Tops of 2 green onions,
  chopped
5 drops Tabasco sauce
White pepper to taste
1¹/₂ pounds cooked
  shrimp, cut into small
  pieces

Shrimp Dip should be made 1 day ahead. Combine all ingredients; mix thoroughly and chill. Serve with crackers.

## MARINATED SHRIMP

1 cup olive oil
¹/₃ cup vinegar
2 large cloves pressed garlic

2 teaspoons tarragon
Cooked shrimp

Place all ingredients except shrimp in blender and blend 1 minute. Remove from blender and add cooked shrimp. Marinate 2 to 4 hours.

*This recipe from Calumet Farm chef, Richard Paul*

## COLD DEVILED SHRIMP

2 pounds raw shrimp, shelled
1 lemon, thinly sliced
1 red onion, thinly sliced

¹/₂ cup pitted black olives, drained
2 tablespoons chopped pimiento

Devein shrimp and cook in 1 quart boiling salted water a scant 3 minutes. Drain at once. Add lemon, onion, olives and pimiento; toss together. Stir Marinade into mixture and mix well. Cover and refrigerate at least 2 hours, stirring twice. Serves 6.

*Marinade*
¹/₄ cup oil
¹/₂ cup fresh lemon juice
1 tablespoon wine vinegar
1 tablespoon dry mustard
1 clove garlic, minced

¹/₂ bay leaf
1 teaspoon salt
1 teaspoon pepper
¹/₄ teaspoon red pepper

Combine all ingredients and mix well.

## DEVILED EGGS

6 large eggs
1¹/₂ tablespoons mayonnaise
1 tablespoon vinegar
1 teaspoon dry mustard

¹/₂ teaspoon salt
¹/₄ teaspoon sugar
Pinch of cayenne pepper
Parsley (for garnish)

Place eggs in a saucepan; cover with cold water. Put pan over medium heat; bring water to boiling point. Reduce heat; allow eggs to simmer for 20 minutes. Immediately place hard-cooked eggs in cold water to prevent discoloration of yolks. Halve eggs lengthwise; remove yolks, being careful not to break whites. Mix all ingredients except parsley in a food processor or with an electric mixer. Using a spoon or pastry tube, lightly mound yolk mixture in egg halves, dividing evenly. Garnish with sprigs of parsley; cover and refrigerate until time to serve. Deviled eggs may be made a day or two ahead. Makes 1 dozen.

## CHEESE TWISTS

| | |
|---|---|
| 1 cup butter or margarine | 2 cups grated sharp |
| 2 cups flour | Cheddar cheese |
| 1 teaspoon baking powder | 6 tablespoons cold water |
| | 2 teaspoons Tabasco |
| | sauce |

Cut butter or margarine into sifted flour and baking powder. Add grated cheese and mix well by hand. Combine water and Tabasco sauce; add to dough while mixing. Chill for 30 minutes. Roll like pie crust on a lightly floured board. Cut into 2½"x ½" strips. Twist each strip and place on an ungreased baking sheet. Bake at 325° for 10 minutes. These can be made weeks ahead and frozen until needed. Makes about 13 dozen.

## ROQUEFORT WAFERS

| | |
|---|---|
| ½ pound Roquefort cheese | 1 egg beaten with ½ |
| ¼ pound butter | teaspoon water |
| 1 teaspoon mustard | 1 cup chopped pecans or |
| ¼ to ½ teaspoon salt | walnuts |
| 1¼ cups flour | |

Cut Roquefort and butter into chunks and put into food processor. Blend until mixed and add mustard, salt and flour. Mix well. Remove from the food processor and form into two 1½" diameter logs. Roll the logs in egg mixture and allow to dry 1 minute. Roll in chopped nuts; wrap each roll in wax paper and chill. Cut in thin slices and bake on unbuttered cookie sheet at 425° for 12 to 15 minutes. Makes 30 wafers.

*Note:* Whole logs can be frozen and then thawed and sliced at baking time.

## CRISPY CHEESE WAFERS

4 ounces sharp Cheddar
cheese
1/2 cup (1 stick) butter
1 cup flour

1 cup Rice Krispies
Cayenne
1 teaspoon paprika

Cream Cheddar cheese and butter in mixer. Add flour and mix. Add rest of ingredients and mix well. Make 1"-size balls, place on sheet pan and press with wet fork. Bake 10 minutes at 400°. Makes 4 dozen.

*This recipe from Calumet Farm chef, Richard Paul*

## CHEESE WAFERS

*...can be made ahead; freezes beautifully*

1/4 pound New York sharp
Cheddar cheese, grated
1/2 cup (1 stick) butter or
margarine, softened

1 cup all-purpose flour
Dash of red pepper
1 egg, beaten
Pecan halves

Cream cheese and butter. Combine flour and red pepper; add to creamed mixture, mixing well. Shape dough into small balls and place on ungreased cookie sheet; flatten to 1/4" thickness. Brush wafers with beaten egg, top each with a pecan half. Bake at 350° for 10 to 12 minutes. Remove from pan while hot; sprinkle lightly with salt.

## PECAN - CHEESE WAFERS

1 pound sharp Cheddar
   cheese, grated
1/2 pound (2 sticks) butter,
   softened

2 cups all-purpose flour
2 teaspoons salt
Dash cayenne pepper
1 cup chopped pecans

Cream cheese and butter together, beating well. Add flour, salt and cayenne pepper, stirring until thoroughly mixed. Work in pecans. Shape dough into 2 long rolls; cover with wax paper. Chill until dough can be easily sliced into thin wafers. Place on cookie sheet and bake at 350° for 12 minutes.

*Note:* These wafers freeze very well.

## CHEESE MOLD

Olives and pimiento strips for
   decoration (optional)
1 pound sharp Cheddar
   cheese, grated

1 1/2 pounds cottage
   cheese, drained
Salt and pepper to taste
1 medium onion, grated
2/3 stick butter, melted

Arrange olives and pimiento strips in a decorative design in a buttered mold. Combine remaining ingredients, mixing well with hands; press firmly into mold. Chill at least 12 hours. Dip mold in warm water to remove. Serve with crackers.

## ROQUEFORT CANAPÉS

1 pound Roquefort cheese, at room temperature
1/2 cup (1 stick) butter (no substitute)
1 (8-ounce) package cream cheese
1 1/2 to 2 ounces Cognac or brandy
2 tablespoons minced chives
3/4 cup almonds, toasted and chopped

Blend Roquefort, butter, cream cheese and brandy until well blended and smooth; add chives. Make a roll of this mixture on wax paper the size of a fifty cent piece in diameter. Chill thoroughly; roll in almonds. Slice thin and put on unsalted crackers or Melba toast rounds.
*Note:* Do not use a food processor (will be too runny).

## CHEESE STRAWS

1 1/2 cups flour
1 teaspoon baking powder
1/2 teaspoon salt
1/4 teaspoon red pepper
1 (10-ounce) package extra sharp Cracker Barrel cheese
1 stick Parkay margarine, softened

Sift together the first 4 ingredients; set aside. Grate or grind cheese; combine with margarine and flour mixture, blending well. Place dough in a pastry tube to make straws or use a 1 1/2" ribbon disk on a cookie press to make ribbons. Cut into 2" lengths on an ungreased cookie sheet. Bake at 350° for 10 to 12 minutes or until edges turn light brown.

## PEPPER JELLY

3/4 cup chopped sweet bell
  peppers
2/3 cup chopped banana
  peppers
1/3 cup chopped hot peppers

1 1/2 cups white wine
  vinegar
6 cups sugar
6 ounces Certo
A few drops of green food
  coloring

Place chopped peppers and 1/2 cup of vinegar in the container of an electric blender; blend and set aside. Bring remaining cup of vinegar and sugar to boil. Add pepper mixture and return to boil; boil for one minute. Remove from heat; add Certo and food coloring. Ladle into sterilized jars, adding lids directly out of boiling water. Secure with tops. Makes about 12 pints.

## WALNUT-CHEESE OLIVES

1/4 cup (1/2 stick) butter,
  softened
4 ounces cream cheese,
  softened
4 ounces Roquefort or blue
  cheese, softened
2 tablespoons minced shallots
2 teaspoons brandy

1/4 teaspoon dry mustard
Salt
White pepper
1 cup chopped
  lightly-toasted walnuts
24 to 36 pitted small green
  olives

In a bowl, combine first 8 ingredients and mix thoroughly. Chill, covered, for 30 minutes or until mixture is firm enough to hold its shape. Finely chop walnuts and put them in a shallow dish. Pat olives dry with paper towels. Coat olives with the cheese mixture and roll them in the walnuts; place on a platter, cover and chill for 30 minutes or until firm.

## PEANUT BARS

1 loaf sandwich bread
1 (12-ounce) jar smooth
   peanut butter
1 1/2 cups salad oil

Dried parsley flakes
Seasoned salt
Red pepper flakes

Trim crusts from bread slices and place crusts on cookie sheet. Cut each slice of bread lengthwise into 4 strips; place strips on another cookie sheet. Bake both sheets at 250° for about 1 hour, until bread has dried out and is light brown. Combine peanut butter and salad oil, mixing until smooth. Crumble bread crusts; add enough parsley to be noticeable; add salt and red pepper to taste. Dip each bread finger into peanut butter mixture; prop against a bowl to drain for a few minutes. Roll fingers in crumb mixture and place on a cookie sheet to dry. Makes 5 dozen.

*Note:* These can be stored in a tight container or frozen.

## WATERCRESS SANDWICHES

1 (3-ounce) package cream
   cheese, softened
1 tablespoon lemon juice
1/2 cup sour cream
1 teaspoon finely chopped
   chives
Cayenne pepper to taste
Salt to taste

Dash of Worcestershire
   sauce
1 cup watercress,
   chopped and lightly
   packed into cup
18 slices white bread,
   crusts removed
2 tablespoons butter,
   softened

Blend cream cheese, lemon juice, sour cream, chives and seasonings. Stir in watercress. Flatten each slice of bread with a rolling pin. Spread bread with butter and then with sandwich filling. Roll each slice up jelly-roll fashion and arrange the sandwiches seam-side down in a shallow pan. Cover with a damp cloth and chill 1 hour or more. To serve, cut each roll in half so it is about 1 1/2" long. Garnish with a sprig of watercress and serve. These may be made a day ahead. Makes 36 small sandwiches.

# BEVERAGES

## THE KENTUCKY JULEP

THE JULEP is not a miser's beverage, and it reaches its height of conviviality only where friends are gathered together to lend the nectar of their charm to the succulent ingredients, which combine to soothe all of the senses of man. Even as friendship is a nurtured emotion…so is a JULEP born.

One does not dash madly to the ice tray; bombard commercial glasses with characterless lumps of cold; splash whiskey, sugar and water into a blasphemous hodgepodge…stirring the whole with a hasty finger that has only just applied some mint to the conglobberation with the gesture one would use to discard parsley from a main course to his butter plate.

Ah, no! The JULEP is a triumph of leisure! First, one should have a prechilled silver tumbler. He then selects a tender sprig of mint ( the sacrificial mint) which is rubbed with firm, though gentle, pressure around the interior walls of the tumbler, being careful not to crush, or mince, the leaves…it is fragrant taste we are seeking.

Crush ice to the size of pebbles from a clear and running brook until each particle sparkles in the late afternoon sun like the eyes of fairies caught in the morning dew.

Pack the tumbler with these joyous creatures, then feed them sweet nectar brewed of equal parts of sugar and water to the consistency of liquid honey. A teaspoon and a half, poured slowly over the ice, should suffice.

Then fill the tumbler with finest Bourbon…from Kentucky, of course.

Now, stir until a frost appears; add fresh, tender, topleaf sprigs of mint about three inches long, and serve.

Did you ever FEEL such a cool caress?

Did you ever SEE a more relaxing picture?

Did you ever HEAR a more pleasing tune?

Did you ever SMELL a more fragrant odor?

Did you ever TASTE a more enjoyable sip?

What more, then, can you possibly need…except a friend to enjoy a JULEP with you?

*By J. Cabell Breckinridge, a long-time resident of Lexington, Kentucky.*

# BEVERAGES

## HOT DRINK FOR COLD WEATHER

9 cups cranberry juice
9 cups pineapple juice
1 cup brown sugar

4 teaspoons whole cloves
4 sticks cinnamon

Pour cranberry and pineapple juices into a large percolator; place sugar, cloves and cinnamon in percolator basket. Cook as you would coffee.

## EGGNOG

6 eggs, separated
1 cup sugar, divided
1 cup Bourbon whiskey

1 pint whipping cream
1 cup milk
Grated nutmeg

Beat egg whites until stiff but not dry; gradually add 1/3 cup sugar, beating continuously. Beat egg yolks, add 1/3 cup sugar, beating until well blended. Add whiskey very slowly; fold in beaten egg whites. Whip cream until almost stiff; add 1/3 cup sugar and beat until cream holds a peak. Gently fold into egg mixture; stir in milk. Serve very cold with grated nutmeg as desired. Makes 5 pints.

## HUMMERS

2 large scoops premium
   vanilla or coffee ice cream
1 1/2 ounces Kahlua

1 1/2 ounces white rum
1/2 cup crushed ice

Place all ingredients in a blender container; blend until all ice crystals are melted and the mixture is as thick as a milkshake. If necessary, add a little more ice.

## MILK PUNCH

1 cup sugar
1 cup water
1/2 gallon milk
1 quart Bourbon, chilled

1/2 (16.9-ounce) bottle
Crème de Cacao,
chilled
1/2 to 1 gallon vanilla ice
cream

Combine sugar and water in a saucepan; boil 5 minutes to make a simple syrup. Set aside to cool. Mix milk, Bourbon and Crème de Cacao in a chilled punch bowl; stir in syrup. Add 1/2 gallon ice cream and refrigerate until time to serve. If punch becomes too thin, more ice cream may be added. Makes 1 1/2 gallons.

## PICK-ME-UP PUNCH

1 (6-ounce) can frozen
   concentrated lemonade or
   limeade, undiluted
12 oz. grapefuit juice

9 ounces dark rum
9 ounces golden rum
Freshly ground nutmeg

Thaw frozen juices; combine with rum. Pineapple juice or Grenadine may be added. Sprinkle each drink with a dash of nutmeg; garnish with fruit, if desired.

## CHRISTMAS TODDY

16 cubes sugar
9 drops of bitters on each of
   the 16 cubes of sugar
8 after-dinner coffee spoons of
   Marischino cherry juice

1 orange peel, cut in strips
26 ounces Bourbon
   whiskey

Mix, leave orange peel in mixture 36 hours. Remove peel and let sit 30 days. Pour over ice and add cherry.

## WASSAIL BOWL

*...a warming winter beverage*

1 gallon apple cider
½ to ¾ cup dark brown
   sugar, firmly packed
¼ teaspoon salt
1 tablespoon whole allspice
1 tablespoon whole cloves
2 sticks cinnamon bark
2 blades mace (¼ teaspoon)

¼ teaspoon powdered
   ginger
¼ teaspoon grated
   nutmeg
3 oranges, thinly sliced
   and seeded
2 lemons, thinly sliced
   and seeded
1 pint Holland gin

Combine cider, ½ cup sugar and salt in a large pot or kettle; bring to a boil. Put spices on a piece of cloth, tie with string and drop into cider; reduce heat and simmer for 15 minutes. Remove from heat and set aside. If mixture is not sweet enough, add more of the remaining sugar. Before serving, bring to a boil again and remove spice bag. Warm a silver or heavy china bowl by placing over a kettle of boiling water. Add fruit slices and gin to bowl; when warm, pour in boiling spiced cider. Ladle into cups or mugs. Serves 32.

## CHRISTMAS COCKTAIL

½ cup lemon juice
2 quarts orange juice
1 quart pineapple juice
1 quart grapefruit juice

1 cup Grenadine
1 quart good Bourbon
   whiskey

Stir mixture and put in refrigerator overnight or longer. Shake before serving. Add more bourbon if you like the drink stronger.

## MINT TEA

2 cups sugar
2½ cups water
1 cup firmly packed mint
  leaves

Juice of 6 lemons
Juice of 2 oranges
Rind of 1 orange, grated

Boil sugar and water 5 minutes. Cool; add remaining ingredients and let stand for 1 hour. Strain and refrigerate. To serve, combine one part juice mixture with two parts brewed tea. Pour over crushed ice in glasses. Serves 36. Omit orange juice and rind for lemonade tea.

## SPICED ICED TEA

½ cup sugar
5 quarts water
6 tablespoons instant tea
1 (6-ounce) can frozen
  concentrated orange juice,
  thawed

1 (12-ounce) can frozen
  concentrated
  lemonade, thawed
2 tablespoons lemon juice
½ teaspoon cinnamon
¼ teaspoon nutmeg

Stir sugar in water until dissolved; add remaining ingredients, mixing well. Serves 25.

## TOMATO JUICE

*Great for aspic and Bloody Marys*

½ bushel firm ripe tomatoes,
  washed and cut in pieces
2 large onions
1 bunch celery, cut up
15 whole cloves
2 teaspoons mustard seed

1 teaspoon whole
  peppercorns
1 bay leaf
½ cup sugar
Salt to taste (about 1
  teaspoon to 1 quart
  juice)

Combine first 7 ingredients; cook until soft and the juice flows freely. Press through a fine sieve. Add sugar and salt to the strained juice; bring to a good boil. Fill sterilized jars and seal at once with sterilized lids.

# BEVERAGES

## HOT TOMATO JUICE

6 cups canned tomatoes
1 cup chicken stock or
   bouillon
2 medium onions, sliced
3 ribs celery, chopped
1 bay leaf

4 sprigs parsley
1/4 teaspoon savory
1/4 teaspoon dried basil
Salt to taste
Mild vinegar or lemon
   juice to taste

Combine ingredients in a saucepan; bring to a boil. Simmer for 10 minutes; strain and serve hot. Serves 10.

## HOT BRICKS

*...an old favorite of the fox hunters, who talk about having one of these drinks before they take off through the early morning mists on a chilly Thanksgiving*

1 quart Bourbon, 100 proof
  (or at least 90 proof)
1 1/2 quarts water, if using 100
   proof (only 1 quart water, if
   using 90 proof)

2/3 cup sugar
1 stick butter (real butter,
  not margarine)
2 teaspoons ground or
  cracked nutmeg

Boil water; add sugar, butter and nutmeg. Reduce heat to simmer and add Bourbon. *Do not boil after adding booze* (it boils out the alcohol). Serves 12.

## HOT CRANBERRY DRINK

4 cups sugar
4 cups water
2 quarts whole cranberries
4 quarts water

3 quarts orange juice
2 quarts pineapple juice
1 cup lemon juice

Combine sugar and 4 cups water; boil for 3 minutes to make a syrup, then set aside. Boil cranberries in 4 quarts water until berries pop. Cool and strain. Combine sugar syrup and cranberry juice with remaining fruit juices and serve hot. Bourbon or rum may be added, if desired. Makes 3 gallons.

## BROCCOLI BISQUE

1 cup sliced leeks
1 cup sliced mushrooms
3 tablespoons butter or
   margarine
3 tablespoons flour

3 cups chicken broth
1 cup broccoli florets
1 cup light cream or milk
1 cup grated Jarlsburg
   cheese

In a large saucepan, sauté leeks and mushrooms until tender (do not brown). Add flour and cook, stirring, until bubbling. Remove from heat and gradually blend in chicken broth. Return to heat; cook and stir until smooth and thick. Add broccoli; reduce heat and simmer 20 minutes or until broccoli is tender. Blend in cream and cheese and cook until cheese melts.

## SOLID SOUP

*...rich and yummy and simple!*

1 (8-ounce) package cream
   cheese, softened
1 teaspoon curry powder
1 teaspoon lemon juice

1 (10½-ounce) can beef
   consommé, divided
Stuffed green olives,
   sliced, or snipped
   parsley

Put cream cheese, curry powder and one-half of consommé in a blender container; process until smooth. Pour into demi-tasse cups and place in refrigerator; chill about 3 hours or until mixture is solid. Dividing equally, add remaining consommé to cups; chill until firm. For color, garnish each cup with an olive slice or a bit of parsley.

# SOUPS

## MUSHROOM BISQUE

4 tablespoons (¹/₂ stick) butter
¹/₂ pound fresh mushrooms, sliced
¹/₃ cup finely chopped onion
1 tablespoon fresh lemon juice
3 tablespoons flour
4 cups chicken consommé
Salt to taste
¹/₂ teaspoon ground black pepper
2 cups heavy cream
2 ounces dry sherry (good grade)
Chopped parsley

Melt butter and sauté mushrooms and onions for 4 to 5 minutes, stirring constantly. Sprinkle with lemon juice. Blend in flour; gradually stir in consommé, salt and pepper. Stir while cooking until mixture is slightly thickened. Add cream and sherry; heat thoroughly. Sprinkle with parsley and serve immediately. Serves 12.

## OYSTER BISQUE

*... this soup is best made the day before*

4 cups oysters
4 tablespoons butter
4 tablespoons minced green onions
4 tablespoons chopped celery
4 tablespoons flour
1 cup chicken stock, heated
3 cups milk, heated
1 teaspoon salt
1 teaspoon freshly ground pepper
Paprika
2 tablespoons minced parsley

Drain oysters and reserve liquor. In a heavy pot, heat the "naked" oysters until the edges curl. Remove oysters from pot and melt butter in it. Add onions and celery and sauté until soft. Add flour and cook 4 to 5 minutes, stirring constantly. Stir in the stock, milk and oyster liquor and cook until thickened slightly. Pureé vegetables and sauce in a food processor or blender. Add seasoning and oysters. When re-heating, use a double boiler. Top each serving with paprika and then parsley.

## CLEAR MUSHROOM BROTH

2 pounds mushrooms
2 quarts water
1 tablespoon beef extract
1/2 teaspoon salt

Pepper to taste
Dash of dry Vermouth

Wash mushrooms and chop finely, including stems. Simmer in water, covered, for 3 hours. Strain, pressing pulp until dry; discard pulp. Reheat broth; add beef extract, salt and pepper. Just before serving, stir in Vermouth. Serves 8.

## CRAB BISQUE

1 onion, minced
2 tablespoons butter
1 tablespoon flour
1 (10 1/2-ounce) can condensed
   tomato soup

1 quart half-and-half
2 (6-ounce) cans crabmeat
Salt and pepper to taste
1/4 cup sherry

Sauté onion in butter; blend in flour. Add tomato soup and gradually stir in half-and-half. Cook 10 minutes but do not boil. Add crabmeat and season to taste; heat thoroughly. Stir in sherry just before serving.

## TOMATO BOUILLON

4 cups tomato juice
2 (10 1/2-ounce) cans beef
   consommé, undiluted
4 whole cloves
8 peppercorns

1/2 bay leaf
1/2 teaspoon salt
1 small onion, quartered
Pinch of basil
Parsley and celery tops

Combine all ingredients and simmer gently for 30 minutes. Strain and correct seasoning. Serve hot or cold. If used hot, put a dollop of whipped cream on top of each serving. Serves 8.

# SOUPS

## KENTUCKY BURGOO

2 pounds beef, cubed
Soup bone
1/2 pound lamb, cubed
1 frying chicken, cut up
4 quarts water
Salt and pepper to taste
Red pepper to taste
2 cups diced potatoes
3 cups chopped onions

2 cups lima beans
4 carrots, diced
2 green peppers, diced
3 cups corn (fresh, if
    possible)
2 cups okra, diced
6 cups tomatoes
1/2 teaspoon garlic
1 cup minced parsley

Put the beef, soup bone, lamb, chicken, water, salt, pepper, and red pepper in a heavy pot with a tight-fitting lid. Bring to a boil, then simmer, covered, for two hours. Remove the chicken skin and bones and cut meat into bite-sized pieces. Return meat to pot. Add potatoes, onions, lima beans, carrots, green peppers, and corn. Simmer two hours. Mixture will be thick but should not stick. Add water sparingly, if necessary. Add okra, tomatoes, and garlic and simmer 1 1/2 hours longer. Add parsley and remove from stove. This soup will keep in refrigerator for a long time. The flavor improves with standing. Makes 10 servings.

## SQUASH SOUP

1 medium onion, chopped
1 tablespoon butter
2 (14 1/2-ounce) cans chicken
    broth

4 to 5 yellow squash
Salt and pepper
Dash of red pepper
1 pint light or heavy
    cream

Sauté onion in butter until transparent. Add broth and squash and cook over medium heat until tender. Cool; process in blender until smooth. Add seasonings and cream. Chill for several hours. Serves 6.

## CHEESE SOUP

³/₄ cup finely chopped carrots
³/₄ cup finely chopped celery
³/₄ cup finely chopped
   scallions
2 cups boiling water
¹/₄ pound (1 stick) butter
1 medium onion, finely
   chopped
³/₄ cup flour
4 cups boiling milk

4 cups boiling chicken
   stock (canned may be
   used)
1¹/₂ pounds sharp
   Cheddar cheese, grated
2 tablespoons Mr.
   Mustard
Black pepper and cayenne
   pepper, to taste
Salt (use very little if
   cheese is salty)

Boil the carrots, celery and scallions in the boiling water for 5 minutes. Melt butter in a large pot and sauté onion for 1 minute; blend in flour. Add broth and milk slowly, stirring constantly, until well blended and smooth. Add cheese, mustard, seasonings, vegetables and cooking liquid. Blend in a blender on medium speed until very smooth; serve hot.

## CARROT SOUP

1 pound carrots, sliced in
   large pieces
2 ounces butter
2 medium onions, coarsely
   chopped
1 small clove garlic, minced
1 potato, diced

1 teaspoon cornstarch
³/₄ pint water
³/₄ pint milk
Salt and freshly ground
   pepper
Parsley, chopped

Place carrots, butter, onions and garlic in a saucepan. Bring to a boil, cover, reduce the heat and cook for 15 minutes. Add the potato, cornstarch, water, and milk, and simmer for 25 minutes. Season to taste with salt and freshly ground pepper. Add chopped parsley and transfer to an electric blender. Blend on high. Garnish with additional chopped parsley and serve hot. May be served chilled. This recipe may be prepared a day ahead or may be frozen.

## CARROT AND ORANGE SOUP

1 1/4 pounds carrots, scraped
   and sliced
1 medium onion, diced
3 1/2 cups orange juice
1 1/2 cups strong chicken broth

1/4 teaspoon cinnamon
1/4 teaspoon mace
1/4 teaspoon nutmeg
Pepper to taste
1 cup sour cream

Combine carrots, onion, orange juice and chicken broth in a saucepan; simmer until vegetables are tender. Add cinnamon, mace, nutmeg and pepper. Pour mixture into a blender container and purée until smooth. Chill well; fold in sour cream.

*Note:* It is important to use sweet carrots. California carrots or those with the tops still on are best.

## CRAB-AVOCADO SOUP

4 large avocados, medium-ripe
1 tablespoon minced onion
1 large clove garlic (optional)
2 3/4 cups heavy cream
1/2 cup sour cream
3 tablespoons instant chicken
   bouillon dissolved in 1/4 cup
   boiling water

2 tablespoons lemon juice
1 tablespoon light rum
1/2 teaspoon salt
1/4 teaspoon white pepper
   or Tabasco sauce
6 ounces fresh or frozen
   crabmeat, well drained
Sour cream

Peel avocados and place pulp in an electric blender container with onion and garlic, if desired; process until puréed. Combine with remaining ingredients, stirring in crabmeat last. This soup is best served cold with a dollop of sour cream but may also be served hot. Serves 3 to 4.

## GREEN ONION SOUP

12 green onions, chopped
  (stems and all)
3 medium potatoes, peeled
  and thinly sliced
4 cups chicken stock
1 (10³/₄-ounce) can cream of
  celery soup, undiluted

³/₄ cup evaporated milk
1 tablespoon butter or
  margarine
¹/₂ teaspoon salt
¹/₄ teaspoon pepper

Cook green onions and potatoes in chicken stock until tender, about 10 minutes. Strain, reserving liquid. Place cooked vegetables, canned soup and milk in the container of a food processor or blender; process until smooth. Add to reserved liquid and heat slowly. Stir in butter, salt and pepper. Serve hot or cold. Makes 4 to 6 servings.

## ONION SOUP

3 tablespoons butter
1 tablespoon oil
1¹/₂ pounds yellow onions,
  thinly sliced
1 teaspoon salt
¹/₄ teaspoon sugar
3 tablespoons flour
2 quarts boiling beef bouillon

¹/₂ cup dry white wine
Salt and pepper to taste
3 tablespoons Cognac
Rounds of French bread,
  toasted hard
1 to 2 cups grated Swiss
  cheese

Heat butter and oil in a saucepan; add onions and cook, covered, over low heat for 15 minutes. Uncover; stir in salt and sugar. Cook over medium heat for 30 to 40 minutes, stirring often. Sprinkle flour on onions and stir for 3 minutes. Turn off heat; add boiling bouillon, wine, salt and pepper. Simmer 30 to 40 minutes longer, partially covered. Just before serving, add Cognac. Place a round of French bread in each cup, fill with soup and serve with cheese. Serves 6.

# SOUPS

## CREAM OF PIMIENTO SOUP

3 tablespoons butter
3 tablespoons flour
3/4 teaspoon salt
Few grains pepper
1 1/2 cups milk

1 (4-ounce) jar whole
    pimientos, drained
1/2 teaspoon grated onion
1 1/2 cups chicken broth,
    fresh or canned

In a 2-quart saucepan, melt butter over low heat; add flour, salt and pepper. Cook and stir for 1 minute; slowly pour in milk, stirring constantly, until sauce is smooth and thickened. Remove any seeds and skin clinging to pimientos. Put pimientos, onion and broth in a blender container and process on "purée" for no more than 10 seconds, just until pimiento is finely minced. Add mixture to sauce in saucepan; re-heat before serving. This soup may also be served cold. Serves 4.

*Note:* For a richer soup, substitute half-and-half for one-third of milk.

## TOMATO-CELERY SOUP

1 small onion, chopped
1/2 cup finely chopped celery
2 tablespoons butter
1 (10 1/2-ounce) can tomato
    soup, diluted with 1 can
    water

1 teaspoon minced
    parsley
1 tablespoon lemon juice
1 teaspoon sugar
1/4 teaspoon salt
1/8 teaspoon pepper
Whipped cream

Sauté onion and celery in butter; do not brown. Add remaining ingredients and simmer for 5 minutes (the celery will remain crisp). Top each cup of soup with a spoonful of unsweetened whipped cream; garnish with additional chopped parsley.

*This is a Shakertown recipe.*

## GAZPACHO

2 cucumbers, peeled,
    quartered and seeded
1 medium-sized onion, peeled
    and quartered
1 medium-sized green pepper,
    quartered and seeded
2 (12-ounce) cans V-8 juice

2 tablespoons white wine
    vinegar
2 tablespoons good olive
    oil
1 teaspoon ground cumin
Salt and coarsely-ground
    black pepper to taste

Put first four ingredients into container of electric blender; cover and process at "chop" until vegetables are finely chopped. Stir in remaining ingredients and chill. Makes 6 servings.

## VICHYSSOISE

¼ cup sliced onions
3 tablespoons butter
2 cups thinly sliced potatoes
2 cups chicken stock
1½ cups milk
1 cup cream
1 teaspoon salt

3 to 4 drops Tabasco
    sauce
Dash of Worcestershire
    sauce
3 tablespoons chopped
    chives

Sauté onions in butter until transparent. Add potatoes and chicken stock; simmer until vegetables are soft. Put the mixture in a food processor or blender and purée. Return to saucepan and add milk; allow to come to a boil. Remove from heat; let cool, then add cream and seasonings. Refrigerate in a sealed glass jar until very cold. Serve in cups; sprinkle with chives. Serves 8.

# SOUPS

## EASY VICHYSSOISE

*This is not only easy but so delicious you will never use another recipe.*

2 (10 ounce) cans condensed chicken broth, Campbell's
1 (3¼ ounce) individual package Pillsbury's "Idaho Mashed Potatoes" Granules (no substitute)
1 teaspoon celery salt
1 teaspoon onion powder
2 cups half-and-half

Put broth in saucepan, add seasonings, bring to a boil. Add potatoes and stir out all lumps. Blend in half-and-half and allow to cool. Refrigerate and serve very cold.

## ZUCCHINI SOUP

1 cup boiling water
1 teaspoon salt
2 pounds young zucchini, diced
2 cups milk
1 cup chopped onion
½ garlic clove, minced
2 tablespoons butter
2 cups light cream
1 teaspoon sugar
Salt and pepper to taste
Sour cream

Add water and salt to zucchini in saucepan. Bring to boil; cover and simmer just until zucchini is tender. Add milk to stop the cooking. Meanwhile, sauté onion and garlic in butter until tender. Blend zucchini and onion in blender just until smooth. Add cream, sugar, salt and pepper. Heat to serving temperature or chill. Serve either hot or very cold with a dollop of sour cream.

## FILET DE BOEUF A LA CRÈME TOMATE

*To make your picnic a special one, include these beef roll-ups*

¹/₄ pound (1 stick) butter,  1 whole beef tenderloin
    softened

To cook tenderloin rare, preheat oven to 500.° Spread butter all over meat; put in a roasting pan and place in hot oven. Immediately reduce the temperature to 350°; bake for 20 minutes or until meat thermometer registers 120.° (The meat will continue to cook a little after it leaves the oven.) Allow meat to cool, then refrigerate. When ready to use, cut into thin slices. Spread each slice with Creme Tomate and roll up.

*Crème Tomate*

¹/₄ cup minced onions  1 bay leaf
2 tablespoons butter  1 (8-ounce) package
4 large, ripe tomatoes, peeled,      cream cheese
    seeded and chopped, *or* 4  2 cloves garlic, peeled and
    canned tomatoes, drained      crushed
¹/₂ teaspoon salt  2 tablespoons basil
¹/₄ teaspoon cracked pepper  ¹/₈ teaspoon Tabasco
¹/₄ teaspoon sugar      sauce
Pinch of thyme  ¹/₂ cup heavy cream

Sauté onions in butter until soft; add tomatoes, salt, pepper, sugar, thyme and bay leaf. Simmer, covered, over low heat for 10 to 12 minutes. Remove cover and cook over medium-high heat for 10 minutes or until much of the liquid has evaporated and the sauce is very thick. Strain through a sieve and cool. Place ³/₄ cup sauce in the container of a blender or food processor; add remaining ingredients and blend for 5 to 6 seconds.

# MEAT

## FOOLPROOF RARE ROAST BEEF

*...can be cooked several hours in advance and re-heated before serving*

1 beef rib roast (3 or 4 ribs)     Salt and pepper

Have roast at room temperature. Trim off excess fat, season with salt and pepper and place, fat side up, on a rack in a roasting pan. Preheat oven to 375°; roast meat for exactly 50 minutes. Turn off heat, leaving meat in oven until shortly before serving time. *Do not open oven door at any time.* To re-heat, set oven temperature at 300.° Heat a 3-rib roast for 25 minutes or a 4-rib roast for 30 to 35 minutes. The roast will be rare and ready to carve immediately.

*Note:* It is important that the oven not be opened from the time the roast is placed in the oven until the final re-heating is completed.

## HENRY CLAY'S FAVORITE POT ROAST

1 (4-pound) boneless rump or      Salt and black pepper
   sirloin tip roast         to taste
2 small onions, stuck with 2      Pinch of allspice
   cloves in each      1/2 teaspoon sugar
2 large carrots      2 tablespoons flour
1 red pepper pod         dissolved in 1/4 cup
1 1/2 cups boiling water         warm water

Place beef in Dutch oven with tight-fitting lid; add onions, carrots, red pepper, salt, pepper and allspice. Pour boiling water over beef. Return to a boil; cover and simmer slowly for 6 hours. Remove beef and vegetables; place on warm platter. Strain pan juices, removing all grease. Place sugar in Dutch oven, stirring until brown; pour strained juices over it. Add dissolved flour, stirring until thick. Slice beef and serve with gravy and vegetables.

## POT ROAST WITH RED WINE

3-4 pounds lean beef
1 1/2 cups red wine (Bordeaux)
2 large onions, sliced
1 lemon, sliced
2 tablespoons sugar
1 teaspoon salt

1 teaspoon ginger (may be
  omitted)
12 whole black
  peppercorns
4 tablespoons fat
2 tablespoons flour

Place meat in a deep bowl and add all ingredients except fat and flour. Meat should be more than half covered with wine. Let stand 18-24 hours in a cold place turning occasionally. Remove the meat, pat dry, then brown in 2 tablespoons of fat in a heavy kettle. Add the wine in which it was soaked. Cover the kettle and simmer 3-4 hours. Add a little water if it cooks dry. When tender, lift out meat. In the kettle melt 2 tablespoons fat, stir in the flour and brown lightly. Add the liquid, stir, and cook until thickened. Put the meat in the gravy and heat 5 minutes longer. Serves 8.

## FILET OF BEEF

2 cloves minced garlic
1/2 cup (1 stick) butter, melted
2 tablespoons medium-grind
  pepper

1/2 cup red wine (optional)
1 filet of beef

Sauté garlic in butter; add pepper and wine, if desired. Pour mixture over beef; let stand until meat is at room temperature. Bake at 425° for 20 minutes until rare or medium rare. If not done enough, return to oven. (Remember that it will continue to cook after it is removed from oven.) Serve with Sauce Maison, page 172.

## TERIYAKI SHISH KABOB

½ cup soy sauce
½ cup honey
¼ cup sherry
1 teaspoon grated orange rind
1 clove garlic, minced
2 pounds sirloin steak, cut
   into 20 large cubes
20 raw, large shrimp, peeled
   (all but tail section)

1 fresh pineapple, cored
   and cut into 20 wedges
5 green onions, cut into
   1½" to 2" pieces
1 large green pepper, cut
   into 20 pieces
2 tablespoons cornstarch

Combine first 5 ingredients to make a marinade; add cubed steak and shrimp. Allow to stand 3 to 4 hours, stirring occasionally; drain, reserving marinade. To prepare small shish kabobs for appetizers, thread a pineapple wedge, a shrimp, a green onion sliver, a steak cube and a piece of green pepper on each cocktail skewer. For dinner portions, prepare 8 long skewers with at least twice the number of ingredients. Mix cornstarch with reserved marinade in a saucepan; boil until clear. Place skewers on the rack of a broiler pan; brush shish kabobs with marinade. Place pan 5" under broiler and broil for 3 minutes until shrimp turns pink. Turn over and brush other side with marinade; broil 5 minutes longer. Serve at once. Makes 20 cocktail portions or 8 dinner portions.

## MEAT LOAF WITH TOMATO SAUCE

1 egg
1 green pepper, chopped
1 onion, chopped
2 pounds ground beef

¼ pound very lean pork
1 cup sour cream
¾ cup finely crushed
   saltine crackers

Combine egg with green pepper and onion. Using 2 forks, lightly mix beef and pork. Add chopped vegetable mixture, sour cream and crushed crackers. Shape mixture into a loaf; place in a lightly greased 1-quart baking dish. Bake at 425° for 45 to 60 minutes.

*Continued...*

## MEAT LOAF WITH TOMATO SAUCE, *Continued*

*Tomato Sauce*

3 tablespoons olive oil
1 Bermuda onion, chopped
1/2 green pepper, chopped
2 ribs celery with leaves, sliced
1 carrot, sliced
4 cups tomatoes, peeled and mashed

1/2 bay leaf
1/2 teaspoon sweet basil
1/2 teaspoon oregano
1 teaspoon brown sugar
1 teaspoon salt
1/8 teaspoon pepper

Heat oil over low heat; stir in onion, pepper, celery and carrot. Sauté for 5 minutes, stirring constantly. Add tomatoes and remaining ingredients. Cook gently for 45 minutes until sauce thickens. Watch carefully to prevent burning. Strain sauce and adjust seasoning; serve hot over meat loaf. Sauce will keep for several days in refrigerator.

## BEEF-EGGPLANT PARMESAN

1 1/2 pounds ground beef
1 onion, chopped
1 (15-ounce) can tomato sauce
1 teaspoon garlic powder
1 teaspoon oregano
1 teaspoon salt
1 teaspoon pepper
1/2 teaspoon basil

1 medium- large eggplant
2 eggs
3 tablespoons water
3 tablespoons flour
1/2 pound mozzarella cheese, grated
4 ounces Parmesan cheese, grated

Brown beef and onion; add tomato sauce and seasonings. Simmer while preparing the eggplant. Peel and slice eggplant in 1/4" slices; place on paper towels to drain. Sprinkle with salt. Beat eggs and water; add flour and beat with a wire whisk until fairly smooth. Heat just enough oil in a large skillet to coat the bottom. Add more, if needed. Dip eggplant slices in batter and fry until brown; drain on paper towels. In a casserole, alternate layers of eggplant, sauce and both cheeses, ending with a layer of cheeses. Cover and refrigerate until ready to heat. Bake at 350° for about 45 minutes. Serves 4.

# MEAT

## SPAGHETTI CASSEROLE

2 tablespoons butter
1 clove garlic
1 teaspoon sugar
1 teaspoon salt
Pepper to taste
1½ pounds lean ground beef
2 (8 ounce) cans tomato sauce
1 (8 ounce) package spaghetti

1 (3 ounce) package cream
   cheese, softened
1½ cups sour cream
6 green onions, chopped
½ pound Cheddar
   cheese, grated

Place butter in a cold skillet; add garlic and mash with sugar, salt and pepper. Cook until butter is melted, then add meat and brown. Add tomato sauce and simmer, uncovered, for 20 minutes. Cook spaghetti according to package directions. Combine cream cheese, sour cream and green onions. Place spaghetti in a greased 13"x9" casserole; top with cream cheese mixture and then meat mixture. Sprinkle with Cheddar cheese. Bake, uncovered, at 350° for about 30 minutes, until hot and bubbly. Serves 6 to 8.

## CHEESE-STUFFED MEATLOAF

½ pound mozzarella cheese,
   not sliced
2 pounds lean ground beef
2 eggs
½ cup packaged seasoned
   bread crumbs
1 cup tomato juice

½ teaspoon salt
1 teaspoon oregano
Freshly ground pepper
   to taste
2 small onions, minced
7 to 8 paper-thin slices
   boiled ham

*Continued...*

## CHEESE-STUFFED MEATLOAF, *Continued*

Grate cheese, set aside. Combine beef, eggs, bread crumbs, tomato juice, salt, oregano and pepper. Sauté onions in a little vegetable oil until golden brown; add to meat mixture; mix well. Turn out on sheet of aluminum foil, flatten into oblong loaf about 1" thick. Place ham slices on meat mixture keeping them about 1" from the edge. Sprinkle grated cheese on the ham. Using foil to help, fold the meat mixture jelly-roll style over the ham and cheese, closing all openings. Turn the loaf from the foil into a baking pan and shape into loaf. Bake at 325° for 1 hour. Serves 6 to 8.

## VEAL PARMIGIANA

| | |
|---|---|
| 1 cup bread crumbs | 2 (8-ounce) cans tomato |
| 3/4 cup grated Parmesan | sauce |
| cheese, divided | 1 1/2 teaspoons basil |
| 12 thin slices veal | 1/2 teaspoon thyme |
| 2 eggs, slightly beaten | 1/2 teaspoon onion salt |
| 1 cup chopped onion | 1/2 teaspoon salt |
| 4 tablespoons olive oil, | Pepper to taste |
| divided | 2 tablespoons butter |
| 4 tomatoes | 8 ounces mozzarella |
| | cheese, sliced |

Combine bread crumbs and 1/4 cup Parmesan cheese. Dip veal slices in egg, then coat well with crumb mixture; let stand. In a saucepan, sauté onion in 2 tablespoons olive oil until crisp-tender; add tomatoes, tomato sauce, herbs and seasonings. Cover and simmer 15 to 20 minutes. Heat butter and remaining olive oil in a skillet; brown veal a few slices at a time. Arrange in a 13"x 9"x 2" baking dish; cover with mozzarella slices and pour sauce over all. Sprinkle with remaining 1/2 cup Parmesan. Bake at 350° for 15 to 20 minutes. Serves 8.

## VEAL SCALLOPINI

1/4 cup flour
1/2 cup grated Parmesan
  cheese
1/2 teaspoon salt
Dash of black pepper
1 1/2 pounds veal cutlets,
  thinly sliced
2 tablespoons olive oil

1 large (or 2 small) cloves
  garlic
1/2 cup dry white wine
1/2 cup stock or
  consommé
1 tablespoon lemon juice
1 tablespoon chopped
  parsley

Combine flour, Parmesan cheese, salt and pepper. Pound into both sides of cutlets. Heat oil in skillet and add garlic. Lightly brown meat on both sides; remove garlic. Add wine, leftover flour-cheese mixture, consommé and lemon juice. Cover and simmer slowly for 20 minutes. Garnish with parsley. Serves 6.

## VEAL MARSALA

1 pound veal, thinly sliced
4 ounces freshly grated
  Parmesan cheese
1/2 pound fresh mushrooms
3 tablespoons butter
1 tablespoon Kitchen Bouquet

5 ounces beef bouillon
2/3 cup Marsala wine
2/3 cup water
2 1/2 tablespoons
  cornstarch

Cut veal into medallions and pound until thin; press the Parmesan cheese into both sides of the meat. Sauté mushrooms in butter, then remove mushrooms and sauté veal medallions until lightly brown. Return mushrooms to pan, add Kitchen Bouquet and beef bouillon. Cook 2 to 3 minutes over low heat. Add Marsala wine and cook 2 more minutes. Add cornstarch dissolved in water and cook until thickened. Serves 4.

## CURRIED VEAL PAPRIKA

4 pounds veal shoulder, cut in
  1 1/2" cubes
1/2 cup (1 stick) butter
2 teaspoons salt
1 tablespoon sugar
4 teaspoons curry powder
1 1/4 teaspoons pepper
1/4 teaspoon paprika
1 (10 1/2-ounce) can condensed
  beef broth, undiluted

2 1/2 cups sour cream
2/3 cup all-purpose flour
2/3 cup water
1 cup snipped parsley
1 (8-ounce) package wide
  noodles, cooked
1/4 cup almond slivers,
  roasted
1/2 teaspoon poppy seed

Brown veal, one-third at a time, in hot butter in a Dutch oven. Remove to plate; sprinkle with salt, sugar, curry powder, pepper and paprika. Add broth and sour cream; stir in flour, blended smooth with water. Add parsley; simmer for 1 hour. Arrange noodles in a large baking dish. Put veal in the center; top with almonds and poppy seed. Cover with foil and bake at 350° for 15 minutes.

## SWEETBREADS SUZANNE

2 pairs sweetbreads
1/2 pound butter
1 heaping tablespoon very
  finely grated onion

2 cups cream
Salt and pepper

Parboil and blanch sweetbreads; cut into 8 equal parts. Put butter in a frying pan over high heat; when butter is frothing, add onion and stir until well blended. Add sweetbreads and sauté them, turning very gently until they are light, golden brown. Remove and drain on paper towels. Pour cream into the frying pan; stir until slightly thickened, then season to taste. Place sweetbreads on a warm serving dish and pour over sauce. Serve at once.

## ROYAL DANIELI CALVES LIVER

¼ cup butter
¼ teaspoon sage
2 cups thinly sliced onions
1 pound calves' liver
¼ cup flour
½ teaspoon salt

⅛ teaspoon pepper
3 tablespoons dry white
   wine
3 tablespoons beef stock
1 tablespoon minced
   parsley

Melt butter in skillet. Add sage and onions; sauté for 10 minutes. Cut liver into thin strips, removing skin and veins. Combine flour, salt and pepper in a brown paper bag. Add liver; shake until coated with flour mixture. Add liver to onions; cook 5 minutes over medium-high heat, stirring constantly. Transfer to a warm serving dish. Put wine, beef stock and parsley in skillet and cook for 1 minute; pour over liver and serve immediately.

## LAMB FRIES

Lamb fries
1 cup milk
1 egg, beaten

1 teaspoon Tabasco sauce
Salt and black pepper to
   taste
Oil for frying

Peel and quarter lamb fries. Soak in salted water for 5 minutes. Combine remaining ingredients. Dip fries in mixture; fry in hot oil. Serve with cream sauce.

*Cream Sauce*
1 tablespoon flour
1 tablespoon butter, melted
1 tablespoon oil used in frying
   fries

1 cup milk
Salt and pepper to taste

Brown flour in butter and oil; gradually add milk, stirring constantly. Season to taste.

## LEG OF LAMB

1 (5- to 6-pound) leg of lamb,
    with little visible fat
Salt
1/4 cup finely-chopped parsley
1 tablespoon dried rosemary
1 tablespoon olive oil

2 cloves garlic, crushed
1/4 teaspoon salt
1 1/4 cups chicken broth
18 to 20 new potatoes,
    parboiled (optional)

Wipe meat with a damp cloth; rub with salt. With a sharp knife, cut several slits in the leg. Combine parsley, rosemary, olive oil, garlic and 1/4 teaspoon salt; insert some of the mixture into each slit and spread the rest all over the leg. Place the meat in a roasting pan skin-side-down on a rack; do not cover. Roast in a 325° oven for 2 1/2 to 3 hours, basting frequently with chicken broth. If desired, place potatoes in pan with meat during the last cooking hour, basting and turning often. For easy carving, allow the leg of lamb to be out of the oven 30 minutes before serving time for it to set. Pour pan juices into a narrow jar; skim off fat, reserving 1/4 cup. Add water to juices if needed to measure 2 cups.

*Gravy*
1/4 cup fat
1/4 cup flour

2 cups pan juices
Salt and pepper

Blend fat and flour; stir and cook until lightly browned. Add pan juices slowly and bring to boiling point, stirring constantly. Lower heat and simmer for 5 minutes. Season to taste and pour into a heated gravy boat or bowl.

## BROILED RACK OF LAMB

6- to 8-chop rack of lamb
Butter

Rosemary

Have the butcher clean the ends of the rib bones of a 6- to 8-chop rack of lamb. Dot the meat with butter and rosemary and brown it under the broiler. Turn it once to brown both sides. This will take 30 minutes, and the bone ends should be well charred. Cover the charred bone ends with paper frills and serve at once. Serves 3.

## BOILED KENTUCKY COUNTRY HAM

1 (12- to 14-pound)  
  sugar-cured Kentucky ham

6 ounces molasses  
2 tablespoons whole  
  cloves

Using a scrub brush, brush ham well in cold water, to remove mold and dirt. Place ham in a lard can, cover with cold water and soak at least 24 hours. Pour off water and cut hock off ham. Place an aluminum foil pie pan in the bottom of the lard can. Put ham in can and add enough fresh, cold water to completely cover. Bring to a boil; add molasses and cloves. Boil, uncovered, for 1 1/2 hours. Put a wooden dough board or chopping block on the floor, then about 4 thicknesses of newspaper. Set ham (still in can) on papers. Be sure ham is completely covered in hot liquid. Press can lid on tightly; pull papers around sides and top of can, and tie with string. Cover with old quilts or blankets. Let sit for 11 to 16 hours, according to size of ham. (A 12-pound ham requires 11 to 12 hours, a 13-pound ham requires 12 to 14 hours, and a 14-pound ham requires 14 to 16 hours.) Unwrap; carefully remove from water, using two large meat forks. Put on a platter; trim skin and fat from ham and remove bone. Spread ham with Glaze.

*Glaze*  
1 cup light brown sugar,  
  firmly packed

1 cup cornmeal  
1/4 cup pineapple juice

Combine ingredients and spread on top of ham; place under a broiler for 2 to 3 minutes until browned.

Cool ham to room temperature before carving. Slice tissue-paper thin; that's the Kentucky way.

## BAKED KENTUCKY COUNTRY HAM

1 country ham, preferably
  about 18 months old
1/2 cup whole cloves

1 cup brown sugar
1 cup vinegar
1 1/2 gallons water

Scrub ham with stiff brush to remove any mold. Immerse, skin side up, in cold water and soak overnight. Sprinkle 1/4 cup cloves in the bottom of a large roaster. Add ham, fat side up, and stick remaining cloves in fat. Add brown sugar, vinegar and water to roaster; cover and bake at 375° for 1 hour. Lower heat to 275° and bake an additional 20 minutes per pound. Cool; trim off fat. If desired, remove bone and tie ham securely with string. Refrigerate overnight. Remove string from ham; cover with Topping and bake at 350° until brown.

*Topping*
1 cup brown sugar
1 cup cornmeal

1 tablespoon ground
  cloves
1 teaspoon cinnamon

Combine ingredients and mix thoroughly.

## HAM WITH SHERRY

1/4 cup butter
1 (1 1/2" thick) slice of cooked
  ham, center cut
1/4 cup brown sugar

1 cup sherry
2 teaspoons cornstarch
1/4 cup water

Melt butter in a heavy skillet and saute ham slice until nicely browned. Remove ham to a platter and place in a low oven to keep warm. Put brown sugar and sherry in the skillet; stir until sugar dissolves. Make a paste of cornstarch and water; add to sherry mixture, stirring constantly until thickened and smooth. Return ham to the skillet; simmer in sauce for 10 minutes, turning to cook both sides evenly. Put ham on platter and pour sauce. Serves 6 to 8, depending on size of ham slice.

# MEAT

## HAM TIMBALES WITH EGG SAUCE

1 cup ground, cooked ham
   (preferably Kentucky
   country ham)
1 cup dry bread crumbs
1 cup milk
4 tablespoons butter, softened
2 egg yolks, beaten
1 tablespoon chopped parsley

1 tablespoon grated onion
   or onion juice
1/8 teaspoon pepper
2 dashes of
   Worcestershire sauce
2 egg whites, stiffly beaten
   with a pinch of salt

Combine all ingredients except egg whites, mixing thoroughly; fold in egg whites. Grease 4 small ramekins and fill two-thirds full with ham mixture. Set in a pan of hot water and bake at 350° about 1/2 hour until set. Unmold onto a warm platter and serve with Egg Sauce. Serves 4.

*Egg Sauce*
2 tablespoons butter
1 tablespoon flour
1 1/2 cups half-and-half

Salt and white pepper
2 hard-cooked eggs, finely
   chopped
Paprika

Melt butter and blend in flour; slowly add half-and-half and cook until sauce is thickened, stirring constantly. Season to taste with salt and white pepper; stir in chopped eggs. Pour sauce over ham timbales and sprinkle with paprika.

## PORK LOIN STUFFED WITH PRUNES

20 prunes, halved and pitted
1 (4- to 5-pound) loin of pork
2 to 3 teaspoons salt

1/2 teaspoon white pepper
1/4 teaspoon ground
   ginger
1 cup commercial prune
   juice

Soak prunes for 1/2 hour in warm water. Trim the meat and make a deep cut into the thickest part; insert the prunes. Rub the meat with seasonings and

*Continued...*

## PORK LOIN STUFFED WITH PRUNES, *Continued*

secure the stuffed roast with string; brown on all sides. Add 1 cup of the water in which prunes were soaked; cover and simmer over low heat about 1 1/2 hours or until tender. Baste occasionally. Add commercial prune juice after the first hour. Before slicing, remove the string and cut away the backbone. Strain the juice and remove the fat (to be used in gravy). Serves 8.

*Gravy*

3 tablespoons fat
3 tablespoons flour
2 cups pan juice

1 cup commercial prune
  juice
Salt and pepper to taste

Heat the fat; add flour and stir until browned. Add pan juice and prune juice. Simmer 10 minutes, stirring occasionally. Season with salt and pepper.

## BARBECUED RIBS

2 cups Kraft Barbecue Sauce
  (not hickory smoked)
2 tablespoons lemon juice
2 bay leaves
3 tablespoons chili powder
3/4 cup Worcestershire sauce
2 teaspoons garlic powder
1/2 cup brown sugar, packed
2 teaspoons pepper
1 1/2 tablespoons salt

1/4 cup Hickory smoke
1 tablespoon oil
1 (16-ounce) can tomatoes
  with juice, mashed
2 (6-ounce) cans tomato
  paste
1 (8-ounce) can tomato
  juice
8 pounds pork spare ribs,
  country-style

In a large saucepan, place all the ingredients except ribs and simmer for 4 hours. About 15 to 20 minutes before sauce is finished, preheat oven to 350°. Put the ribs in a shallow baking dish and cover with the sauce. Bake uncovered for 1 1/2 hours.

# MEAT

## BAKED PORK CHOPS

1 large onion, thinly sliced
1 large orange, thinly sliced
4 to 6 pork chops, preferably
   center-cut

Salt and freshly ground
   pepper

In a shallow baking dish, place a layer of onion and orange; add chops, which have been salted and peppered on both sides. Top with a layer of onion and orange; cover. Bake, covered, at 350° for 1½ to 2 hours. Remove cover when done; brown under broiler if necessary.

## CHICKEN IN A BAG

1 whole frying chicken
Juice of 1 lemon
¼ cup melted butter or
   margarine
Salt
Freshly ground pepper
½ carrot, scraped
½ rib celery (top half with
   leaves)

½ small onion
3 sprigs parsley
¼ teaspoon thyme
1 Reynolds oven cooking
   bag
Flour
½ cup sautéed sliced
   mushrooms

Rinse chicken; dry thoroughly. Rub inside and out with lemon juice, then with melted butter or margarine; sprinkle with seasonings. Stuff cavity with carrot, celery, onion and parsley; sprinkle thyme on top of chicken. Place chicken in cooking bag according to directions on box; set in a 10"x 6"x 2" baking dish. Put in a preheated oven and bake at 325° to 350° for 1 to 2 hours, depending on size of chicken. (It cannot be overcooked.) Remove from oven, cut 1 corner of bag and drain juices into a pan for gravy. Remove chicken from bag and return to oven to brown while making gravy. Skim fat from broth; make a paste of flour and water and add enough to broth to thicken it. Stir in sautéed mushrooms and pour over chicken. Serves 4.

## SOUTHERN FRIED CHICKEN

*...time-honored crusty chicken*

| | |
|---|---|
| 1 cup all-purpose flour | 3 pounds chicken pieces |
| 2 teaspoons salt | Milk |
| 1 teaspoon pepper | Lard or shortening |

Combine flour, salt and pepper in a shallow bowl, mixing well. Dip each piece of chicken in milk, then roll in flour, coating heavily. In a heavy skillet, melt fat to a depth of ½." When fat is moderately hot, gently lower chicken into it, placing skin side down. Do not crowd the pieces; turn and fry until golden brown on all sides. Cover skillet and reduce heat; simmer until fork-tender. The meatier pieces will take from 25 to 30 minutes; wings and backs will cook more quickly. Remove cover for last 5 minutes for a crisp crust. Drain chicken on paper towels; keep warm while making gravy. Serves 4.

*Cream Gravy*

| | |
|---|---|
| 3 tablespoons drippings | ½ cup cream |
| 3 tablespoons flour | Salt and pepper |
| 2½ cups milk | |

Pour all drippings from skillet into a small bowl; measure and return 3 tablespoons. Stir in flour until well blended; cook over medium heat for 2 to 3 minutes, until bubbly. Gradually add milk and cream; boil until thick and smooth, stirring constantly. Season with salt and pepper to taste. Serve in a hot gravy boat or bowl.

*Note:* Half butter and half vegetable oil or lard gives a delicate flavor to fried chicken, but any fat may be used satisfactorily.

## CORDON BLEU CHICKEN BREAST

*Per serving:*
1 chicken breast half, skinned
    and boned
1 slice baked ham
1 slice aged Swiss cheese
Dijon mustard
Salt and pepper
Flour

*Coating:*
1 egg beaten with 2
    tablespoons heavy
    cream
1/2 cup fine breadcrumbs
    mixed with 1/2 cup
    cracker crumbs
Melted butter
Sauterne
Paprika

Split breast; place ham slice and cheese slice on one side. Spread with mustard and sprinkle with salt and pepper. Press both sides together and seal edges with flour. Flour lightly and dip in egg-cream mixture, then in crumb mixture; place on a buttered cooking tray. Drizzle with melted butter and a small amount of sauterne; sprinkle with paprika. Bake at 375° for 35 to 40 minutes. Serve with Creamy Sauce.

*Creamy Sauce*
3 tablespoons butter
3 tablespoons all-purpose
    flour
1/2 cup half-and-half
1/3 cup heavy cream

3 egg yolks, beaten
Salt and pepper
1/3 cup dry white wine or
    Cognac

Melt butter in a saucepan; blend in flour and cook over low heat until bubbly. Gradually pour in half-and-half and cream, stirring until well blended. Add a little cream sauce to egg yolks, mixing well; return mixture to sauce in pan. Add salt, pepper and wine; cook, stirring constantly, until smooth and thickened. This is enough sauce for 8 servings of chicken.

## CHICKEN KIEV

| | |
|---|---|
| 4 teaspoons chives | 4 (6-ounce) chicken |
| 8 tablespoons butter | breasts, skinned |
| 4 slices bread, cut in quarters | 8 tablespoons milk |

Combine chives and butter; refrigerate 30 minutes. Roll into finger shape about 2"x¼"; chill in freezer 30 minutes. Put bread in blender. Run at medium speed 30 seconds or until bread is in fine crumbs. Pour crumbs in an even layer in shallow baking pan or pie plate. With mallet or flat side of knife, flatten chicken breasts between sheets of waxed paper to ⅛" thickness. Place butter fingers at long side of chicken breast; roll tightly, tucking in ends of chicken. Secure with toothpicks. Dip rolled chicken breast in milk, then roll in crumbs. Repeat. Place in baking dish and bake at 375° 45 minutes. If crumbs brown before baking time is up, cover with foil. Serves 4.

## CHICKEN BAKED WITH GRAPES

| | |
|---|---|
| 5 whole chicken breasts, split, or 2 (2½-pound) fryers, cut up | 2 tablespoons minced onion |
| Salt and pepper | 1 cup dry white wine |
| 6 tablespoons butter | 2 cups seedless grapes |
| | 10 slices country or "city" ham, warmed |

Season chicken pieces with salt and pepper; brown on both sides in butter. Place pieces in a single layer in a casserole. Brown onion in remaining butter; add wine and heat. Pour wine mixture over chicken. Bake at 350° covered, for 30 minutes. Add grapes and bake another 30 minutes. To serve, place chicken pieces on warmed slices of ham and pour sauce over all. Serves 10.

*Note:* Chicken may be baked 30 minutes, cooled and refrigerated. To reheat, bring to room temperature, add grapes, cover and bake at 350° for 30 minutes.

## PARTY CHICKEN BREASTS

12 chicken breast halves,
  boned
1 large onion, halved
2 carrots
4 sprigs of parsley
1 tablespoon salt
4 cups water
2 tablespoons butter

1/2 cup chopped onion
8 ounces fresh
  mushrooms, chopped
1 cup sour cream
1 cup cream
1/8 teaspoon cayenne
  pepper

Gently boil chicken breasts, onion, carrots, parsley and salt in 4 cups water, covered, for 25 minutes and drain. Melt butter in a heavy skillet and sauté onions and mushrooms for 8 minutes. Remove from heat and drain off any excess liquid. Combine sour cream and cream; stir in caynenne pepper, onions and mushrooms. Arrange chicken breasts in a greased baking dish; spoon the sauce evenly over all and cover with foil. Place on the middle rack of a preheated 300° oven for 20 minutes. (Oven must be at very low temperature or the creams will curdle.) Serves 10 to 12. Serves 10 to 12.

## DIVINE CHICKEN BREAST

8 chicken breast halves,
  boned
4 to 6 tablespoons butter,
  melted
1 cup cashew nuts

1/4 cup water
1 cup cream
1 tablespoon brandy

Make fine crumbs of cashew nuts. Roll chicken pieces in 1/4 cup melted butter, then in nut crumbs. Place in a skillet, adding remaining butter, if needed; brown carefully so nuts do not burn. Remove pieces to a baking dish; pour in water, cover and bake for 40 minutes. Add cream and brandy; bake 20 minutes longer.

## CHICKEN BREASTS MADEIRA

4 whole chicken breasts,
    skinned and boned
Salt and pepper to taste
Flour
Clarified butter
1 cup fresh mushroom caps
1 (14-ounce) can artichoke
    hearts, drained
½ cup julienne-cut ham
1 tablespoon butter
1 tablespoon flour
1 cup water
1 teaspoon Kitchen
    Bouquet
Salt and pepper to taste
½ cup Madeira wine
Chopped fresh parsley

Sprinkle chicken with salt and pepper; dust with flour. Shake off excess flour and sauté breasts in clarified butter on both sides until brown and tender. Remove from skillet. Add mushroom caps to skillet and sauté for 3 minutes; stir in artichoke hearts and ham. Melt butter; add flour, stirring until smooth. Gradually add water and seasonings, cooking over low heat until thickened. Pour into skillet, add wine and stir until well mixed. Return chicken breasts to skillet; cover and simmer for 20 to 30 minutes. Sprinkle with parsley.

## MUENSTER CHICKEN

8 chicken breast halves,
    skinned and boned
Salt and pepper
2 eggs, beaten
¾ cup flour, mixed with ¾
    cup bread crumbs
¼ to ½ cup butter
½ pound Muenster
    cheese, sliced
½ cup butter
2 tablespoons chopped
    parsley
1 teaspoon marjoram
½ teaspoon thyme
½ cup sherry

Sprinkle chicken with salt and pepper. Dip each piece in beaten egg, then coat with flour-crumb mixture. Melt enough butter to cover bottom of skillet; brown chicken on all sides. Place pieces in a single layer in a shallow baking dish; top with cheese slices. In sauce pan, heat ½ cup butter, herbs and ½ cup of sherry, pour over chicken. Bake uncovered at 350° for 30 minutes or until tender. May be prepared a day ahead, covered and refrigerated. Serves 4 to 6.

## CHINESE BARBECUED CHICKEN

3 whole chicken breasts,
   boned, skinned and diced
2½ tablespoons dry sherry
2 tablespoons soy sauce
2 teaspoons cornstarch
1 cup sliced water chestnuts
1 cup diced green pepper
1 cup sliced fresh mushrooms

3 to 4 tablespoons
   vegetable oil
4 to 6 tablespoons Hoisin
   sauce
½ cup whole roasted
   almonds
1 teaspoon salt
Hot cooked rice

Marinate diced chicken in sherry, soy sauce and cornstarch for 15 minutes or more. Sauté water chestnuts, green pepper and mushrooms in 2 tablespoons oil and salt for 2 minutes. Remove from pan and keep warm. Add 1 to 2 tablespoons oil; stir-fry chicken until it turns white. Add vegetables, almonds and Hoisin sauce; mix thoroughly. Serve immediately over hot fluffy rice. Serves 4 to 6.

## CREAM DE VOLAILLE

3 cups cooked chicken,
   ground with ½ cup fresh
   mushrooms
1 cup thick white sauce
1 tablespoon butter

3 eggs, beaten
2 teaspoons salt
⅓ teaspoon red pepper
Chopped parsley

Combine chicken-mushroom mixture with white sauce. Add butter and eggs; beat mixture very hard. Add seasoning and a little chopped parsley. Pour mixture into a greased mold; cover tightly with foil. Place mold in a shallow pan filled with about ½" water; place in an oven and steam at 400° for 1½ hours. Serve with Mushroom Cream Sauce, page 174.

*This is a Shakertown recipe.*

## POLLO CON TOCINO

3 slices bacon, spread with
   chili powder
1 large stewing chicken
2 large onions, sliced
2 garlic cloves, minced
1 medium green pepper,
   chopped

1 (6-ounce) can tomato
   purée
3 tablespoons chopped
   parsley
1 1/2 tablespoons sugar
1 teaspoon salt
2 teaspoons chili powder
Cornstarch

Roll up each slice of bacon and place in cavity of chicken. Put into a large pot, breast side down, with giblets. Sauté onions, garlic and green pepper in butter until soft. Add tomato purée, parsley, sugar, salt and chili powder. When sauce boils, pour over chicken and add enough boiling water to cover three-fourths of chicken. Simmer until tender, approximately 2 hours, always keeping liquid at three-quarter level. Remove meat from bones in large pieces. Strain sauce and thicken with cornstarch mixed with water. Serve half of sauce with chicken and half in a separate bowl. Serve chicken with Rice Ring, page 199.

## CHICKEN KEENE

1/3 cup butter
1/3 cup flour
1 cup chicken broth
1 1/2 cups milk or cream
2 teaspoons salt
1/8 teaspoon pepper
Meat from 1 cooked hen,
   cubed

1/2 pound mushrooms,
   sliced
1 pimiento, cut in strips
1 green pepper, cut in
   strips
Sherry
Pastry tart shells

Melt butter in top of double boiler; stir flour in slowly. Gradually add chicken broth and milk, stirring constantly. Season. Add chicken, mushrooms, pimiento, green pepper and sherry to taste. Serve in tart shells; sprinkle with paprika.

*This is a Shakertown recipe.*

## CHICKEN PANCAKES

*Crêpes*

4 eggs
1/2 cup milk
1/2 cup chicken stock
1/2 teaspoon salt

2 tablespoons butter,
  melted
1 cup flour, sifted

Combine all ingredients except flour in a mixing bowl, beating until well blended. Gradually add flour, mixing well. Prepare crêpes in a small frying pan or an electric crêpe maker.

*Cream Sauce*

6 tablespoons butter
6 tablespoons flour
3 cups chicken broth

3/4 teaspoon salt
3/4 teaspoon pepper

Melt butter over low heat; add flour, stirring 3 to 4 minutes until blended. Stir in broth slowly; season with salt and pepper. Simmer, stirring with a wire whisk until thickened and smooth. Measure 2 cups of sauce to put in filling, reserving the remainder for the Topping.

*Filling*

2 cups cooked chicken, cut in
  bite-size pieces
1 tablespoon chopped fresh
  parsley
1 teaspoon grated onion
1/2 cup half-and-half
1 egg yolk, beaten

2 cups Cream Sauce
3 slices bacon, crisply
  cooked and crumbled
1/2 cup grated Swiss
  cheese, mixed with 1/2
  cup grated Parmesan
  cheese

Combine chicken, parsley, onion and half-and-half in a saucepan; simmer for 8 minutes. Stir egg into cream sauce, then add chicken mixture, cooking until thickened. Add bacon and one-half of cheese mixture. Reserve remaining cheese mixture for Topping. Spread a generous amount of filling down the center of each crêpe. Roll up crêpe, leaving ends open; place seam-side down in a buttered baking dish.

*Continued...*

## CHICKEN PANCAKES, *Continued*

*Topping*
Reserved Cream Sauce
1 to 2 tablespoons
  half-and-half

Reserved cheese mixture

Combine cream sauce and half-and-half; pour over crêpes in baking dish and sprinkle with remaining cheese mixture. Bake at 350° for 20 minutes.

*Note:* The crêpes with sauce freeze well but must be defrosted completely before cooking.

## COUNTRY CAPTAIN

1/4 cup all-purpose flour
2 teaspoons salt
1 teaspoon white pepper
8 chicken breast halves,
  skinned and boned
1/2 cup (1 stick) butter
3/4 cup chopped onion
2 medium green peppers,
  seeded and chopped
2 small cloves garlic or 1/2
  teaspoon garlic powder
2 (14 1/2-ounce) cans tomato
  wedges or 1 (28-ounce) can
  whole tomatoes, quartered

1 (14 1/4-ounce) can
  seasoned tomato sauce
1 1/2 to 2 teaspoons curry
  powder
1/2 cup raisins
1 (3 1/4 ounce) package
  slivered almonds,
  toasted
Chopped parsley
Hot cooked rice
Chutney

Combine flour with 1 teaspoon salt and 1/4 teaspoon pepper in a plastic bag. Shake chicken, one piece at a time, in flour mixture to coat. Brown chicken in butter in a large skillet; remove and keep warm. Add onion, green pepper and garlic to skillet; sauté until soft. Add tomatoes, tomato sauce, curry powder, remaining teaspoon salt and 3/4 teaspoon pepper; simmer, uncovered, for 10 minutes. Place chicken in a 13"x 9"x 2" baking dish; add raisins and sauce. Cover and bake at 325° for 1 1/2 hours. Garnish with almonds and parsley; serve with hot fluffy rice and chutney.

# POULTRY

## CURRY OF CHICKEN

1 (4-pound) chicken
3 tablespoons butter, melted
2 large slices onion
2 tablespoons raisins
1/2 cup diced sour apples
2 teaspoons curry powder
3/4 teaspoon salt
2 cups chicken stock (fat removed)
3 tablespoons butter, melted
3 heaping tablespoons flour

1 cup heavy cream
Hot cooked rice
*Condiments*
  Slivered almonds
  Grated fresh coconut
  Chutney
  Chopped hard-cooked egg
  Diced onion
  Crumbled crisp bacon
  Guava jelly

Boil chicken until barely tender; debone while warm; cut into large pieces and keep hot in a double boiler. Combine butter in a saucepan with onion, raisins and apples; cook slowly for 10 minutes. Add curry powder and salt and blend in chicken stock; boil 10 minutes. Strain through a colander, pressing onion, raisins and apples through with stock. In a large saucepan combine butter and flour. Cook until bubbly; add stock mixture and cream. Cook until thick and smooth. Pour over chicken in the double boiler. Serve with hot, fluffy rice and bowls of condiments.

## CHINESE CHICKEN

8 chicken breast halves, skinned and boned
1 (6-ounce) package frozen Chinese pea pods, thawed, or 6 ounces fresh pea pods
1/2 pound fresh mushrooms, washed and sliced

1 pound fresh broccoli, washed and cut into florets
1/4 teaspoon oregano
3 tablespoons soy sauce
1 teaspoon cornstarch
1 chicken bouillon cube
1 cup water

Cut chicken into bite-size pieces. Sauté in vegetable oil in a wok or large skillet until thoroughly cooked, about 8 minutes. Add pea pods, mushrooms and broccoli; cook about 2 minutes. Add remaining ingredients; simmer until vegetables are crisp-tender. Serve immediately.

## CHICKEN TETRAZZINI GLENCREST

1 (5½- to 6-pound) hen
4 tablespoons butter
4 tablespoons flour
2 cups hot chicken broth
1½ cups cream
¼ cup sherry
1 teaspoon lemon juice
Salt and pepper to taste

1 onion, chopped
½ green pepper, chopped
1 pound mushrooms,
  sliced
2 tablespoons butter
½ pound thin spaghetti
1 cup grated Parmesan
  cheese

Simmer hen until tender; let cool in broth. Pull skin from hen and slip meat from bones. Chill meat and dice. Reserve 2 cups of broth. Melt butter over low heat; add flour, stirring about 3 to 4 minutes until well blended. Slowly stir in broth, cream and sherry. Season with lemon juice, salt and pepper. Simmer and stir sauce with a wire whisk until thick, smooth and hot. Sauté onion and green pepper in butter; remove. Sauté mushrooms. Add onion, green pepper and mushrooms to sauce. Cook spaghetti as directed, using any leftover broth. Place spaghetti in the bottom of a greased shallow casserole; cover with chicken and sauce. Sprinkle with Parmesan cheese. Bake at 325° to 350° for 30 minutes until bubbly. Serves 8 to 10.

## CHICKEN OR TURKEY VANDERBILT

½ cup finely chopped
  shallots
4 cups finely chopped
  mushrooms (about 1
  pound)
4 tablespoons butter

8 slices cooked breast of
  chicken or turkey
8 slices baked country
  ham
1 cup Mornay Sauce,
  page 171

Sauté shallots and mushrooms in butter until soft, adding more butter if necessary; season to taste with salt and pepper. Spread mixture in the bottom of an oblong baking dish; cover with rows of ham slices topped with chicken breast slices. Pour Mornay Sauce over all and bake at 350° for 30 minutes or until golden brown.

# POULTRY

## CHICKEN TARRAGON

1 (3 pound) frying chicken
   split in half
3 tablespoons butter
1 teaspoon flour

1 cup white wine
1 teaspoon tarragon
Salt and pepper to taste

In a heavy skillet, brown chicken in butter. Remove to a casserole while adding the flour, wine and tarragon to the pan juices. Blend all together to deglaze. Pour over the chicken, cover and bake in a 325° oven for 1 1/2 hours.

## CHICKEN AND SAUSAGE SUPREME

1/2 pound hot-seasoned
   ground sausage meat
5 tablespoons butter
12 large mushrooms, sliced
1/4 cup flour
1 teaspoon salt

Freshly ground pepper
   to taste
2 cups chicken broth
2/3 cup half-and-half
2 cups diced, cooked
   chicken

Roll sausage into small balls; sauté in a skillet until brown. Remove and set aside. Drain fat from skillet. Melt 1 tablespoon butter in skillet and sauté mushrooms; remove and set aside. Add remaining 4 tablespoons butter to skillet and stir in flour, salt and pepper; let bubble 1 minute. Gradually add broth and half-and-half, stirring constantly; bring to a boil, reduce heat and simmer 1 minute or until sauce is thickened. Add sausage, mushrooms and chicken. Serve over rice or noodles, in patty shells or on rounds of pie crust which have been seasoned with celery seed and paprika. Serves 6.

## CHICKEN AND ASPARAGUS IN PATTY SHELLS

Yolks of 2 hard-cooked eggs
1 tablespoon butter
1 cup cream
Salt and pepper

2 cups diced cooked
chicken breast
1 cup cooked asparagus
tips
6 baked patty shells

Rub yolks through a sieve or ricer; combine with butter to form a paste. Add cream and blend thoroughly. Season with salt and pepper; stir in chicken. Carefully fold in asparagus tips. Warm over low heat or in a double boiler. Spoon into hot patty shells. Serves 6.

## CHICKEN NOODLE SURPRISE

1 (5-pound) hen
5 small onions, chopped
2 green peppers, chopped
3 tablespoons butter
1 1/2 tablespoons flour
2 cups chicken broth
2 cups tomatoes, fresh or
canned
1 (6-ounce) can pitted ripe
olives, sliced

1 (8-ounce) can sliced
mushrooms
1 (8-ounce) package thin
noodles
1 pound sharp Cheddar
cheese, diced
1 cup buttered bread
crumbs

Stew hen until tender; remove skin and bones and cut meat into 1 1/2" pieces. Reserve 2 cups chicken broth. Sauté onions and green peppers in butter until tender; add flour, stirring until smooth. Add broth and bring to a boil, stirring constantly, until sauce is thickened. Add tomatoes, olives and mushrooms. Cook noodles and drain well. Layer half of noodles, chicken, sauce and cheese in a greased 3-quart casserole. Repeat, making another layer; top with buttered bread crumbs. Bake at 325° for 1 hour. Serves 10.

## CHICKEN AND SPINACH CASSEROLE

1 clove garlic, minced
1 tablespoon butter
1 tablespoon flour
1/3 cup milk
2 (10-ounce) packages frozen
   chopped spinach, cooked
   and drained
2 (2 1/2-pound) frying
   chickens, cooked, boned
   and cubed

3 tablespoons butter
3 tablespoons flour
3/4 cup cream
3/4 cup chicken stock
Salt and pepper to taste
1 cup grated Parmesan
   cheese

Sauté garlic in 1 tablespoon butter for 1 minute; blend in flour and cook 1 minute. Add milk and boil 1 minute, stirring constantly; stir in spinach. Spread mixture on the bottom of a casserole; cover with chicken. Melt 3 tablespoons butter; add flour, blending well. Stir in cream and broth slowly; season with salt and pepper. Simmer and stir with a wire whisk until thick and smooth. Pour sauce over chicken; sprinkle with cheese. Bake at 400° for 20 minutes or until bubbly. Serves 6 to 8.

*Note:* This may be frozen. Thaw and bring to room temperature before baking.

## SCALLOPED CHICKEN AND SWEETBREADS

2 tablespoons butter or
   chicken fat
1 tablespoon chopped onion
1/4 pound mushrooms, sliced
1/4 cup flour
1 cup chicken stock
1/2 cup milk
1/2 cup cream

1 cup cubed, cooked
   chicken
1/2 cup cooked
   sweetbreads
1/3 cup blanched almonds
1 teaspoon salt
1/4 cup bread crumbs
2 teaspoons butter, melted

Melt butter or chicken fat; add onion and mushrooms and sauté. Stir in flour until smooth. Add chicken stock, milk and cream; cook until thick. Add chicken, sweetbreads, almonds and salt; put in a 1-quart casserole. Sprinkle buttered crumbs on top and brown in oven.

## CHICKEN AND WILD RICE CASSEROLE

1 cup uncooked wild rice or a mixture of wild and white rice
½ cup chopped onion
½ cup (1 stick) butter
½ cup flour
1 (6-ounce) can sliced mushrooms (broiled type)
1 cup chicken broth
1½ cups half-and-half
3 cups diced chicken or turkey
2 tablespoons dried parsley
1½ teaspoons salt
¼ teaspoon pepper
½ cup slivered almonds

Cook the rice according to directions on package. Sauté onion in butter until tender but not brown; remove from heat and stir in flour. Drain mushrooms, saving liquid. Add enough chicken broth to mushroom liquid to make 1½ cups; gradually stir into onion mixture. Slowly add half-and-half; cook and stir until mixture is thickened. Add cooked rice, mushrooms, chicken, parsley, salt and pepper. Place in an ungreased 2-quart casserole; sprinkle with almonds. Bake uncovered at 350° for 25 to 30 minutes. Serves 6 to 8.

## CHICKEN AND ARTICHOKE CASSEROLE

1 (3-pound) chicken
3 chicken breast halves
1 cup butter
½ cup flour
3 ½ cups sweet milk
3 ounces Gruyère or Swiss cheese
⅛ pound rat cheese
1 tablespoon Accent
2 cloves garlic, pressed
½ tablespoon red pepper
2 (8-ounce) cans button mushrooms, drained
2 (14-ounce) cans artichoke hearts, drained and quartered
Hot buttered noodles

Boil chicken in well-seasoned water until tender. Cut meat into large pieces and set aside. Melt butter in skillet and blend in flour; add milk slowly, stirring constantly, until thickened. Cut cheeses into small pieces and add to sauce, stirring until melted. Add chicken, seasonings, mushrooms and artichoke hearts. Pour into a greased casserole; bake at 350° for 30 minutes. Serve over buttered noodles. Serves 12.

## MEXICAN CHICKEN CASSEROLE

1 (4 to 5-pound) chicken,
cut up
3 cups water
1 tablespoon salt
4 tablespoons butter
1 cup chopped onion
3 tablespoons flour
2 cups milk
1 cup chicken broth

1 1/2 (4-ounce) cans
chopped green chilies,
drained
1 1/2 teaspoons salt
6 tortillas, cut or torn in
bite-size pieces
1 pound Cheddar cheese,
grated

Put chicken in a pot with water and salt; cover and simmer until tender, about 1 hour. Cool in broth. Remove meat from bones and cut into large pieces. Reserve 1 cup of broth for sauce. Melt butter; add onion and sauté until limp. Add flour and cook for 1 minute. Pour in milk and chicken broth; cook until thickened, stirring constantly. Add green chilies and 1 1/2 teaspoons salt. In a greased 3-quart casserole, put layers of chicken, tortillas, sauce and cheese. Repeat until all are used, ending with cheese on top. Bake at 375° for 1 hour or until hot clear through. This may be refrigerated for a day or frozen and thawed before baking. If cold when put into oven, allow 45 minutes additional baking time. Serve with Hot Mexican Sauce (page 174). Serves 10.

## TURKEY IN A BAG

Using a large brown grocery bag, spray the inside with vegetable cooking spray. Rinse and dry the turkey; place one large onion and one rib of celery inside the cavity. Place the turkey in the bag which has been placed on a broiler pan. Melt one stick butter and pour over the turkey while it is in the bag. Season with salt and pepper and fold over the ends of the bag and secure with either staple or paper clips. Bake in a pre-heated oven at 300° for 30 minutes per pound.

## CHICKEN CROQUETTES

8 slices white bread
1 cup chicken stock
1 cup (2 sticks) butter
4 eggs, beaten light
½ onion, finely chopped
1 teaspoon salt
1 teaspoon pepper

4 sprigs parsley, chopped
1 pound ground cooked
chicken (both white
and dark meat)
Egg whites
Fine bread crumbs

Place bread slices on a large platter and pour chicken stock over them. When bread has absorbed the stock and softened (about 30 minutes), add butter, eggs, onion, salt, pepper and parsley. Place mixture into a large saucepan and cook until thickened, stirring frequently. Pour out onto the large platter and cool. Mix in ground chicken. Shape into croquettes; roll in egg whites, then in bread crumbs. Fry in hot lard until browned. Serve with Mushroom Cream Sauce, page 174.

## BRUNSWICK STEW

2 fat hens, disjointed
6 (28-ounce) cans tomatoes
5 pounds onions, chopped
10 pounds potatoes, cubed
4 (10-ounce) packages frozen
baby lima beans
4 (17-ounce) cans cream-style
corn

3 (10 ounce) packages
frozen cut okra
4 red pepper pods
2 (20-ounce) cans tomato
purée
1 (5-ounce) bottle
Worcestershire sauce
1 pound butter (no
substitute)

Cook hens in plenty of water over medium-low heat until they are tender enough to fall from bones. Remove chicken and let cool. Add tomatoes and onions to broth; cook 1 to 1½ hours. Meanwhile, remove meat from bones and return to broth. Add potatoes, lima beans, corn, okra and pepper pods; reduce heat and cook 1 hour longer, stirring occasionally. Add tomato purée, Worcestershire sauce and butter; simmer another ½ hour. Stir frequently to prevent sticking. Remove pepper pods before serving. Makes 25 servings.

## ORIGINAL HOT BROWN

*Cheese Sauce*

2 tablespoons butter
1/4 cup flour
2 cups milk
1/4 cup grated sharp Cheddar
   cheese

1/4 cup grated Parmesan
   cheese
1/4 teaspoon salt
1/2 teaspoon
   Worcestershire sauce

Melt butter in a saucepan; blend in flour. Add milk, cheeses and seasonings, stirring constantly until smooth and thickened. Set aside.

*Sandwiches*

8 slices trimmed toast
1 pound sliced turkey breast
8 slices tomato
8 slices bacon, partially
   cooked, or 1/4 pound baked
   country ham, thinly sliced

4 ounces grated Parmesan
   cheese
Sprigs of parsley

Cut toast into triangles and put in baking dishes. Arrange turkey slices on toast and cover with hot cheese sauce; top with tomato and bacon or ham. Sprinkle with Parmesan cheese and bake at 400° until bubbly. Garnish with parsley.

*Note:* To freeze Hot Browns, omit tomato slices and wrap sandwiches in aluminum foil. When ready to bake, remove foil and bake at 375° until hot and bubbly.

## HOT BROWN

*Sauce*

2 tablespoons butter
2 tablespoons flour
Salt to taste
Dash of cayenne pepper
1/4 teaspoon curry powder
   (optional)
1 cup milk

1 (3 1/2-ounce) can sliced
   mushrooms, drained, or
   1/4 pound fresh, sliced
   mushrooms, sautéed
1 chicken bouillon cube
1 tablespoon sherry

Melt butter in a small skillet; blend in flour, salt, cayenne and curry. Remove from heat; add milk slowly, stirring until smooth. Return to heat; stir in mushrooms and bouillon cube. Cook until bouillon cube is dissolved and sauce is thickened; add sherry last.

*Sandwiches*

4 slices bread, lightly toasted
4 chicken breast halves,
   cooked and sliced, or 8
   large slices cooked turkey

4 slices bacon, partially
   cooked and cut in half
1 cup grated Cheddar
   cheese

Place toast on 4 ovenware dishes; cover with sliced chicken or turkey. Pour over sauce, sprinkle with cheese and place pieces of bacon crisscross on top. Place under a broiler and broil slowly until bacon is crisp.

## TURKEY HASH

1/2 cup chopped celery
1/2 cup chopped onion
1/4 cup chopped bell pepper
4 tablespoons (1/2 stick) butter
1 1/2 cups chopped cooked
   turkey

1 cup turkey gravy
1 tablespoon chopped
   parsley
Salt and pepper to taste

Sauté vegetables in butter until limp. Add remaining ingredients and simmer until blended, about 15 to 20 minutes. The hash is better if made the day before, and it freezes well. Serves 6 to 8.

## TURKEY A LA KING

| | |
|---|---|
| 1 (8-pound) turkey | 1/2 cup chopped green |
| 2 cups strong broth | pepper |
| 1/2 cup (1 stick) butter | 1/4 cup chopped pimiento |
| 1/2 cup all-purpose flour | 1/2 pound fresh |
| 3/4 cup cream | mushrooms, sliced and |
| 2 egg yolks, beaten | sautéed |
| Salt and red pepper | 1/2 cup sherry |
| to taste | |

Stew turkey; cool and cut into 1″ bite-size pieces. Set aside 6 cups of cut-up turkey. Cook down broth until it measures 2 cups. In a large saucepan, melt butter; blend in flour and cook for 3 minutes. Slowly add broth, stirring constantly until thick and smooth; stir in cream. Cool; add egg yolks and season with salt and red pepper. Stir in turkey, green pepper, pimiento and mushrooms. Keep mixture hot by placing the saucepan in a larger pan of hot water. Before serving, add sherry.

## TURKEY-POTATO HASH

| | |
|---|---|
| 2 cups cubed potatoes | 4 tablespoons flour |
| 1/2 cup chopped onion | 2 cups cooked, diced |
| 3 cups of turkey or chicken | turkey |
| broth | Salt and pepper |

Cook potatoes and onion in broth until tender. Mix flour with enough water to make a paste; stir into potato mixture and cook until thickened. Add turkey and season to taste. The hash can be served over corn griddle cakes.

*Variation:* Chopped green pepper or pimiento or sliced mushrooms may be added to hash in desired amounts.

*This recipe from Lexington caterer, Mary Ellen Hardin*

## DOVES CYNTHIANA

12 doves
Salt and pepper
1 cup plus 2 tablespoons
   butter
2 tablespoons bacon grease

Paprika
1 cup water
½ cup sherry
¼ to ½ cup soy sauce

Clean the doves thoroughly. Cover with salted water; place in the refrigerator and soak overnight. Drain; sprinkle with salt and pepper. In a heavy skillet, melt 6 tablespoons butter with bacon grease. Brown doves on all sides and sprinkle with paprika. Pour off grease; add ¾ cup butter to skillet. After butter is melted, pour in water and cover. Place skillet in a hot oven; bake at 250° for about 2½ hours or until doves are tender. Baste every 15 minutes. In the last half hour, add sherry and soy sauce. Serve doves with pan juices.

## DOVES IN WINE

24 doves
Salt and pepper
Flour
1 cup butter

2 cups red wine
¼ cup vinegar
¼ cup Worcestershire
   sauce

Sprinkle doves with salt and pepper and lightly dust with flour; brown in butter. Add other ingredients. Cook, covered, very slowly for 1 hour. Thicken pan juices with flour and serve with doves.

# GAME

## DUCK AND WILD RICE CASSEROLE

2 large wild ducks, cleaned
3 stalks celery, cut into 2"
    pieces
2 carrots, scraped and cut into
    2" pieces
1 onion, halved
2 bay leaves
1 1/2 teaspoons salt
1/4 teaspoon pepper
1 (6-ounce) package long grain
    and wild rice mix

1 (4-ounce) can sliced
    mushrooms
1/2 cup chopped onion
1/2 cup melted margarine
1/4 cup all-purpose flour
1 1/2 cups half-and-half
1 tablespoon chopped
    fresh parsley
1/2 cup slivered almonds

Combine first 7 ingredients in a large Dutch oven; cover with water and bring to a boil. Reduce heat; cover and simmer 1 hour or until ducks are tender. Remove ducks from stock; strain stock and reserve. When ducks cool, remove meat from bones; cut into bite-size pieces and set aside. Cook rice mix according to directions on the package. Drain mushrooms, reserving liquid. Add enough duck broth to mushroom liquid to make 1 1/2 cups. Sauté chopped onion in margarine until tender; add flour, stirring until smooth. Add mushrooms; cook 1 minute, stirring constantly. Gradually stir in mushroom liquid-broth mixture; cook over medium heat, stirring constantly, until thickened and bubbly. Stir in duck, rice, half-and-half and parsley; spoon into a greased 2-quart shallow casserole. Sprinkle almonds over top. Cover and bake at 350° for 15 to 20 minutes; uncover and bake 5 to 10 additional minutes or until thoroughly heated. Serves 6 to 8.

## BARBECUE SAUCE FOR CHICKEN

1/2 cup catsup
1 cup vinegar
1/2 cup Worcestershire sauce
3 tablespoons lemon juice

1 lemon, thinly sliced
1 cup water
1 stick butter
1 teaspoon salt
Red pepper to taste

Simmer all together for 10 minutes; keep hot. Cover chicken with sauce and cook for 20 minutes covered and 30 minutes uncovered. Baste often.

# GAME

## ROAST DUCK WITH CUMBERLAND SAUCE

2 Mallards or 4 Teal
Salt
3 oranges, quartered
3 onions, quartered
1 1/2 cups orange juice

3 tablespoons butter,
  melted
1/2 cup honey
1 tablespoon
  Worcestershire sauce
1/4 cup dry sherry

Parboil ducks in salted water for 45 minutes. Salt cavity and fill with quartered oranges and onions. Place breast down in a tight-fitting pan. Combine juice, butter, honey, Worcestershire sauce and sherry. Baste duck with juice mixture and bake at 375° for 45 minutes. Baste again after 1/2 hour, checking to see if pan needs a little water to prevent duck from sticking. Reduce heat to 275° and roast for an additional 2 1/2 to 3 1/2 hours, depending on size of ducks. Baste every 30 minutes. To make gravy, thicken pan juices with mixture of 1 tablespoon butter and 1 tablespoon flour per cup of juice or serve with Cumberland Sauce.

*Cumberland Sauce*
6 tablespoons currant jelly
3 tablespoons sugar
2 tablespoons lemon juice

2 tablespoons dry sherry
Pinch of salt

Combine ingredients in a saucepan; heat and stir until blended.

## MARINADE FOR SHISH KABOBS

1/2 cup olive oil
2/3 cup sherry
1 large onion, chopped
2 to 3 large garlic cloves,
  pressed
2 teaspoons salt

2 teaspoons oregano
1/2 teaspoon freshly
  ground pepper
1/4 cup chopped fresh
  parsley

Mix ingredients well; pour over cubed meat. Cover and refrigerate at least 8 hours (overnight is best). Baste kabobs several times with marinade while grilling. This recipe makes enough marinade for 5 1/2 pounds cubed meat.

# SAUCES AND GRAVIES

## MARINADE FOR STEAKS AND CHOPS

1 1/2 cups salad oil
3/4 cup soy sauce
1/2 cup wine vinegar
1/3 cup lemon juice (fresh is best)
1/4 cup Worcestershire sauce

2 garlic cloves, crushed
2 tablespoons dry mustard
1 tablespoon black pepper
2 1/4 teaspoons salt
1 1/2 teaspoons dried parsley

Combine all ingredients and mix well. Cover meat with marinade and chill for several hours. Turn meat several times to allow the flavor to penetrate more evenly. If a stronger flavor is preferred, refrigerate overnight. Let meat come to room temperature before cooking. Save leftover marinade to use another time. It may be stored, tightly covered, in the refrigerator for two weeks or in the freezer indefinitely. Makes 3 1/2 cups.

## SAVORY SAUCE FOR BREAST OF CHICKEN

*...makes chicken taste like pheasant!*

2 tablespoons butter
2 tablespoons flour
2 cups chicken stock or chicken bouillon
3 cloves garlic, minced
2 tablespoons chopped onion
2 tablespoons chopped country ham

1 bay leaf
1 tablespoon Worcestershire sauce
1 tablespoon tomato catsup
1/2 teaspoon celery salt
2 tablespoons sherry

Brown butter and stir in flour; gradually add chicken stock, stirring until smooth. Add remaining ingredients, except sherry; simmer for 10 minutes. Stir in sherry. Serve over chicken breasts on slices of country ham. This is enough sauce for 10 to 12 chicken breast halves.

# SAUCES AND GRAVIES

## MORNAY SAUCE

2 tablespoons butter
2 tablespoons flour
1 cup milk
1 egg yolk

2 tablespoons cream
4 tablespoons grated
   Gruyère cheese
Salt and pepper

Melt butter; add flour and blend over low heat about 5 minutes. Slowly stir in milk; cook over low heat until thick and smooth. Beat egg yolk with cream; add to sauce mixture, stirring. Stir in cheese until melted. Season to taste.

## SAUCE FOR CHICKEN-CORN BREAD

*Here's a flavorful answer for leftover chicken or turkey*

1/2 cup (1 stick) butter
1/4 cup flour
2 cups half-and-half or milk
1/2 teaspoon salt
1/8 teaspoon pepper

1 tablespoon
   Worcestershire sauce
1/2 teaspoon A.1. steak
   sauce
2 tablespoons grated
   onion

Melt butter; blend in flour and cook until bubbly. Add half-and-half, stirring until thickened; stir in remaining ingredients. Serve the sauce over split squares of buttered homemade corn bread filled with a thick layer of chicken or turkey slices.

## HORSERADISH SAUCE

1/2 cup mayonnaise
1/2 cup heavy cream, whipped
1/8 teaspoon dry mustard

1/3 cup prepared
   horseradish, drained
Tabasco sauce to taste
Worcestershire sauce to
   taste

Combine mayonnaise and whipped cream; stir in dry mustard and horse-radish. Season lightly with Tabasco and Worcestershire sauce.

# SAUCES AND GRAVIES

## LAMB GRAVY

1 pint tomato catsup
1 (12-ounce) glass currant jelly
1/2 cup brown sugar
1/2 cup Bourbon whiskey
1 cup sherry
1/2 teaspoon cinnamon
1/2 teaspoon ground cloves
1 teaspoon paprika
1/2 bay leaf
1 teaspoon Worcestershire
3 tablespoons chopped chutney
bunch of fresh, or dried mint

Boil, stirring often, until the mixture thickens.

## HENRY BAIN SAUCE

*...serve with steak or roast beef*

1 (14-ounce) bottle catsup
1 (12-ounce) bottle chili sauce
1 (10-ounce) bottle A.1. steak sauce
1 (10-ounce) bottle Worcestershire sauce
1 (8-ounce) jar Major Grey's chutney
2 tablespoons Tabasco sauce

Combine all ingredients, mixing well and pour into bottles. The sauce will keep for months in refrigerator.

## SAUCE MAISON

*...serve with filet of beef*

1/2 cup chopped green onions
1 1/2 cups red wine
1/2 cup (1 stick) butter
1 1/2 teaspoons salt
2 teaspoons minced parsley
1/4 teaspoon ground pepper

Boil the green onions and wine for 7 minutes until reduced in volume. When slightly cool, add the remaining ingredients.

# SAUCES AND GRAVIES

## HOLIDAY CRANBERRY SAUCE

1 cup water
1 cup sugar
1 medium-size piece fresh
   ginger root, peeled

1 large hard green pear,
   peeled and diced
2 cups fresh cranberries,
   washed
Juice and rind of 1 lemon

Place water and sugar in a saucepan; stir until sugar is dissolved. Boil the syrup for 5 minutes. Add pear; cook 5 minutes more. Add cranberries; boil without stirring until all skins pop open, about 15 minutes. Remove from heat and cool. Before serving, remove ginger root and add lemon juice and rind. This sauce will keep 2 weeks in the refrigerator.

## STUFFING FOR TURKEY OR CHICKEN

5 cups bread cubes
3/4 cup chopped celery
1 cup sausage meat
12 mushrooms, sliced
1 turkey or chicken liver,
   cooked and chopped
1/4 cup butter, melted
1 cup chicken broth
6 tablespoons Madeira wine

1/4 cup chopped parsley
2 eggs, beaten
2 (3-ounce) cans water
   chestnuts, drained and
   sliced
Salt and pepper to taste
1/2 teaspoon thyme
1/4 teaspoon sage

Bake 5 cups of bread cubes at 250°, turning frequently, until dried out and crisp, but not brown. Sauté celery, sausage and mushrooms separately in butter. Mix the bread cubes, celery, sausage, mushrooms and liver with remaining ingredients. Stuff turkey or chicken.

*Note:* This is more than enough for a 12-pound turkey or two 5-pound capons. Put excess in foil and bake in oven with the turkey or chicken.

# SAUCES AND GRAVIES

## MUSHROOM CREAM SAUCE

*...serve with Cream de Volaille or chicken croquettes*

3 tablespoons butter
1/4 cup flour
Salt and pepper to taste
Dash of paprika
1 1/2 cups warm milk

1 1/2 cups canned
   unsweetened
   condensed milk
Sliced mushroom buttons
   (if fresh, brown lightly
   in butter)

Melt butter in top of double boiler; add flour, salt, pepper and paprika while stirring with a wire whisk until smooth. Add milk slowly, stirring constantly. Cook until smooth, stirring constantly. Add the desired amount of mushrooms.

*This a Shakertown recipe.*

## GENERAL ROBINSON SAUCE

*...serve with lamb*

1/2 cup brown sugar
1 cup tomato catsup
1 (10-ounce) jar mint *or*
   currant jelly
2 cups lamb broth (pan
   drippings)

1 teaspoon cinnamon
1/2 teaspoon salt
1/2 teaspoon pepper
1/4 cup sherry

Mix all ingredients except sherry in a 2-quart pan; simmer uncovered until thick, 45 minutes to 1 hour. Add sherry and serve. Makes 3 cups.

## HOT MEXICAN SAUCE

1 (4-ounce) can chopped
   green chilies
2 (10-ounce) cans tomatoes
   and green chilies

1 teaspoon salt
1 tablespoon vinegar
1 tablespoon sugar
1 onion, chopped

Combine all ingredients. Serve with tacos or other Mexican dishes.

## BAKED FISH WITH SWISS CHEESE

*this is a wonderful recipe when the fish you're using isn't the best*

| | |
|---|---|
| 4 fish fillets (any kind) | 4 slices Swiss cheese |
| Salt and freshly ground black pepper, to taste | 1 cup sour cream |

Place fish fillets, not over-lapping, in a buttered shallow 8"x 10" baking dish. Season with salt and pepper. Place a slice of cheese on each fillet; sprinkle with a bit more pepper. Spread sour cream over all. Bake at 300° for 30 minutes. Large fillets require 8 minutes more cooking time. Serve at once. Serves 4.

## FRIED CATFISH

| | |
|---|---|
| 6 small catfish, cleaned and dressed | ¼ teaspoon pepper |
| 1 teaspoon salt | 2 cups self-rising cornmeal |

Sprinkle catfish with salt and pepper. Place cornmeal in a paper bag; drop in catfish one at a time, and shake until coated completely. Fry in deep, hot salad oil over high heat until fish float to the top and are golden brown. Drain well. Serve hot. Serves 4 to 6.

# FISH AND SHELLFISH

## SALMON LOAF

1 (15½-ounce) can red
  salmon, drained and
  crumbled
1 cup mashed potatoes
¼ cup chopped celery

1 tablespoon grated onion
2 tablespoons mayonnaise
1 tablespoon lemon juice
1 teaspoon parsley
Salt and pepper to taste

Combine all ingredients, mixing thoroughly; shape into an oval loaf. Place on an oven-to-table platter. Cover with Meringue and bake at 350° for 30 minutes or until meringue is puffed and golden. Serves 6.

*Meringue*
1 egg white

¼ cup mayonnaise

Beat egg white until stiff but not dry; gently fold in mayonnaise. Spread evenly over salmon loaf.

## AVOCADO CRAB MORNAY

½ cup (1 stick) butter
¼ cup flour
1 cup light cream
½ cup chicken broth
½ cup sherry
¼ cup grated Parmesan
  cheese
2 tablespoons shredded Swiss
  or Gruyère cheese
Dash of nutmeg

Dash of cayenne pepper
Dash of salt
6 scallions, minced
3 ripe avocados, peeled,
  pitted and diced
1½ pounds crabmeat,
  preferably lump
Freshly grated Parmesan
  cheese

Melt ¼ cup butter in a heavy saucepan over low heat; add flour, stirring until smooth. Gradually add the next 8 ingredients. Remove from heat. Gently sauté scallions in remaining butter until barely limp; add avocados and crabmeat, stirring constantly. Combine with sauce and cook over low heat; do not boil. Place in large scallop shells; sprinkle with cheese. Bake at 500° for 5 minutes; serve immediately. Serves 8 to 10.

## CRABMEAT CUTLETS

2 pounds fresh crabmeat
1/4 cup fresh lemon juice
6 tablespoons butter
6 tablespoons flour
1 pint half-and-half
1 teaspoon salt
Dash of red pepper

4 teaspoons
  Worcestershire sauce
1 egg-sized onion, grated
3 eggs, beaten with small
  amount of water
Bread crumbs

Preparations for crabmeat cutlets must begin 1 day ahead. Pick over crabmeat to remove any bits of shell. Put into shallow dish; sprinkle with lemon juice. Refrigerate while making cream sauce. Melt butter over low heat; stir in flour and blend. Add half-and-half gradually; cook slowly until thickened, stirring constantly. Add seasonings, onion and crabmeat. Refrigerate overnight. Dividing the mixture evenly, shape into 10 cutlets. Dip each into bread crumbs, then into egg and once again in bread crumbs. Fry in deep fat until golden brown. Serve hot with tartar sauce. Serves 10.

## CRAB IMPERIAL

2 cups lump crabmeat
1 cup mayonnaise (homemade
  or Hellmann's)
1 tablespoon Dijon mustard
1 teaspoon Worcestershire
  sauce
2 tablespoons chopped
  pimiento

1/4 cup minced green
  pepper
Tabasco sauce
Salt and pepper
1/4 cup fine fresh bread
  crumbs
2 tablespoons butter,
  melted

Remove all bits of shell from crabmeat. Combine mayonnaise, mustard, Worcestershire, pimiento and green pepper; season to taste with Tabasco, salt, and pepper. Add crabmeat; toss gently to blend. Fill 6 shells or ramekins equally with crabmeat mixture; sprinkle with crumbs. Drizzle 1 teaspoon of melted butter over each one. Place all on a baking sheet and bake at 350° for 20 minutes. Serves 6.

## CRAB SUPREME

1/2 cup (1 stick) butter, melted
1 onion, chopped
2 ribs celery, chopped
2 pounds fresh crabmeat
1 hard-cooked egg, chopped
1 cup mayonnaise
1/2 teaspoon prepared mustard
1/4 teaspoon salt
1/4 teaspoon pepper
1/2 (7-ounce) box corn flakes, crushed
Paprika

In half of the melted butter, sauté onion and celery until tender. Add crabmeat, egg, mayonnaise, mustard and seasonings; mix thoroughly and pour into a casserole. Combine corn flakes and remainder of butter; put on top. Sprinkle with paprika. Bake at 350° for 20 minutes until bubbly. Serves 8 to 10.

## SHRIMP STEW

1/2 cup flour
3 tablespoons cooking oil
2 medium onions, chopped
2 ribs celery, chopped
1/2 cup chopped green bell pepper
4 small cloves garlic, mashed and centers removed
1 1/2 quarts water
2 (6-ounce) cans tomato paste *or* 2 fresh tomatoes, chopped
2 bay leaves
2 pounds raw medium shrimp, peeled and deveined (approximately 40 )
Salt and pepper
Hot cooked rice

Make a roux by combining flour and oil in a heavy 4-quart saucepan. Brown over medium heat, stirring constantly to prevent scorching. Add onions, celery, green pepper and garlic; stir and cook until vegetables are softened. Add water, tomato paste and bay leaves; simmer slowly for 1 1/2 hours. Remove bay leaves after first 30 minutes. Add shrimp and simmer for 15 minutes; do not overcook. Season to taste with salt and pepper; serve immediately over hot cooked rice. Serves 6 to 8.

*This recipe is from Big Sink Farm chef, Morgan Bradley*

## SHRIMP CASSEROLE

2 1/2 tablespoons butter
1/2 pound mushrooms

2 pounds shrimp
1 (14-ounce) can artichoke
hearts

Sauté mushrooms in butter. Set aside. Boil, shell and devein shrimp. In a 2-quart casserole, layer artichoke hearts, shrimp and mushrooms.

*Sauce*
4 1/2 tablespoons butter
4 1/2 tablespoons flour
3/4 cup milk
3/4 cup whipping cream
1/2 cup dry sherry

1 tablespoon
Worcestershire sauce
Salt and pepper to taste
1/2 cup grated Parmesan
cheese
Paprika

Blend flour in melted butter; add milk and cream, stirring constantly. Continue stirring until thick, then add sherry, Worcestershire, salt and pepper and pour over layered ingredients. Sprinkle with paprika and bake at 375° for 20 to 30 minutes. Serve over rice. Better if made the day before. Serves 8 to 10.

## SHRIMP AND GREEN NOODLE CASSEROLE

1 (8-ounce) package green
noodles
1 bunch spring onions, finely
chopped
3 pounds shrimp, barely
cooked and cleaned
1 cup mayonnaise
1 cup sour cream

1 (10 3/4-ounce) can cream
of mushroom soup
2 tablespoons prepared
mustard
2 eggs, beaten
1 cup sharp Cheddar
cheese, grated
1/2 cup melted butter

Cook noodles al dente and drain. While still hot, toss with spring onions. Place noodles in a buttered 2-quart casserole; top with shrimp. Combine mayonnaise, sour cream, soup, mustard and eggs; pour over shrimp. Combine cheese and melted butter; sprinkle on top and bake at 350° for 30 minutes. Serves 8 to 10.

# FISH AND SHELLFISH

## SHRIMP LOUISIANE

1 quart water
1 rib celery with leaves
1 bay leaf
1/2 teaspoon whole allspice

1/2 lemon, sliced
1 pound fresh raw,
   headless, unpeeled
   shrimp
Hot cooked rice

Boil water, celery, bay leaf and allspice. Add lemon slices and shrimp; return to boil. Remove from heat; cover and let stand for 2 minutes or until shells are barely pink. Drain shrimp and immediately rinse under cold running water. Peel and devein. Cut each shrimp in half; add to Sauce. Heat through and serve over rice. Serves 4.

*Sauce*
1 teaspoon minced onion
2 tablespoons butter
3 tablespoons catsup

2/3 cup cream
1/2 teaspoon salt
1/4 teaspoon celery salt

Sauté onion in butter until lightly browned; stir in catsup, cream and seasonings.

## SHRIMP NEWBURG

6 tablespoons butter
2 tablespoons flour
1 teaspoon salt
1/2 teaspoon nutmeg
Dash of paprika
2 cups half-and-half

3 egg yolks, well beaten
3 tablespoons sherry
2 pounds shrimp, boiled,
   and shelled
Toast points

Melt butter in saucepan over low heat; add flour, salt, nutmeg and paprika, stirring constantly. Gradually stir in half-and-half, egg yolks and sherry; cook over medium heat, stirring constantly, until sauce is thickened and bubbly. Add shrimp and serve over toast points. Serves 4.

## SHRIMP AND RICE ROCKEFELLER

1 cup chopped onion
2 tablespoons margarine
3/4 pound raw, peeled,
   deveined shrimp, cut in half
1 (10¾-ounce) can cream of
   mushroom soup, undiluted
1 cup grated Swiss cheese
¼ cup dry sherry
3 cups cooked rice

1 (8-ounce) can water
   chestnuts, drained and
   sliced
2 (10-ounce) packages
   frozen chopped
   spinach, cooked and
   well drained
1 tablespoon lemon juice
¼ cup grated Parmesan
   cheese
Salt and pepper to taste

Sauté onion in margarine until tender but not browned. Add shrimp and continue cooking until shrimp is slightly pink, about 2 minutes. Stir in soup, Swiss cheese and sherry; heat just until warm. Add rice, water chestnuts, spinach, lemon juice and 2 tablespoons Parmesan cheese; season with salt and pepper. Spoon into a lightly greased baking dish; sprinkle with remaining Parmesan. Bake, uncovered, at 350° for 20 minutes or until hot and bubbly. Serves 6 to 8.

## OVEN BARBECUED SHRIMP

1 pound butter
1 pound margarine
1 teaspoon rosemary
3/4 cup Worcestershire sauce
5 tablespoons black pepper
4 teaspoons salt

4 lemons, thinly sliced
1 teaspoon Tabasco sauce
10 pounds raw, unpeeled,
   headless, medium-
   to-large shrimp

Combine all ingredients except shrimp and heat to boiling point. Place shrimp in a large shallow pan and pour the sauce over them. Bake, uncovered, at 400° for 20 minutes, stirring twice during cooking. Serve with the sauce and buttered French bread. Serves 16.

# FISH AND SHELLFISH

## SHAKERTOWN SCALLOPED OYSTERS

1 pint oysters
6 tablespoons cream and
   oyster liquor

1 1/2 cups coarse cracker
   crumbs
Salt and pepper
1/2 cup melted butter

Pick over oysters and drain. Grease the baking dish and cover with a third of the crumbs. Cover with half of the oysters and season. Add half the oyster liquor and cream. Repeat. Cover the top with remaining crumbs. Pour melted butter over all. Bake at 400° for about 30 minutes. Serves 6.

## FRIED OYSTERS

1 (12-ounce) can select oysters
4 eggs, slightly beaten

Bread crumbs, finely
   grated, or fine cracker
   crumbs
Salt and pepper to taste

Drain oysters; dry thoroughly between paper towels. Season the eggs lightly with salt and pepper. Dip each oyster into eggs, then into crumbs; place on a cutting board for 1/2 hour to dry again. Deep fry in hot Crisco (365° to 375°) for 2 to 3 minutes until browned. Drain on paper towels. Serves 4.

## CUCUMBER SAUCE

1 cup sour cream
2 teaspoons chopped chives
1 teaspoon dill weed

1/2 cup seeded and finely
   chopped cucumber
Salt and pepper to taste

Mix all together and serve very cold with salmon.

## ASPARAGUS-CHEESE SOUFFLÉ

| | |
|---|---|
| 4 tablespoons butter | 1 cup grated Cheddar |
| 6 tablespoons flour |   cheese |
| 2 cups milk | 6 egg yolks, beaten |
| 1/2 teaspoon salt | 6 egg whites, stiffly beaten |
| 1/4 teaspoon pepper | 2 (15-ounce) cans |
| 1 1/2 cups bread crumbs, |   asparagus, drained and |
|   packed |   cut |

Melt butter and blend in flour; add milk gradually, stirring constantly. Reduce heat and cook 3 minutes longer. Add seasonings, bread crumbs and cheese, stirring until cheese is melted. Cool; stir in egg yolks. Fold in egg whites, then asparagus. Pour mixture into a greased large ring mold, set in a pan of hot water and bake at 325° for about 1 hour.

## KENTUCKY LEMON ASPARAGUS

3 pounds fresh asparagus

Wash and trim asparagus to equal length. Tie in 6 bundles using cotton string and stand in bottom of double boiler with tips up. The pan should be half full of boiling water. Turn double boiler top upside down and place over asparagus. Cook until tender (8 to 10 minutes) and remove strings. Or, asparagus may be steamed about 10 minutes.

*Topping*
| | |
|---|---|
| 1/2 cup butter | 1 1/2 teaspoons grated |
| 1 cup bread crumbs |   lemon rind |
| | Salt to taste |

Brown bread crumbs in butter over medium heat. Add lemon rind, salt and sprinkle on hot asparagus. Serves 12.

## COUNTRY GREEN BEANS

1/2 small ham hock (4" long),
plus extra strip ham fat if
hock is lean
4 cups water — to barely
cover beans
1/4 teaspoon crushed dried red
pepper
1 teaspoon salt
1/2 teaspoon dried cloves
1 1/2 tablespoons brown
sugar
1/2 small onion

Bring all the above to a boil and cook for 15 to 20 minutes. *Add:* Three pounds green snap beans. Bring back to a boil. Turn heat to medium low and put the lid half on. Simmer for three hours, or more until the liquid has evaporated. Remove the ham hock and break up the ham into small pieces. Add pieces to beans. If doubled, use less water. Serves 6 to 8.

## TANGY GREEN BEANS

1/2 cup finely minced scallions
2 tablespoons butter
1 pound young green beans
1 tablespoon raspberry
vinegar, or to taste
Salt and freshly ground
pepper to taste

Sauté scallions in butter until transparent; set aside. Cook beans in boiling water until tender but still crisp; rinse with cold water and drain well. Add vinegar to scallions, season with salt and pepper and combine with beans. Serve hot or chilled. Serves 4.

## BROCCOLI RING

3 tablespoons butter
3 tablespoons flour
1 cup milk
1/4 teaspoon salt
6 eggs, separated
2 cups cooked chopped
broccoli

6 tablespoons chopped
celery
3 tablespoons onion juice
Juice of 1/2 lemon
1 cup mayonnaise

Melt butter over low heat; blend in flour. Slowly stir in milk; add salt and cook, stirring constantly, until sauce is smooth. Beat egg yolks and stir into sauce; add broccoli, celery, onion juice and lemon juice. Cool; add mayonnaise and mix thoroughly. Beat egg whites until stiff and fold into broccoli mixture. Spoon into a ring mold; set in a pan of water in oven. Bake at 350° for 1 hour.

## BROCCOLI AU GRATIN

1 pound fresh broccoli, cut
into florets with 1/2" to 1"
stem remaining
3 tablespoons butter
3 tablespoons flour
1 scant teaspoon salt
1/4 teaspoon dry mustard

1 cup plus 2 tablespoons
milk
3/4 cup grated sharp
Cheddar cheese
3 tablespoons grated
Parmesan cheese
(optional)

Steam broccoli until just tender. Meanwhile melt butter; stir in flour, salt and dry mustard and cook until blended. Gradually add milk; cook over medium heat, stirring constantly, until thick. Add cheese and stir until it is melted. Place broccoli in a greased casserole and pour over cheese sauce. Sprinkle Parmesan cheese on top. Bake at 350° for 20 minutes. Serves 4 to 6.

# VEGETABLES

## BROCCOLI CASSEROLE

2 (10-ounce) packages frozen
  broccoli
1 cup mayonnaise
2 eggs, beaten
2 teaspoons onion, chopped

1 (10¾-ounce) can cream
  of celery soup
1 cup grated sharp
  Cheddar cheese
¾ cup dry bread crumbs

To thaw broccoli, heat in water, bringing it just to a boil. Drain, cool and chop; mix with remaining ingredients, except bread crumbs. Place mixture in a 2-quart casserole and cover with bread crumbs. Bake, uncovered, at 350° for 45 minutes.

## CARROT SOUFFLÉ

½ pound carrots
  (5 medium-size)
2 tablespoons minced onion
4 tablespoons butter or
  margarine
3 tablespoons flour

½ teaspoon salt
¼ teaspoon nutmeg
Red pepper to taste
1 cup milk
3 eggs, separated

Wash, but do not scrape, carrots; cut into 1½" pieces. Cook, covered, in boiling salted water until very tender; drain and purée in an electric blender, making three-fourths of a cup. Sauté onion in butter until limp but not brown; stir in flour and seasonings. Slowly add milk, stirring until thickened. Add puréed carrots and cool slightly. Add beaten egg yolks and cool to lukewarm; fold in beaten egg whites. Pour into an ungreased 1-quart casserole; bake at 350° for 35 to 40 minutes until center is firm. Serves 4 to 6.

## CARROTS WITH GRAPES

*This dish is not only good but has great eye appeal*

8 medium-size carrots, cut on
  diagonal
2 tablespoons butter
3 tablespoons brown sugar
3 tablespoons Vermouth

2 teaspoons cornstarch
3 tablespoons water
3/4 cup green grapes,
  halved
3/4 cup red grapes, halved

Cook carrots for 8 minutes. Meanwhile, melt butter and stir in sugar and Vermouth. Mix cornstarch and water until blended; add to sauce. Cook over low heat, stirring constantly, until smooth and slightly thickened. Add more water if needed. Stir in carrots and heat through. *Add grapes only when ready to serve.* Serves 4.

## CARROT RING

3 cups cooked carrots
3 tablespoons minced celery
2 tablespoons minced onion
2 tablespoons sugar
3 egg yolks, beaten
1 cup bread crumbs
1 cup cream

1 teaspoon
  Worcestershire sauce
1 teaspoon salt
2 tablespoons melted
  butter
3 egg whites, beaten until
  stiff but not dry

Mix all ingredients together, folding in beaten egg whites last. Pour into a greased ring mold and place in a shallow pan of water in the oven. Bake at 350° for 30 to 40 minutes until firm. Invert carrot ring onto a platter and fill center with creamed fresh peas.

# VEGETABLES

## INDIAN CELERY CASSEROLE

4 cups celery, cut in 1" pieces
1 (6-ounce) can sliced water
   chestnuts, drained
1/4 cup chopped pimiento
1 (10¾-ounce) can cream of
   chicken soup

1/2 cup sliced, toasted
   almonds
1 cup croutons
2 tablespoons butter,
   melted

Put celery in boiling, salted water and cook 8 minutes; drain. Layer celery, water chestnuts, pimiento and chicken soup in a buttered 2-quart casserole. Toss almonds and croutons in melted butter; sprinkle on top. Cover and bake at 350° for 30 minutes until bubbly.

*Variation:* To serve as a main dish, add 2 to 3 cups chopped, cooked chicken.

## FRESH CORN PUDDING

3 cups fresh corn cut from
   cob
6 whole eggs, stirred well (not
   beaten)
3 cups heavy cream
1/2 cup sugar

1 teaspoon salt
1 teaspoon flour
1/2 teaspoon baking
   powder
2 teaspoons butter

Using a sharp paring knife, barely cut through the tips of the corn kernels, then scrape the cob to remove the remaining juice and pulp. Stir in eggs and cream. Combine dry ingredients and add to corn mixture; stir in melted butter and mix well. Pour into a greased baking dish and bake at 350° for about 1 hour until knife inserted in center comes out clean. Serves 8.

*From Lexington caterer, Christine Gilmore*

## CORN PUDDING

2 cups fresh corn cut from
    cob, or frozen or canned
1 tablespoon flour
3 tablespoons sugar
1 teaspoon salt

2 eggs
3/4 cup milk
2 tablespoons butter,
    melted

Combine ingredients in order listed; pour into a 1-quart baking dish. Place in a larger pan of water and bake at 350° for 30 to 45 minutes. Can be mixed a day ahead and baked when needed. Serves 4 to 6.

## LARGE CORN PUDDING

6 cups fresh corn cut from
    cob
6 tablespoons sugar
1/4 teaspoon salt
6 tablespoons cornstarch

8 eggs, beaten
5 cups whole milk
1 cup half-and-half

Mix corn, sugar, salt and cornstarch; stir in eggs. Pour in milk and half-and-half, mixing thoroughly. Pour into a 13"x 9"x 2" baking dish; bake at 350° for about 1 1/2 hours. Serves 10.

## CUSHAW

1 medium cushaw
1/2 cup brown sugar
1 teaspoon cinnamon

1/4 teaspoon nutmeg
1/2 cup (1 stick) butter
1/3 cup heavy cream

Peel cushaw. Using only the tenderest pieces, dice and cook, covered, in boiling water until tender. Drain well. Return to pot and add remaining ingredients in order listed. Cover and keep warm until serving time. This can also be baked in a casserole in which case the cushaw should be boiled until just barely tender. Serves 6 to 8.

# VEGETABLES

## STUFFED EGGPLANT

1 large eggplant or 2 medium
 ones
1 large onion, chopped
1 green pepper, seeded and
 chopped
1/2 cup (1 stick) butter
1 (16-ounce) can tomatoes,
 drained
1 (5-ounce) jar Old English
 cheese spread
1 cup butter cracker
 crumbs
Worcestershire sauce
 to taste
Cayenne pepper to taste
1 cup bread crumbs
Grated Parmesan cheese
Paprika

Cut eggplant in half lengthwise; scoop out the pulp, leaving a 1/2" shell. Chop pulp and boil about 15 minutes. Drain thoroughly. Sauté onion and green pepper in butter until golden brown. Add tomatoes, cheese spread, cracker crumbs and cooked eggplant pulp. Season with Worcestershire sauce and cayenne. Fill shell with mixture; sprinkle with bread crumbs, Parmesan cheese and paprika. Bake at 350° for 30 to 40 minutes.

## EGGPLANT CASSEROLE

1 large eggplant
1/2 onion, chopped
1/2 green pepper, chopped
1 tablespoon bacon fat
1 cup canned tomatoes,
 chopped, and juice
1 cup fine fresh bread
 crumbs
1 teaspoon salt
1/2 teaspoon pepper
1 tablespoon butter
1 teaspoon
 Worcestershire sauce

Boil eggplant for 30 minutes in shell. Cool; remove pulp and place in bowl. Sauté onion and green pepper in skillet with bacon fat. Add chopped tomatoes and juice; simmer for 10 minutes. Add bread crumbs, salt, pepper, butter, Worcestershire sauce and eggplant pulp. Pour into a greased baking dish; sprinkle with more bread crumbs and dot with extra butter. Bake at 375° until crumbs are brown. Serves 6.

## HOMINY RING

1 cup milk
2 tablespoons butter
2 cups cold boiled hominy,
    drained

2 eggs, beaten
1 teaspoon salt
1/4 teaspoon pepper

Heat milk and butter; add hominy and mix until smooth. Stir in eggs and seasonings; pour into a buttered 1-quart ring mold and bake at 350° until firm and brown on top, about 30 to 40 minutes.

## BAKED MUSHROOMS

3 pounds mushrooms
Lemon juice
2 to 3 tablespoons minced
    onion
4 tablespoons butter
Steak seasoning to taste
2 tablespoons flour

4 tablespoons grated
    Parmesan cheese
1 cup milk or cream
3 egg yolks, lightly beaten
4 tablespoons Pepperidge
    Farm herb dressing,
    crushed fine

Clean, trim and slice mushrooms; sprinkle with lemon juice to keep white. Simmer with onion and butter for about 2 minutes, add seasonings to taste. Stir in flour and cheese, cooking an additional 2 minutes. Place in a buttered baking dish. Mix milk or cream with egg yolks and pour over mushrooms; sprinkle with crumbs and dot with butter. Bake at 425° for 15 to 20 minutes until golden brown.

## MUSHROOMS AU GRATIN

2 pounds mushrooms,
  washed, dried and sliced
4 tablespoons butter
2 tablespoons flour
1/2 teaspoon salt

1/8 teaspoon freshly
  ground pepper
2/3 cup sour cream
1/2 cup chopped parsley
1 cup shredded Gruyère
  or Swiss cheese

Sauté sliced mushrooms in butter for 1 minute. Cover skillet and cook until mushrooms are juicy, about 3 to 5 minutes. In a bowl, blend flour, salt and pepper with sour cream; mix gently with the mushrooms and heat to boiling. Immediately remove from heat; pour into a shallow ungreased 8"x 12" casserole. Combine parsley and cheese and sprinkle on top. Bake uncovered at 425° for 10 minutes. Prepare ahead and bake later. Serves 8.

*Note:* To make uniform mushroom slices quickly and easily, use an egg slicer.

## ONION RINGS

3 to 4 large onions
3 cups buttermilk or milk
1 egg
1 teaspoon salt
1 1/2 teaspoons baking powder

1 cup all-purpose flour
2/3 cup water
1/4 cup milk
1 tablespoon vegetable oil
1/4 teaspoon cayenne
  pepper

Slice onions 1/4" thick and soak in buttermilk for 30 minutes. Drain onion rings on paper towels, having them as dry as possible so that the batter will stick. Combine remaining ingredients. Dip each ring in batter and drop into hot fat (350° to 370°); fry until brown. Drain on paper towels.

## CREAMED ONIONS

1 pound baby white onions
4 tablespoons butter
2 tablespoons flour

1 cup milk, heated
1/2 teaspoon salt
1/8 teaspoon freshly
   ground pepper

To make peeling of onions easier, place them in a pot of boiling water and cook for 2 minutes. Drain and peel. Melt butter and blend in flour; add warm milk gradually, stirring constantly. Reduce heat and cook 3 minutes longer; add seasonings and onions.

## CREAMED PEAS AND NEW POTATOES

8 to 10 very small new
   potatoes, peeled

2 (17-ounce) cans smallest
   early peas

Cook potatoes, covered, in boiling salted water 10 to 15 minutes or until tender; drain. Drain and rinse peas. Vegetables should be dry. Combine with Sauce in top of double boiler; heat 10 to 15 minutes. Serves 6.

*Sauce*
1/4 cup butter
1/4 cup all-purpose flour
1 cup chicken broth

1 cup milk
1 teaspoon salt
1/8 teaspoon pepper

Melt butter in a heavy saucepan over low heat; blend in flour. Cook 1 minute, stirring constantly. Gradually add chicken broth and milk; cook over medium heat, stirring constantly until thickened. Stir in salt and pepper. This sauce can be made one day ahead.

*Note:* 1 1/2 pounds of fresh English peas may be substituted for canned. Shell and wash; add to a small amount of boiling salted water. Reduce heat; cover and cook 8 to 12 minutes or until peas are tender. Drain.

# VEGETABLES

## FRESH BLACK-EYED PEAS

2 ham hocks
1 quart water
1 quart shelled fresh
   blackeyed peas

1 small onion, minced
1 to 1 1/2 teaspoons salt
1/4 teaspoon pepper

Place ham hocks in a 4-quart Dutch oven with water; bring to a boil. Reduce heat; cover and simmer 30 minutes. Add peas, onion and seasonings; cook 30 to 40 minutes longer or until peas are tender. Add more water if needed. Meat from hocks may be cut up and added to peas. Serves 6 to 8.

## FRIED BANANA PEPPERS

12 banana peppers
1 egg, beaten
3/4 cup milk

1 1/2 cups cornmeal
1/3 cup fresh saltine
   cracker crumbs

Cut peppers in half lengthwise and remove seeds. In a large bowl, beat egg and milk; add peppers and soak 1 hour. (If peppers are very hot, soak longer.) Mix cornmeal and cracker crumbs; lift peppers from milk mixture and put in cornmeal mixture, pressing the meal onto peppers to coat heavily. Repeat the procedure, coating peppers twice. This can be done early in the day, refrigerating until ready to fry. In a heavy skillet, put enough oil to cover the peppers (they should not be turned while cooking). The oil is hot when a drop of water makes it sizzle. Fry peppers until golden brown; remove and drain on paper towels. If they brown too fast, reduce heat to medium high.

## NOISETTE POTATOES

Potatoes
Clarified butter or salad oil

Salt and pepper to taste

With a ball cutter, scoop out rounds of potatoes the size of hazelnuts. Sauté the potatoes in clarified butter or salad oil until they are golden and soft. Season with salt and pepper.

## NEW POTATO CASSEROLE

10 large new potatoes or
    Russet potatoes
1/2 cup grated Cheddar cheese
1 cup mayonnaise

1/2 cup chopped onion
1 pound bacon, cooked
   and crumbled

Boil unpeeled potatoes; slice. Combine cheese, mayonnaise and onion; gently stir into potatoes. Place in a greased casserole and top with bacon. Bake at 350° for 20 to 30 minutes or until bubbly.

## SWISS SCALLOPED POTATOES

1 cup shredded Swiss cheese
1/2 cup sliced green onions,
   including tops
1 tablespoon dill weed
2 tablespoons butter
2 tablespoons flour

1 teaspoon salt
1 cup milk
1 cup sour cream
6 to 7 cups cooked,
   peeled, sliced potatoes

In a small saucepan, toss cheese, onions and dill weed. Set aside. In a 1-quart pan, melt butter; stir in flour and salt. Gradually add milk; cook, stirring constantly, until thickened, about 2 minutes. Remove from heat and add sour cream. In a buttered shallow 3-quart baking dish, layer one-third of potatoes, one-half of cheese mixture and one-half of sour cream mixture. Repeat, making a second layer. For the top layer, use the remaining one-third of potatoes and sprinkle with Topping. Bake in a pre-heated oven at 350° for 30 to 35 minutes. Makes 8 to 10 servings.

*Topping*
1/2 cup Swiss cheese
1/4 cup fine dry bread crumbs

1/4 cup melted butter

Mix all ingredients.

*Note:* To make a main dish casserole, add 3 cups of diced cooked ham to layers and double the amount of sour cream sauce.

## ESCALLOPED POTATOES

2 tablespoons minced parsley
1 1/2 cups thinly-sliced onions
4 1/2 cups thinly-sliced
   potatoes
3 teaspoons salt
3 tablespoons butter

2 tablespoons plus 1
   teaspoon flour
1 3/4 cups milk
1/8 teaspoon pepper
1/8 teaspoon paprika

Bring 1" of water to boil in a pan; add parsley, onions, potatoes and 2 teaspoons salt. Boil for 5 minutes; drain. Melt butter, blend in flour, pepper and remaining teaspoon of salt. Add milk and cook until thickened, stirring constantly. Combine vegetables and cream sauce; place in a shallow casserole and bake, uncovered, at 400° for about 35 minutes. Cheese or bread crumbs may be put on top if desired. Serves 4 to 5.

## CREAMED POTATOES

3 pounds Idaho potatoes
1 1/2 sticks butter or margarine

3/4 teaspoon salt
Scant 1/2 cup milk

Peel and slice potatoes in 3/4" slices; boil in 1 quart water about 7 minutes, covered, or until barely soft when pierced with a fork. Drain all water from potatoes. In the bowl of an electric mixer, place 1 stick of butter. Put potatoes into bowl; mix slowly at first to break up potatoes, then beat fast for several minutes. Slowly add salt and milk, beating until fluffy. Dot with remaining butter; bake 15 to 20 minutes at 350.°

## SWEET POTATO CASSEROLE

3 cups sweet potatoes, cooked
   and mashed
$^1/_2$ cup sugar
$^1/_3$ cup cream
2 eggs
1 $^1/_2$ teaspoons vanilla extract

1 cup butter, melted
$^1/_8$ teaspoon ground
   cinnamon
$^1/_{16}$ teaspoon ground
   allspice
$^1/_4$ teaspoon salt

Combine all ingredients and put in a greased casserole. Sprinkle evenly with topping and bake at 350° for 30 minutes.

*Topping*
$^1/_3$ cup butter, melted
1 cup brown sugar

$^1/_3$ cup flour
1 cup chopped pecans

## SWEET POTATO BALLS

1 (12-ounce) can sweet
   potatoes
1 egg, separated
$^1/_2$ teaspoon salt
$^1/_2$ teaspoon cinnamon

2 tablespoons melted
   butter
6 marshmallows
Crushed corn flakes

Mash potatoes thoroughly; add egg yolk, salt, cinnamon and butter, mixing well. Mold potato mixture around marshmallows, forming 6 balls with a marshmallow in the center of each. Beat egg white until foamy. Roll balls in egg white, then in corn flakes. Place in a baking dish; bake at 350° for 10 to 12 minutes until golden brown. Serves 6.

# VEGETABLES

## RATATOUILLE

*... a low-calorie, no-salt vegetable casserole*

8 medium tomatoes
1 ½ pounds zucchini, peeled and sliced
3 ribs of celery, sliced
1 large green pepper, cut into large squares
1 large eggplant, cut into large cubes
1 large onion, cut into large squares
¼ cup corn oil margarine
3 cloves garlic, minced
1 tablespoon oregano
1 tablespoon basil
1 teaspoon pepper
4 tablespoons grated Parmesan or Sapsago cheese

Scald tomatoes in boiling water for 1 minute; drain, peel and cut in half. Squeeze out and discard tomato juice; cut each half into 4 pieces and set aside. Blanch separately in boiling water the zucchini, celery, green pepper and eggplant. Drain and set aside. Sauté onion in margarine for 4 to 5 minutes; add garlic, oregano, basil and pepper. Continue cooking until onion is transparent. Combine all ingredients, mixing thoroughly; spoon into a greased shallow casserole and sprinkle with cheese. Bake at 350° for 25 to 30 minutes. Serves 8 to 10.

## RISOTTO

1 small onion, chopped
3 tablespoons butter
1 cup raw rice
2 cups chicken stock or bouillon, heated
Salt and pepper to taste

Sauté chopped onion in butter until tender. Add rice and sauté, stirring, until each grain of rice is golden and coated with butter. Heat chicken stock in a saucepan until boiling; add rice and onions and return to a boil. Cover, lower heat and simmer for 15 to 25 minutes or until all liquid is absorbed. Serves 6 to 7 .

## WILD RICE AND CHEESE CASSEROLE
*....wonderful with duck, dove and other game*

1 cup raw wild rice
1 cup grated Cheddar cheese
1 (4-ounce) can sliced
  mushrooms
½ (6-ounce) can pitted ripe
  olives, finely chopped

1 (16-ounce) can stewed
  tomatoes
½ cup chopped onion
½ cup vegetable oil
1 cup hot water

Cook wild rice and drain; mix with other ingredients. Pour into a greased casserole and bake at 350° for 1 hour. Serves 8.

## HERB RICE

8 to 10 slices bacon
3 tablespoons bacon drippings
1 small onion, chopped
1 cup chopped celery

1 cup canned, sliced
  mushrooms
2½ cups cooked rice
2 tablespoons soy sauce
1 egg, beaten

Fry bacon; crumble and set aside. Sauté onion and celery in bacon drippings. Add mushrooms, cooked rice and soy sauce. Before serving, reheat and stir in beaten egg and crumbled bacon. Makes 6 servings.

## RICE RING WITH CHEESE

2 cups uncooked rice
½ pound sharp Cheddar
  cheese, grated

4 tablespoons (½ stick)
  butter
Salt to taste

Cook rice; put into a warm bowl and add remaining ingredients, stirring until cheese and butter are melted. Pack in a very well greased 10" ring mold, or solid mold. One hour before serving, set mold in a pan of boiling water in oven. Bake at 350°.

# VEGETABLES

## WILD RICE CASSEROLE

1 cup wild rice, soaked
  overnight
1 (10½-ounce) can
  consommé, undiluted
4 tablespoons butter
¾ pound fresh mushrooms,
  sliced

1½ cups finely chopped
  celery
6 to 8 green onions, sliced
1 (6-ounce) can water
  chestnuts, drained and
  sliced
½ cup vermouth

Wash and drain soaked rice and combine with consommé in a large saucepan. Simmer, covered for about 30 minutes or until liquid is absorbed. Melt butter in a skillet and sauté mushrooms, onions and celery until limp. Mix with water chestnuts and rice and put in a buttered 2 quart casserole. Refrigerate until ready to use. When ready to reheat add vermouth and dot top with butter. Bake at 350° for 30 to 40 minutes.

## RICE SOUFFLÉ

3 eggs, separated
1 cup cold cooked rice
½ cup milk

2 tablespoons butter
¼ pound grated Cheddar
  cheese
Dash of salt

Beat egg yolks; add to rice. Add milk, butter and cheese, stirring well. Fold in beaten egg whites. Pour into a greased 1-quart casserole and bake at 300° for 30 to 45 minutes. Serves 4 to 6.

## GREEN RICE

6 cups cooked rice
1 cup cooked, chopped
  spinach, drained

2 tablespoons chopped
  parsley
1 teaspoon nutmeg
1 tablespoon butter

Combine all ingredients and heat; place in a warm serving bowl. Serves 12.

## SPINACH ARTICHOKE CASSEROLE

2 packages frozen chopped
   spinach, thawed
1 square Philadelphia cream
   cheese

1 stick butter
1 can artichokes
1 can water chestnuts

Cook spinach, drain and chop. Put in butter and cream cheese, sliced water chestnuts, sliced artichokes. Season with Worcestershire, Tabasco, and Parmesan cheese. Put in casserole, cover and heat 350.°

## SPINACH MUSHROOM CASSEROLE

2 pounds fresh spinach, or 3
   packages frozen leaf
   spinach
3/4 pound sliced mushrooms
1/2 stick butter, or margarine
1 cup grated Cheddar or
   Parmesan cheese

1 cup medium cream
   sauce (page 213)
Salt
Nutmeg
1/2 cup buttered cracker
   crumbs

Cook spinach and drain well. Sauté mushrooms in butter. Add salt and nutmeg to taste. Mix mushrooms and spinach with the cream sauce and place in buttered shallow casserole. Put crumbs on top. Bake in pre-heated 350° oven until hot and bubbly, approximately 30 minutes. This may be prepared a day ahead of time. Serves 6.

# VEGETABLES

## SPINACH ROULADE

3 pounds fresh spinach or 3
   (10-ounce) packages frozen
   spinach
6 tablespoons butter
4 eggs, separated

Salt
Pepper, freshly ground
Nutmeg, freshly grated
Bread crumbs
1/4 cup grated Parmesan
   cheese

Cook spinach. (If using fresh spinach, wash well and cook just until wilted.) Drain and squeeze out water. Put spinach in a large bowl; beat in butter and egg yolks. Add seasonings to taste. Beat egg whites until peaks form; fold into spinach mixture. Spread on a buttered 15"x 10" jellyroll pan lined with wax paper, having an extra inch at each end. Sprinkle with bread crumbs and cheese. Bake at 350° for 12 to 16 minutes. Unmold onto foil or a dish towel. (If not using immediately, roll up in foil and refrigerate.) This may be prepared a day ahead. Unroll roulade; spread evenly with Mushroom Filling or Brunch Filling and roll up again. Serve at room temperature or warm with a side dish of Creme Fraiche (page 304).

*Mushroom Filling*

1/2 pound mushrooms, finely
   minced
3 tablespoons finely-minced
   scallions
2 tablespoons butter
1 tablespoon fresh dill

8 ounces cream cheese,
   softened
2 to 3 tablespoons sour
   cream
Salt
Pepper, freshly ground

Sauté mushrooms and scallions in butter. Blend cream cheese and sour cream; add mushroom-scallion mixture and seasonings.

*Brunch Filling*

3 tablespoons butter
4 eggs, beaten
1/4 pound smoked salmon,
   minced

1 tablespoon minced
   chives
Salt
Pepper, freshly ground

Melt butter; add eggs and lightly scramble. Add remaining ingredients.

## SPINACH RING

1 1/2 pounds fresh spinach or 1
  (10-ounce) package frozen
  chopped spinach
1 tablespoon minced onion
3 tablespoons butter
3 tablespoons flour

1 cup light cream *or* 1/2
  cup cream and 1/2 cup
  chicken stock
3 eggs, separated
Salt and pepper to taste
Dash of nutmeg

Cook spinach and drain well. (If using fresh, chop finely.) Sauté onion in butter until transparent; add flour and stir for 1 minute until blended. Slowly add cream (or cream and chicken stock); bring to a boil, stirring constantly, and cook 1 minute over low heat. Beat egg yolks and slowly add to sauce, stirring constantly. Cook 1 minute longer until sauce is thickened. Season with salt, pepper and nutmeg and add to spinach. Beat egg whites until stiff but not dry; fold into spinach mixture. Pour into a greased 9" ring mold. Set in a pan of hot water and bake at 325° until set, about 30 minutes. Unmold onto a platter and serve hot. Serves 4.

*Note:* The center of the spinach ring may be filled with hot, cooked vegetables, chicken, fish or eggs.

## SPINACH CASSEROLE

3 (10-ounce) packages frozen
  chopped spinach
1/2 cup chopped onion
4 tablespoons butter
2 tablespoons flour
2 cups milk

1/2 teaspoon salt
1/2 cup sherry
6 hard-cooked eggs,
  grated
1 cup bread crumbs
1 cup grated Cheddar
  cheese

Cook spinach until thawed; drain well. Sauté onion in butter until lightly browned; blend in flour. Slowly add milk, stirring until mixture is thickened. Stir in salt, sherry and grated eggs; add spinach. Pour into a greased baking dish; sprinkle with bread crumbs and cheese. Bake at 350° until hot and bubbly.

## SPINACH MORNAY

2 (10-ounce) packages frozen
   chopped spinach
2 tablespoons butter
1/4 pound mushrooms, sliced
2 tablespoons flour
1/2 cup milk
1 teaspoon salt

1/4 teaspoon pepper
1 teaspoon
   Worcestershire sauce
1/4 cup plus 1 tablespoon
   grated Parmesan cheese
1 tablespoon fresh bread
   crumbs

Cook spinach just until thawed; drain. Melt butter, add mushrooms and sauté for 5 minutes. Blend in flour and gradually add milk; cook over low heat, stirring constantly until thickened. Stir in spinach, seasonings and 1/4 cup Parmesan cheese. Turn mixture into a buttered 1-quart casserole. Combine crumbs and 1 tablespoon cheese; sprinkle over top. Bake at 375° for 20 minutes. Serves 6.

## SUMMER SQUASH CASSEROLE

2 pounds small, yellow squash
1 egg, beaten
1/4 cup cream or evaporated
   milk
1 tablespoon sugar, mixed
   with 5 teaspoons
   cornstarch

1/2 cup (1 stick) butter or
   margarine, melted
1 small onion, finely
   chopped
Salt and pepper to taste

Pare squash and cut into cubes. Heat 1/2 cup water to boiling, add squash and cover pan tightly. Reduce heat and simmer until barely tender; drain well and mash. Beat egg with cream or milk; add sugar-cornstarch mixture and blend thoroughly. Stir in melted butter and chopped onion; fold in mashed squash and season with salt and pepper. Pour into a greased 2-quart casserole; bake at 325° for 30 minutes.

## SUMMER CREAMED SQUASH

1½ pounds yellow squash, sliced
1 tablespoon bacon drippings
4 tablespoons butter
2 tablespoons cream

2 teaspoons grated onion
¼ teaspoon salt
⅛ teaspoon coarsely ground black pepper

Boil squash until barely tender and drain well. Heat bacon drippings in heavy skillet and add squash when very hot. Stir until moisture is gone and the squash is in smaller pieces. Reduce heat; add butter, cream, onion, salt and pepper. Simmer for 10 to 15 minutes. Serves 4.

## TOMATOES FILLED WITH CRAB MEAT AND CHEESE

8 tomatoes, unpeeled
1½ tablespoons butter
3 tablespoons finely chopped green pepper
3 tablespoons finely chopped onion
1½ tablespoons flour
1½ cups milk

1½ cups crab meat
1 cup grated Cheddar cheese
2 tablespoons Worcestershire sauce
⅓ teaspoon salt
Cayenne pepper to taste

Scoop out tomatoes; turn upside down to drain while preparing filling. Melt butter over low heat; add green pepper and onion and cook for 3 minutes. Blend in flour; slowly stir in milk. When sauce is thick and boiling, add remaining ingredients and cook until cheese is melted. Spoon filling into tomatoes and place in a pan with enough water to keep them from scorching. Bake at 325° for 15 to 20 minutes until hot throughout.

# VEGETABLES

## SCALLOPED TOMATOES

1/2 cup minced onion
1/4 cup chopped green pepper
3 tablespoons butter
1/4 cup chopped celery
3 tablespoons brown sugar
2 cups French bread cubes,
  browned in 1/4 cup butter
1 bay leaf, crumbled

1/4 teaspoon oregano
1/8 teaspoon cayenne
Salt and pepper to taste
3 1/2 cups fresh tomatoes
  or 1 (28-ounce) can
  tomatoes, drained
1/4 cup bread crumbs,
  buttered

Sauté onion, green pepper and celery in butter until tender. Add brown sugar, buttered bread cubes, bay leaf, oregano, cayenne, salt and pepper. Add tomatoes, mixing thoroughly; pour into a greased casserole. Sprinkle buttered bread crumbs on top and bake at 375° for 45 minutes. Serves 6.

## BROILED TOMATOES

6 ripe tomatoes
Salt, pepper and cayenne
  to taste

Dry bread crumbs mixed
  with basil or oregano
Butter

Halve 6 ripe tomatoes and sprinkle each half lightly with salt, pepper and cayenne. Top the tomatoes with fine dry bread crumbs or mix crumbs with the basil or oregano and put butter bits on top. Broil the tomatoes 3" from the heat for about 6 minutes or until tomatoes are brown and hot.

## DALY DOZEN TOMATOES

12 firm, ripe, medium
  tomatoes
Salt
4 tablespoons minced onion
2 stalks celery, finely chopped
1 teaspoon salt

$^{1}/_{2}$ teaspoon pepper
3 cups coarsely crushed
  cereal (wheat bran,
  Team or cornflakes)
Butter
12 teaspoons maple syrup
  or pancake syrup

Cut large hollows in unpeeled tomatoes. Salt them and invert on a rack to drain for about 15 minutes. Combine onion, celery, salt, pepper and cereal. Place tomato cases in a baking dish; fill and mound with the mixture. Dot each tomato with butter and drizzle with a teaspoon of syrup. Add enough water to the baking dish to keep the tomatoes from scorching; bake at 350° for 20 minutes.

## TOMATOES WITH BROCCOLI-CHEESE TOPPING

3 large tomatoes, unpeeled
Salt
1 cup shredded Swiss cheese

1 (10-ounce) package
  frozen chopped
  broccoli, cooked and
  drained
$^{1}/_{4}$ cup chopped onion

Slice tomatoes $^{3}/_{4}$" thick; sprinkle with salt. Combine all but 2 tablespoons cheese with broccoli and onion; spoon mixture onto tomato slices. Place on a baking sheet and sprinkle with reserved cheese. Broil for about 10 minutes or until cheese bubbles and tomatoes are hot. Serves 6.

# VEGETABLES

## FRESH CRISP ZUCCHINI

6 small fresh zucchini
2 tablespoons butter
6 green onions, chopped

Salt and fresh pepper
  to taste
Nutmeg (optional)
Freshly grated Parmesan
  cheese

Using the coarse blade of a food processor or hand grater, grate unpeeled zucchini; drain on paper towels. Melt butter in a large skillet or saucepan. Add zucchini and onions; cook over high heat, tossing constantly until hot. Remove from heat; add seasonings, top with Parmesan cheese and serve immediately. Serves 6.

## ZUCCHINI MEAT SAUCE

*A salt-free, low-calorie sauce*

1/2 cup fat-free chicken or
  vegetable stock
3/4 cup chopped onion
1 clove garlic, minced
2 cups cubed zucchini
1/2 pound very lean ground
  beef
2 cups tomato sauce

1 tablespoon fresh basil or
  1/2 teaspoon dried basil
1/2 cup chopped fresh
  mint or 1/4 cup dried
  mint
1/4 teaspoon dried chili
  pepper
Freshly ground pepper

Heat stock in saucepan; add onions and garlic and cook until tender. Add zucchini; cover and simmer until tender, approximately 5 minutes. Brown meat in skillet and drain off all fat. Add meat, tomato sauce and seasonings to zucchini mixture; simmer over low heat for 10 minutes. Serve over rice or pasta. Serves 4.

## STUFFED ZUCCHINI

6 medium zucchini
3 cups butter crackers,
    crumbled
1/2 cup grated Parmesan
    cheese
1 small onion, minced

3 tablespoons minced
    parsley
1/8 teaspoon pepper
1 teaspoon salt
2 eggs, beaten
2 tablespoons butter

Wash zucchini and cut off ends, but do not peel. Cook in boiling salted water for 5 minutes or until tender. Halve lengthwise; remove pulp with spoon. Combine pulp, crackers, cheese, onion, parsley, salt, pepper and eggs. Fill zucchini shells with mixture and dot with butter. Sprinkle with additional cheese and bake at 350° for 30 minutes.

## ZUCCHINI CASSEROLE

2 tablespoons olive oil
1/2 cup chopped onion
4 zucchini (about 1 1/4
    pounds), unpeeled and
    sliced
4 tomatoes, peeled and sliced,
    or 1 (1-pound) can whole
    tomatoes

1/2 (6-ounce) can tomato
    paste
1 cup pitted ripe olives,
    sliced, and juice
1/2 cup grated Parmesan
    cheese
1/4 cup seasoned bread
    crumbs

In a large saucepan, heat oil; add onions and cook slowly until softened. Add zucchini and tomatoes; cook gently until zucchini is soft. Add tomato paste, olives and juice; turn into a greased 2-quart baking dish. Mix cheese and crumbs; sprinkle on top. Bake at 350° for 20 minutes or until bubbly hot. Serves 6.

## SPICED APPLE RINGS

3 medium apples
1/4 cup butter
1/4 cup brown sugar, packed
1 teaspoon cinnamon

1/8 teaspoon ground
  cloves
1/8 teaspoon ground
  ginger
1/4 teaspoon salt

Core apples and slice in 1/2" crosswise slices. Melt butter in a skillet; stir in brown sugar, spices and salt. Sauté apple rings in mixture over low heat, turning occasionally, until apples are tender. This is a good brunch dish. Makes approximately 12 apple rings.

## APPLE FRITTERS

3 large tart apples
Sugar
Cinnamon
Few drops rum or Kirsch
3/4 cup flour
1 tablespoon sugar
1 tablespoon melted butter

1/4 cup warm water
1 egg white, stiffly beaten
Pinch of salt
2 tablespoons cognac
1 egg yolk, beaten
Chopped pistachio nuts

Peel and core apples; cut into thin slices and sprinkle with sugar, cinnamon and rum or Kirsch. Cover and let stand for about 1 hour. Drain apples well, reserving juice. Sift flour and 1 tablespoon sugar into a mixing bowl; stir in melted butter and about 1/4 cup warm water, or enough to form a smooth batter. Batter should be just thick enough to coat apple slices; if it is too thick, thin with a little of the reserved juice. Just before using batter, fold in egg white, salt, cognac and beaten egg yolk. Dip apple slices into fritter batter and fry, a few at a time, in hot deep fat (370°) until golden brown; drain on absorbent paper. Put fritters on a cookie sheet, sprinkle with sugar and set in a 400° oven for about 5 minutes to glaze. Sprinkle with nuts.

## BAKED APPLES WITH SPICED SWEET POTATOES

6 firm apples (Golden
  Delicious suggested)

*Per apple:*
¹/₂ teaspoon sugar
¹/₈ teaspoon grated lemon
  rind
1¹/₂ teaspoons butter

Wash and core apples without cutting all the way through. Cut slice off bottom, so apple will sit firmly; pare the upper one-third of each apple. Place them in a shallow pan. Fill each center with sugar, lemon rind and butter. Put 6 tablespoons water in bottom of pan; bake at 400° until tender, basting often. After 30 minutes, test with a straw to see if done.

2 medium sweet potatoes,
  cooked, peeled and mashed
3 tablespoons butter
Salt to taste
¹/₈ teaspoon nutmeg, freshly
  grated

1 teaspoon cinnamon
2 tablespoons cream
2 tablespoons brown
  sugar
¹/₄ cup chopped pecans
¹/₄ cup raisins
6 marshmallows

In a mixing bowl, beat potatoes until fluffy. Add butter, salt, nutmeg, cinnamon, cream and brown sugar; beat until well mixed. Fold in pecans and raisins. Fill each baked apple with potato mixture; top with a marshmallow. In a 350° oven, warm apples several minutes; then place under broiler to brown marshmallows. Serve warm. Serves 6.

## SCALLOPED PINEAPPLE

*...is great served as a side dish with ham or turkey dinners*

1 cup margarine
2 cups sugar
4 eggs, beaten
1/4 cup milk

4 cups white bread cubes
1 (20-ounce) can crushed
   pineapple

Cream together margarine, sugar and eggs. Add remaining ingredients and mix well. Place in a buttered oblong casserole; bake at 375° for 15 minutes, then at 350° for 1 hour. Serves 6 to 8 .

## SAUCE FOR VEGETABLES

3 egg whites, lightly beaten
1/2 cup Hellmann's
   mayonnaise
2 tablespoons lemon juice
1/4 teaspoon salt

2 tablespoons chopped
   parsley
1/2 cup grated Parmesan
   cheese

Mix all ingredients together and pour over any cooked vegetable. Put in a buttered casserole; bake at 350° until bubbly and brown. The sauce is very good on chopped broccoli, spinach or cauliflower. This is a wonderful way to use left-over egg white.

## BASIC CREAM SAUCE

*Thin* (for soups)

| | |
|---|---|
| 1 tablespoon butter | ¹/₂ teaspoon salt |
| 1 tablespoon flour | ¹/₈ teaspoon pepper |
| | 1 cup light cream or whole milk |

*Medium* (for gravies, sauces, creamed and scalloped dishes)

| | |
|---|---|
| 2 tablespoons butter | ¹/₈ teaspoon pepper |
| 2 tablespoons flour | 1 cup light cream or |
| ¹/₂ teaspoon salt | whole milk |

*Thick* (for soufflés)

| | |
|---|---|
| 3 tablespoons butter | ¹/₈ teaspoon pepper |
| 3 tablespoons flour | 1 cup light cream or |
| ¹/₂ teaspoon salt | whole milk |

*Very thick* (for croquettes)

| | |
|---|---|
| 4 tablespoons butter | ¹/₈ teaspoon pepper |
| 4 tablespoons flour | 1 cup light cream or |
| ¹/₂ teaspoon salt | whole milk |

Melt butter over low heat; add flour, salt and pepper, stirring until well blended. Remove from heat; gradually stir in cream or milk. Return to heat and cook, stirring constantly, until thick and smooth. Makes 2 cups.

# VEGETABLES

## HERBED GARLIC BUTTER FOR VEGETABLES

1 teaspoon dried basil
$1/4$ teaspoon thyme
$1/2$ teaspoon tarragon leaves
2 teaspoons chopped parsley
$1/2$ teaspoon grated lemon
   peel

1 clove garlic, crushed
1 green onion, chopped
Dash of cayenne pepper
Dash of salt
$1/2$ cup soft butter

Combine spices. With back of wooden spoon, press herbs and seasonings together. Add butter; mix to combine thoroughly. Serve over hot cooked vegetables such as carrots, broccoli, green beans or cauliflower.

## HOLLANDAISE SAUCE

3 egg yolks
2 tablespoons lemon juice
$1/2$ teaspoon salt
Dash of pepper

$1/2$ cup (1 stick) butter or
   margarine, softened
$1/2$ cup boiling water

Place all ingredients, except water, in a blender container and process for a few seconds. With the blender running, slowly add boiling water. Pour sauce into the top of a double boiler, stirring constantly until sauce reaches the consistency of soft custard.

## EGG-MUSHROOM CASSEROLE

14 large eggs

Put eggs in saucepan, cover with cold water and heat until water just begins to boil. Turn off heat; cover and let stand 25 minutes. Crack eggs; immediately plunge into cold water and let stand until cooled. Peel and quarter eggs. In a casserole, layer eggs and Mushroom Sauce, ending with sauce. Cover with Cheese-crumb Topping; bake at 350° for 10 to 15 minutes or until bubbly. Makes 12 servings.

*Mushroom Sauce*

| | |
|---|---|
| 2 pounds fresh mushrooms | 1 teaspoon lemon pepper |
| 1/2 cup (1 stick) butter | 1/2 teaspoon onion |
| 5 tablespoons flour | powder |
| 3 cups cream | 1 teaspoon thyme leaves |
| 3/4 teaspoon salt | 1 teaspoon Parmesan |
| 1/2 teaspoon black pepper | cheese |
| | 1/4 teaspoon Tabasco |
| | sauce |

Wash, slice and sauté mushrooms in half of butter; set aside. Melt remaining butter over low heat; blend in flour. Gradually add cream, stirring constantly. Cook 3 minutes; stir in remaining ingredients and mushrooms.

*Cheese-crumb Topping*

| | |
|---|---|
| 1 1/2 cups shredded Cheddar cheese | 1 cup saltine cracker crumbs |
| | 1/4 cup (1/2 stick) butter, cut in small pieces |

Combine and mix well.

*This recipe is from Lexington caterer, Christine Gilmore*

# EGGS, CHEESE AND PASTA

## BÉCHAMEL EGGS

1 loaf French bread
18 eggs
1 pound fresh mushrooms, sliced
1/2 cup (1 stick) butter, melted
3/4 cup flour
2 cups chicken broth
2 cups half-and-half
2 teaspoons salt

Red pepper to taste
Juice of 1 lemon
1/4 pound medium-sharp Cheddar cheese, grated
1 (3-ounce) jar stuffed olives, drained and sliced
1 (3 to 4-ounce) can shrimp, crabmeat or lobster (optional)

Cut bread in 1/2" slices; leave in loaf shape and heat in a very hot oven until crusty on the outside. Hard-cook the eggs and keep in warm water. Sauté mushrooms in melted butter just until tender; add flour and stir until smooth. Gradually add broth, half-and-half, salt, red pepper, lemon juice and cheese, stirring constantly until cheese is melted. Carefully fold in olives and add seafood, if desired. Halve eggs lengthwise; place cut-side up in a large baking or chafing dish. Pour sauce over all and keep hot over a burner. To serve, place a slice of hot bread on each plate and cover with several egg halves and sauce. Serves 8 to 10.

## CRABMEAT QUICHE

1/2 cup mayonnaise
2 tablespoons all-purpose flour
2 eggs, beaten
1/2 cup milk
1 (6-ounce) package frozen crabmeat, thawed and drained

2 cups shredded Swiss cheese (8 ounces)
1/3 cup chopped green onion
Dash of cayenne pepper
9" Pastry Shell for Quiche (see page 219)

Combine mayonnaise, flour, eggs and milk, mixing thoroughly. Stir in crabmeat, cheese, onion and cayenne pepper. Spoon into pastry shell; bake at 350° for 30 to 40 minutes or until firm in center. Makes 6 servings.

# EGGS, CHEESE AND PASTA

## EGG AND SHRIMP CASSEROLE

8 hard-cooked eggs
1/3 cup mayonnaise
1/2 teaspoon dry mustard
1 tablespoon curry powder
Salt and pepper to taste
1 (4¼-ounce) can
   medium-sized shrimp,
   drained

2 tablespoons butter
2 tablespoons flour
1 cup milk
1 (10¾-ounce) can cream
   of shrimp soup,
   undiluted
1/2 cup grated, aged
   Cheddar cheese

Slice eggs in half lengthwise; scoop out yolks and add to mixture of mayonnaise, mustard, curry, salt and pepper. Stuff egg whites with mixture. Lay eggs in single layer in shallow casserole. Melt butter; add flour, stirring until smooth and creamy. Slowly add milk; cook until thick. Add soup and cheese, stirring over low heat until cheese melts. Devein shrimp and soak in cold water for 10 minutes. Drain thoroughly. Place around eggs in casserole. Pour sauce on top. Sprinkle with paprika; bake at 350° for 25 to 30 minutes.

## SHRIMP AND CHEDDAR PIE

1 (8-ounce) can crescent rolls
1 tablespoon butter
1 cup raw medium shrimp,
   cleaned and cut in half
1 cup Hellmann's mayonnaise

1 cup grated sharp
   Cheddar cheese
1/2 cup chopped green
   pepper
1/2 cup chopped green
   onions

Remove rolls from refrigerator and let stand at room temperature for 30 minutes before using. Grease a quiche pan with butter; line with rolls to form a crust. Mix remaining ingredients; pour into crust. Bake at 350° for 1 hour; let stand 8 to 10 minutes before slicing. Serves 4 to 5 .

# EGGS, CHEESE AND PASTA

## HAMBURGER QUICHE

1 pound ground beef
1 medium onion, chopped
1/2 green pepper, chopped
1/4 pound fresh mushrooms,
  chopped (optional)
1 tablespoon Worcestershire
  sauce
Salt and pepper to taste
12 ounces Cheddar cheese,
  grated

1 egg plus enough milk to
  measure 1/2 cup
5 to 6 slices of bacon,
  crisply cooked and
  crumbled (optional)
2 to 3 fresh tomatoes,
  sliced (in season only)
1 unbaked 9" pastry shell

Brown meat; add onion, green pepper and mushrooms. Cook until onions are transparent, about 4 to 6 minutes; add Worcestershire sauce, salt and pepper. Mix three-fourths of the cheese with the egg and milk; fold into meat mixture. Add crumbled bacon; stir well. Pour into pastry shell; top with remaining cheese and sliced tomatoes, if desired. Bake at 350° for 30 minutes. The quiche filling may be baked with no pastry; just pour into a greased pie plate.

## GARLIC CHEESE GRITS

6 cups water
2 teaspoons salt
1 1/2 cups grits
1/2 cup (1 stick) butter
3 eggs, well beaten

1 pound sharp Cheddar
  cheese, grated (about 4
  cups)
1 to 3 cloves garlic,
  minced
Cayenne pepper to taste

Bring water to a rapid boil with salt; gradually stir in grits with a fork. Cook until all water is absorbed. Stir in butter bit by bit; carefully add eggs, cheese, garlic and cayenne pepper. Put into a greased 2 1/2-quart casserole; bake at 350° for 1 hour and 20 minutes. Serves 8.

*Note:* This dish may be frozen before baking, then thawed and baked.

# EGGS, CHEESE AND PASTA

## PASTRY SHELL FOR QUICHE

1 1/2 cups all-purpose flour
1/4 teaspoon salt
6 tablespoons cold butter

2 tablespoons cold
vegetable shortening
3 to 5 tablespoons ice
water

Sift flour with salt into a large, chilled mixing bowl. Cut in butter and shortening with pastry blender or fingers until the consistency of coarse meal. Pour 3 tablespoons of ice water over the mixture all at once; toss together lightly and gather the dough into a ball. If dough seems crumbly, add more ice water by drops. Wrap in wax paper or plastic bag; chill until firm. Place dough on a floured board; roll into a circle 1/8" thick. Press the pastry into a 9" quiche pan or pie pan; trim off excess around edge. Place a piece of buttered aluminum foil, buttered side down, over pastry; gently press into pastry shell. This will keep the sides of the shell from collapsing. Cover foil with a layer of dried peas or beans. Bake at 400° for 10 minutes; remove foil and peas. Prick bottom of shell thoroughly with a fork; return to oven for 3 to 5 minutes or until it begins to brown. Remove and cool.

*Note:* The baking instructions may be used also for a frozen 9" deep-dish pie shell.

## COTTAGE CHEESE SANDWICH SPREAD

1 pound dry cottage cheese
1/4 pound Cheddar cheese,
grated
1/2 cup chopped Spanish
olives
1 heaping tablespoon grated
onion

1/4 teaspoon salt
Dash of Worcestershire
sauce
Dash of red pepper
Mayonnaise

Combine all ingredients; add just enough mayonnaise to hold mixture together. Delicious as a sandwich spread, or served with tomato aspic or celery stuffing.

# EGGS, CHEESE AND PASTA

## TOMATO PIE

| | |
|---|---|
| 1 unbaked 10" pastry shell or 9" deep dish pastry shell | 1 cup sliced spring onions |
| | 1/2 cup sliced ripe olives |
| 2 large ripe tomatoes, cut into 1/2" slices | 3 slices Provolone cheese |
| | 2 eggs, slightly beaten |
| Salt and pepper | 1 cup shredded Cheddar cheese |
| Flour | |
| 2 tablespoons salad oil | 1 cup evaporated milk |

Prick bottom and sides of pastry shell; bake at 350° for 8 minutes or until lightly browned. Set aside to cool. Sprinkle tomato slices with salt and pepper and coat both sides with flour. Sauté in hot oil until golden brown. Reserve 1 tablespoon onions; sprinkle remaining onions and olives in pastry shell. Top with cheese slices and then tomatoes. Combine eggs, Cheddar cheese and milk; mix well and pour over tomatoes. Bake at 375° for 40 to 45 minutes until filling is set. Remove from oven, sprinkle with reserved onion and let stand 5 minutes before cutting. Serves 6.

## WELSH RAREBIT

| | |
|---|---|
| 2 cups beer | 5 pounds aged Cheddar cheese, grated |
| 1/4 pound (1 stick) butter (no substitute) | 12 eggs, beaten |
| 1 teaspoon Tabasco sauce | 4 tablespoons Worcestershire sauce |
| 1 teaspoon dry mustard | |

Put beer, butter, Tabasco sauce and mustard in a saucepan and slowly heat to a simmer. Gradually add cheese, stirring until it is completely melted. Stir in eggs and cook for 2 to 3 minutes; add Worcestershire sauce. Serve on toast or crackers. Serves 20.

*Note:* For a smaller number of servings, use one-fourth or one-half of the recipe.

*Variations:* At cocktail parties, serve from a chafing dish. Seafood may be added. For hot sandwiches, arrange sliced tomatoes on toast, pour over rarebit and top with cooked bacon strips.

# EGGS, CHEESE AND PASTA

## CHEESE SOUFFLÉ

4 tablespoons (½ stick) butter
2 tablespoons flour
1 cup milk
½ teaspoon salt
A few grains of cayenne
   pepper

½ cup grated cheese
4 egg yolks, beaten light
4 egg whites, very stiffly
   beaten

Melt butter and blend in flour. Gradually stir in milk; cook stirring constantly, until thickened. Add salt, cayenne pepper and cheese, stirring until cheese is melted. Remove from heat and beat in egg yolks. Cool mixture and gently fold in egg whites. Pour into a buttered soufflé dish; bake at 350° for 30 to 40 minutes. Serve immediately. Serves 4.

## CHEESE-NOODLE CASSEROLE

1 pound fresh mushrooms,
   sliced
½ cup chopped onion
¼ cup chopped green onions
1 clove garlic, chopped
¼ cup melted butter

1 (8-ounce) package
   medium egg noodles,
   cooked and drained
2 cups grated Cheddar
   cheese
½ cup half-and-half
¼ cup chopped parsley
1 teaspoon salt

Sauté mushrooms, onions, green onions and garlic in butter until tender; drain. Place cooked noodles in a saucepan; add cheese, half-and-half, parsley and salt. Cook over low heat, stirring constantly, until cheese is melted. Add sautéed vegetables, mixing thoroughly. Serve immediately or place in a casserole to reheat and serve later.

## CHEESE GRITS SOUFFLÉ

1 cup grits
1/2 cup (1 stick) butter
3 cups grated sharp Cheddar
    cheese
4 egg yolks, slightly beaten

1/4 cup half-and-half
Dash of Worcestershire
    sauce
Salt and pepper to taste
4 eggs whites, stiffly
    beaten

Cook grits until thick and smooth according to directions on package. Stir in butter, 2 cups cheese, egg yolks, half-and-half, Worcestershire sauce and seasoning. This can be done up to 1 hour ahead, but do not let mixture get cold. Just before baking, fold in egg whites; spoon into a greased 2-quart casserole. Bake at 350° for 30 minutes; sprinkle with remaining cheese and bake 15 minutes longer. Serves 8 to 10.

## WOODCHUCK

*...a wonderful dish for brunch*

4 cups Medium Cream Sauce
    (recipe on page 213)
Salt and pepper to taste
Cayenne pepper to taste
1 pound grated sharp
    Cheddar cheese

1 pound mushrooms,
    sliced
4 tablespoons butter
6 hard-cooked eggs,
    halved lengthwise
1 (5-ounce) can Chinese
    fried noodles

Season Cream Sauce highly with salt, pepper and cayenne pepper; add cheese, stirring until melted. Sauté mushrooms in butter for 5 minutes. Add mushrooms and eggs to sauce; stir in one-half of the noodles. Pour into a buttered 2-quart casserole; top with remaining noodles. Bake at 350° for 30 minutes. Serves 12.

*Variation:* Two cups of chunky, cooked chicken may be added to Woodchuck, either with or without the eggs. Another nice addition is 1/4 cup pimiento strips.

# EGGS, CHEESE AND PASTA

## BAKED CHEESE FONDUE

10 slices good bread, crusts
removed, cubed
½ pound sharp Cheddar
cheese, grated

2 cups milk
3 eggs, beaten
1 teaspoon salt
Red pepper to taste

Place bread cubes in the bottom of a buttered 1½-quart casserole; cover with cheese. Put 1 cup of milk into a blender container. While blender is running, remove small cap in cover and add eggs, seasonings and remaining cup of milk. Process until blended; pour over bread and cheese. Cover and refrigerate overnight or at least 6 hours. Bake at 350° for 35 to 40 minutes or until golden and puffy. Serves 6.

## FETTUCCINI ALFREDO

1 pound fettuccine noodles
¾ stick of butter
1½ cups heavy cream

1 cup grated Romano Cheese,
best quality
Fresh ground black pepper,
to taste

Cook fettuccini in boiling salted water for 7-8 minutes or until al dente. Drain but do not rinse. Melt butter in large saucepan. Add fettuccini and toss until coated. Add 1½ cups heavy cream and stir over medium heat. Add 1 cup grated Romano and black pepper to taste. Serves 8-10.

From Lexington caterer, Phil Dunn

# EGGS, CHEESE AND PASTA

## TOMATO AND CHEESE SANDWICHES

4 slices bread, with crusts
   removed
Mayonnaise

2 tomatoes, sliced
4 strips bacon, cooked

Toast slices of bread on both sides; spread with mayonnaise and cover with tomato slices. Lay bacon on top and cut sandwiches in half diagonally. Spoon Hot Cheese Sauce over top. Serves 4.

*Note:* Sliced chicken and sliced onion may be added to sandwiches to make a luncheon or supper dish.

*Hot Cheese Sauce*
1 tablespoon butter
1 1/2 tablespoons flour
3/4 cup milk
Salt and pepper to taste

1 teaspoon Worcestershire
   sauce
1 (8-ounce) package
   Velveeta cheese, broken
   in pieces

Melt butter in top of a double boiler; blend in flour. Slowly add milk, stirring until thickened. Season to taste and add cheese. Lower heat and cook until cheese is melted.

## SPAGHETTI MOUSSE

1 cup broken spaghetti
1 teaspoon salt
1 bay leaf
1 onion, chopped
1/2 cup (1 stick) butter
1 1/2 cups grated Cheddar
   cheese

1 1/2 cups milk, scalded
3 eggs, well beaten
1 cup soft bread crumbs
2 tablespoons chopped
   pimiento
1 teaspoon grated onion

*Continued*

## SPAGHETTI MOUSSE, *Continued*

Cook spaghetti with salt, bay leaf and onion in boiling water. When barely done, drain. Remove and discard bay leaf; add remaining ingredients and mix well. Put mixture in a greased ring mold; place in a pan of hot water. Steam for 45 minutes in an oven preheated to 350°. Serve with Mushroom Sauce. Serves 6 to 8.

*Mushroom Sauce*

| | |
|---|---|
| 1/2 pound fresh mushrooms, sliced | 1 cup milk |
| 2 tablespoons butter | 1/4 teaspoon salt |
| 2 tablespoons flour | 1/8 teaspoon paprika |
| | Fresh lemon juice to taste |

Sauté mushrooms in butter about 5 minutes; blend in flour. Add milk gradually; cook until thickened, stirring constantly. Add seasonings and lemon juice.

## PASTA WITH RED SAUCE

*Suggested pasta: penne*

| | |
|---|---|
| 3 to 4 cloves garlic, finely chopped | 1/4 teaspoon sugar |
| 1/4 cup olive oil | Salt and pepper to taste |
| 2 (28-ounce) cans Italian peeled tomatoes | 1 pound penne or other tube pasta |
| | Freshly grated Parmesan cheese |
| | Basil leaf or Italian parsley |

Sauté garlic in olive oil until garlic is golden brown; remove from pan. Let olive oil cool. Add tomatoes; cook for 30 minutes on low heat, adding sugar, salt and pepper. Cook pasta and drain; toss with a little butter and mix with sauce. Sprinkle Parmesan on top and garnish with basil leaf or Italian parsley. Serves 4.

# EGGS, CHEESE AND PASTA

## PASTA WITH WHITE SAUCE

*Suggested pasta: rigatoni*

1 pound rigatoni
1 to 1½ sticks butter
½ cup heavy cream
½ cup freshly grated
    Parmesan cheese

1 (16-ounce) package
    whole-milk mozzarella,
    cut into small cubes
1 cup ricotta cheese,
    softened with a little
    warm water

Cook pasta al dente; drain. Toss with all but a small amount of butter and heavy cream. Lightly butter a large baking pan and add a layer of pasta. Follow with a layer of Parmesan cheese, then mozzarella and ricotta. Repeat process until all cheese is used up, ending with Parmesan on top. Place pan in preheated oven and bake at 350° for 20 minutes. Serve hot, topped with freshly ground black pepper. Serves 4.

## PASTA WITH PESTO (GREEN SAUCE)

*Suggested pasta: linguine*

2 large bunches fresh basil
    leaves, washed and dried
½ cup Italian pignoli nuts
2 cloves garlic
½ cup olive oil
¼ cup butter, softened

¼ cup freshly grated
    Parmesan cheese
Salt and pepper to taste
1 tablespoon butter
1 pound linguine
Basil, capers or pignoli
    nuts (for garnish)

Put all ingredients except pasta and garnishes into the container of a blender or food processor; mix until puréed. Cook pasta al dente, drain and toss with a little butter. Mix thoroughly with sauce and garnish with a basil leaf, capers or pignoli nuts. Serves 4.

# EGGS, CHEESE AND PASTA

## LINGUINE WITH BROCCOLI, CAULIFLOWER AND MUSHROOMS

1 cup ricotta cheese
1/3 cup grated Romano cheese
1 teaspoon salt
1 bunch fresh broccoli,
    trimmed and cut into
    florets
1 cup olive oil
1 medium head cauliflower,
    trimmed and cut into
    florets

6 garlic cloves, minced
1 pound mushrooms,
    thickly sliced
2 teaspoons salt
1/2 teaspoon crushed red
    pepper
1 pound linguine
Grated Romano cheese

Combine ricotta and Romano cheeses; set aside. Bring a large stockpot of water to a rolling boil; add salt, broccoli and cauliflower. Cover and return to boil. Uncover and cook until vegetables are crisp-tender, about 7 minutes. Remove vegetables with a slotted spoon; reserve liquid for cooking linguine. Heat olive oil and garlic in a large skillet. When garlic is lightly browned, stir in mushrooms, salt and red pepper; sauté about 5 minutes. Stir in broccoli and cauliflower and continue cooking for 10 minutes. If mixture becomes too dry, add some of the reserved cooking liquid. Bring cooking liquid to a rapid boil, adding water if needed. Add linguine, stirring with a fork to prevent sticking. Cook until al dente, about 10 to 12 minutes; drain well. Reheat vegetable mixture; stir in linguine. Divide among shallow bowls and top with mixture of cheeses. Dust with extra Romano. Serves 8.

## PASTA PRIMAVERA

| | |
|---|---|
| ¹/₂ pound fettuccine | ³/₄ cup fresh green beans, |
| 1 cup broccoli florets | cut in 1" pieces |
| 3/4 cup asparagus tips | ¹/₂ cup sliced mushrooms |
| 2 small zucchini, sliced | 1 cup cherry tomatoes |

Put 2 quarts water in the bottom of a tiered steamer; bring to a boil. Add fettuccine and steam for 8 minutes. Add a second basket, containing all vegetables except cherry tomatoes. Allow to steam for 6 minutes. (If the dish is to be served hot, add tomatoes for the final 2 minutes.) To serve hot, combine vegetables and sauce; toss with fettuccine on a large, buttered pasta dish. To serve cold, toss cooled vegetables and pasta in an Italian salad dressing.

*Sauce*

| | |
|---|---|
| 2 cloves garlic, minced | ³/₄ cup heavy cream |
| ¹/₄ cup butter | ²/₃ cup grated Parmesan |
| 2 tablespoons chicken broth | cheese |
| | Salt and pepper |

Sauté garlic in butter; add remaining ingredients, mixing well.

## ASPARAGUS VINAIGRETTE

1 pound fresh asparagus      1 teaspoon Beau Monde
Seasoning

Trim and wash asparagus; scrape off scales. (Frozen asparagus may be used when fresh is not available). Place in enough water to cover; add Beau Monde Seasoning. Cook until barely tender; drain and chill.

*Sauce*

1 teaspoon Beau Monde
  Seasoning
1/2 teaspoon cracked black
  pepper
1/8 teaspoon garlic powder
1/4 teaspoon Dijon mustard
1 tablespoon sour cream

2 tablespoons tarragon
  white wine vinegar
5 tablespoons olive oil
1 hard-cooked egg, finely
  chopped
1 teaspoon finely chopped
  parsley

In a small bowl, combine Beau Monde Seasoning, pepper, garlic powder, mustard, sour cream, vinegar and olive oil. Beat well to thoroughly mix. Stir in egg and parsley. Refrigerate until very cold; spoon over chilled asparagus. This may be prepared 1 day ahead. Serves 4.

# SALADS AND SALAD DRESSINGS

## MARINATED GREEN BEANS

2 pounds fresh green beans        French dressing

Use firm beans that will snap when broken. Wash and remove stem ends; break in half or, if small, leave whole. Bring a small amount of water to a boil and drop in beans slowly. Quickly return water to boiling and reduce heat to moderate. Boil, uncovered, about 10 to 15 minutes, depending on size and age of beans. Beans should be tender but crisp. Begin sampling after 8 minutes of cooking. Rinse beans under cold water and drain; put in a shallow dish, marinate with French dressing and chill overnight. Before serving, drain off excess dressing.

*Note:* Three (16-ounce) cans of whole Blue Lake green beans may be substituted.

## MARINATED FRESH GREEN BEAN SALAD

1 pound fresh pole beans or        1/3 cup thinly-sliced
   any other good green beans        radishes
1/4 cup minced scallions        1/3 cup chopped walnuts
Salad Dressing (see below)        (optional)

Remove ends from beans; steam or boil just until barely tender. Drain and cool under cold water to stop further cooking. Place beans in a bowl with the scallions; pour over the Salad Dressing. Refrigerate 2 hours. Before serving, add radishes and walnuts, if desired. Serves 4 to 6.

*Salad Dressing*
1/3 cup olive oil        3 tablespoons dill weed
1 tablespoon cider vinegar        1 tablespoon finely
2 tablespoons fresh lemon           chopped parsley
   juice        2 teaspoons sugar
2 tablespoons Dijon mustard        Salt and pepper to taste

Place all ingredients in a jar with tight-fitting lid; shake vigorously.

# SALADS AND SALAD DRESSINGS

## BROCCOLI SALAD VINAIGRETTE

2 1/2 pounds fresh broccoli,
    cut into florets
2 tomatoes, cut into wedges
1/4 pound mushrooms,
    quartered
1 medium red onion, sliced

1 cup toasted, slivered
    almonds
1 tablespoon Lawry's
    seasoned salt
1 teaspoon pepper
1 cup salad oil
3/4 cup red wine vinegar

Steam broccoli 3 to 5 minutes or until barely tender; run under cold water; drain well. Combine broccoli, tomatoes, mushrooms, onions and almonds. Sprinkle with seasoned salt and pepper; toss gently. Combine oil and vinegar in jar, shaking vigorously; pour over salad and toss to mix. Cover and chill before serving. This may be done up to 1 hour in advance.

## LAYERED SALAD DELUXE

1 pound fresh spinach, torn in
    pieces
1 medium head of lettuce,
    torn in pieces
6 hard-cooked eggs, sliced
1 pound bacon, cooked and
    crumbled
1 (8-ounce) can water
    chestnuts, drained and
    sliced

1 (10-ounce) package
    frozen peas, thawed
1/2 pound fresh
    mushrooms, sliced
1 cup mayonnaise
1/2 cup sour cream
1 (0.4-ounce) package
    buttermilk-mayonnaise
    dressing mix
Chopped parsley or
    watercress

Layer the first 7 ingredients in order given in a large salad bowl. Combine mayonnaise, sour cream and dressing mix; spread over top of vegetables and seal to edge of bowl. Garnish with parsley and refrigerate overnight, covered. Toss gently before serving. Serves 10 to 12.

# SALADS AND SALAD DRESSINGS

## CAESAR SALAD

Romaine or Bibb lettuce,
  or a mixture of both

Croutons
Grated Parmesan cheese

Wash lettuce in cold water; drain well. Tear into bite-sized pieces; roll in a towel to dry. Place lettuce in a plastic bag; chill to crisp. At serving time, place lettuce in a large bowl and pour over just enough Caesar Dressing to coat (do not drench); toss gently. Add croutons and cheese to taste: toss again and serve immediately.

*Caesar Dressing*
1 large egg
¼ cup olive oil
Juice of ½ lemon
1 tablespoon red wine vinegar
4 anchovy filets
½ teaspoon Worcestershire
  sauce

¼ teaspoon prepared
  horseradish
¼ teaspoon dry mustard
⅛ teaspoon black pepper,
  freshly ground

Cook egg gently in simmering water for 45 seconds; remove, break open and spoon contents from shell into container of electric blender. Add remaining ingredients; cover and process until well blended. Pour into bottle or jar and refrigerate. Makes about 1 cup.

## CUCUMBERS IN SOUR CREAM

4 cucumbers, thinly sliced
½ medium white onion,
  chopped fine
1 cup sour cream

¼ cup lemon juice
2 tablespoons sugar
Salt and pepper to taste

Combine all the ingredients, mixing well. Chill for an hour before serving. Serves 6.

# SALADS AND SALAD DRESSINGS

## WATER CHESTNUT SALAD

1 cup water
1/2 cup white vinegar
2/3 cup sugar
1/2 teaspoon salt
2 envelopes unflavored gelatin
1 (15-ounce) can asparagus
   spears, cut in small pieces

1 (8-ounce) can sliced
   water chestnuts,
   drained
1 cup finely chopped
   celery
1/4 cup chopped pimiento
1 teaspoon grated onion
Juice of 1 lemon

Combine water, vinegar, sugar and salt; bring to a boil and simmer until sugar is dissolved. Sprinkle gelatin on 1/2 cup cold water to soften; stir into hot mixture until thoroughly dissolved. Chill until the consistency of unbeaten egg white. Fold in remaining ingredients; pour into a large mold and chill until set.

## COLD RICE SALAD

2 cups uncooked long grain
   white rice
5 cups chicken broth
3 (6-ounce) jars oil-marinated
   artichoke hearts
5 green onions, chopped
1 (4-ounce) jar pimientos,
   chopped
Stuffed olives, sliced
   (optional)
1 large green pepper, diced

3 large ribs celery, diced
1/4 cup chopped fresh
   parsley
Reserved artichoke
   marinade
2 cups mayonnaise
1 teaspoon curry powder
Salt and freshly-ground
   pepper to taste

Cook rice in chicken broth for 20 minutes or until liquid is absorbed and the rice is tender. Cool. Drain artichokes, reserving marinade, and chop. Add to rice with onions, pimientos, olives, green pepper, celery and parsley. Combine reserved marinade with mayonnaise, curry powder, salt and pepper; toss with rice and mix thoroughly. Refrigerate until ready to serve.

# SALADS AND SALAD DRESSINGS

## TOSSED SALAD WITH
## MARINATED OLIVES AND DILL

1 (3½-ounce) can pitted ripe
   olives, drained and sliced
3 tablespoons diced pimiento,
   drained
¼ cup salad oil (1 teaspoon or
   more may be olive oil,
   to taste)
1 tablespoon vinegar

½ teaspoon salt
¼ teaspoon dried
   marjoram leaves
¼ teaspoon snipped fresh
   dill
⅛ teaspoon pepper
½ head iceberg lettuce,
   torn into bite-size
   pieces

Combine all ingredients except lettuce; allow time to marinate. Arrange lettuce in a large salad bowl; top with marinated olive mixture. Serves 4.

## TOMATOES AND CUCUMBERS WITH
## FRESH MINT DRESSING

6 ripe tomatoes
2 to 3 cucumbers
½ cup tarragon vinegar
⅔ cup salad oil
¼ cup sugar
½ teaspoon salt

⅛ teaspoon pepper
½ cup chopped fresh
   mint, or ¼ cup dried
   Spice Islands Spearmint
Romaine lettuce
Fresh mint for garnish

Cut tomatoes in ⅛" slices; run sharp tines of fork down length of cucumbers; cut in ⅛" slices. Combine next 6 ingredients in jar; shake well. Place vegetables in 13"x 9"x 2" glass dish, grouping tomatoes in one end, cucumbers in the other. Pour dressing evenly over all. Cover and refrigerate at least 1 hour. Spoon dressing over vegetables occasionally. To serve, line shallow platter with romaine leaves. Arrange tomatoes around edge, cucumbers in center. Spoon dressing on top. Garnish with mint. Serves 10 to 12.

# SALADS AND SALAD DRESSINGS

## COOKED VEGETABLES IN CELERY SEED MARINADE

Either cook or reserve from prior servings an assortment of a few of these vegetables:

Potatoes, sliced crosswise, or pasta
Green beans
Carrots
Broccoli
Green peas
Asparagus
Grated Parmesan cheese
(optional)

Drain cooked vegetables and place in a container with marinade; chill. Before serving, add cherry tomatoes or quartered whole tomatoes and chopped celery. Sprinkle with Parmesan cheese, if desired.

*Marinade*
1 tablespoon celery seed, covered with water and set aside overnight
4 teaspoons grated onion
3/4 cup sugar
1 teaspoon salt
1 teaspoon paprika
1 cup vegetable oil
1/2 cup red wine vinegar

Drain celery seed; mix with onion and sugar. Add remaining ingredients in order given. Place in a jar; cover and shake well before serving.

*Note:* Any favorite salad dressing could be substituted for the marinade.

## SHAKERTOWN COLESLAW

1 quart shredded cabbage
1/4 cup shredded carrot
1/4 cup chopped onion
1/4 cup chopped celery
1/2 cup commercial slaw dressing
1/4 cup Country Dressing
1/4 cup mayonnaise
1/2 to 3/4 teaspoon salt

Mix all together. If too dry, add more Country Dressing (page 257).

# SALADS AND SALAD DRESSINGS

## SPINACH SALAD WITH TANGY DRESSING

1 pound fresh spinach, torn
    into bite-sized pieces
1 cup thinly-sliced hearts of
    palm
1 (8½-ounce) can artichoke
    hearts, drained and
    quartered

6 slices bacon, cooked
    and crumbled
4 green onions, thinly
    sliced
2 to 3 tomatoes, peeled
    and cut into wedges
2 hard-cooked eggs,
    chopped

Combine all ingredients in large salad bowl; toss lightly. Cover and chill until serving time. Serve with Tangy Salad Dressing. Serves 6 to 8.

*Tangy Dressing*
1 small onion, minced
³/₄ cup sugar
¹/₂ cup vinegar
¹/₃ cup catsup

¹/₄ cup vegetable oil
2 tablespoons
    Worcestershire sauce

Combine all ingredients in container of electric blender or food processor; blend until smooth. Chill well before serving.

## SPINACH WITH MUSTARD FRENCH DRESSING

1 (10-ounce) package fresh
    spinach

1 (11-ounce) can mandarin
    oranges, drained
    (optional)

Wash spinach and dry thoroughly; chill. When ready to serve, pour over Mustard French Dressing and toss until all leaves are covered. Serves 6 to 8.

*Mustard French Dressing*
¹/₂ cup olive oil
2 tablespoons fresh lemon
    juice
2 tablespoons Dijon mustard

1 tablespoon chopped
    Italian onion (purple)
Salt and pepper to taste

Combine and beat or shake thoroughly before using.

# SALADS AND SALAD DRESSINGS

## SALAD PLATTER WITH ANCHOVY DRESSING

Bibb lettuce
2 avocados, sliced and dipped
    in lemon juice
2 cups asparagus tips, cooked
    and drained
2 (6-ounce) jars marinated,
    quartered artichoke hearts,
    drained

2 large tomatoes, sliced
    (optional)
1 large Spanish onion,
    sliced and separated
    into rings (optional)

In the center of the platter, place a bowl of Anchovy Dressing; surround with a layer of Bibb lettuce leaves. Arrange prepared vegetables in groups around the bowl. Serves 6 to 8.

*Anchovy Dressing*
1/2 cup grated onion
1/2 cup chopped parsley
1/2 cup anchovies, chopped
2/3 cup whipped cream

1 1/2 cups mayonnaise
2 tablespoons chopped
    chives

Combine first 3 ingredients; mixing thoroughly. Fold whipped cream into mayonnaise; stir in onion mixture and sprinkle with chives.

## FRESH GREEN PEA SALAD

3 cups fresh young peas or 2
    (10-ounce) packages frozen
    peas, thawed
4 slices crisply cooked bacon,
    crumbled
1 cup sour cream or yogurt

1/4 cup chopped green
    onions or chives
Salt and pepper to taste
Garlic powder or fresh
    mint or fresh dill, as
    desired

Cook peas until barely tender; drain and chill. Combine all ingredients and refrigerate until ready to serve. Serve on lettuce.

# SALADS AND SALAD DRESSINGS

## POTATO SALAD

5 medium potatoes, cooked,
 peeled and diced
1 small onion, chopped
6 hard-cooked eggs, grated
1 cup finely-chopped celery
Hellmann's mayonnaise

Catsup
Mustard
1/2 cup slivered almonds,
 toasted and salted
 (optional)

Combine the first 4 ingredients with enough mayonnaise to hold the mixture together. Add enough catsup and mustard to create a creamy color. Garnish with almonds, if desired.

## NEW POTATO SALAD

1 1/2 pounds new potatoes
Spring onions or chives
6 tablespoons olive oil or
 vegetable oil
2 tablespoons white wine
 vinegar

2 tablespoons mayonnaise
1 teaspoon dry mustard
1 teaspoon sugar
Salt and freshly ground
 pepper to taste
A squeeze of lemon juice

Cook potatoes in salted water just until tender, being careful not to overcook. Drain in a colander for several minutes. Slice thinly while still warm and put into a bowl with a handful of spring onions or chives. Put remaining ingredients into a small screw-top jar and shake vigorously until well blended. Pour over the potatoes and toss carefully, using 2 spoons. Cover and chill until needed. Serves 4.

# SALADS AND SALAD DRESSINGS

## CHICKEN SALAD SUPREME

4$^{1}/_{2}$ to 5 pounds chicken
   breasts
Melted butter
Salt and pepper
3 (3$^{1}/_{4}$-ounce) packages
   slivered almonds
2 cups homemade
   mayonnaise
1 tablespoon curry powder

2 tablespoons soy sauce
2 cups sliced celery
3 (6-ounce) cans water
   chestnuts, drained and
   sliced
2 pounds seedless grapes
Boston or Bibb lettuce

Brush chicken breasts with melted butter and sprinkle with salt and pepper. Wrap in heavy-duty aluminum foil; seal edges tightly. Place in shallow pan and bake at 350° for 1 hour. Cool; remove meat from bones and cut in bite-size pieces. Coat almonds with melted butter; spread on cookie sheet. Roast at 350° about 30 minutes or until a mellow brown. Spread on paper towels; sprinkle with salt. A few hours before serving, mix mayonnaise with curry powder and soy sauce; combine with chicken, celery, water chestnuts and grapes. Chill. Arrange lettuce leaves around edge of large platter; mound chicken salad in center. Sprinkle almonds on top. Serves 12.

*Note:* Hellmann's mayonnaise plus the juice of 1 lemon may be substituted for homemade mayonnaise. The chicken may be cooked and the almonds roasted a day ahead.

## SHAKERTOWN CHICKEN SALAD

1 pound cooked chicken
$^{3}/_{4}$ cup chopped celery
$^{3}/_{4}$ cup Country Dressing,
   page 257
$^{1}/_{4}$ cup mayonnaise

$^{1}/_{4}$ cup chopped pecans
$^{1}/_{4}$ teaspoon seasoning salt
$^{1}/_{4}$ teaspoon salt
$^{1}/_{4}$ teaspoon red pepper

Cut chicken in cubes with scissors; mix with celery. Fold in remaining ingredients; top with additional mayonnaise when serving.

# SALADS AND SALAD DRESSINGS

## CALIFORNIA CHICKEN SALAD

4 cups shredded cooked
    chicken breasts
2 cups seedless green grapes

¹/₂ cup toasted slivered
    almonds
Lettuce leaves

Combine chicken, grapes and almonds; arrange on lettuce leaves. Pour Dressing on top; sprinkle with paprika. Serves 4.

*Dressing*
¹/₂ cup (1 stick) butter
2 cups mayonnaise
¹/₄ cup minced parsley
¹/₄ teaspoon minced garlic

¹/₂ teaspoon curry powder
    (more, if desired)
Pinch of marjoram
Salt and pepper to taste

Melt butter; cool to room temperature. Combine remaining ingredients; gently stir in butter.

## MAURICE SALAD

³/₄ heart of crisp iceberg
    lettuce, shredded
¹/₂ cup cooked chicken,
    julienne cut
¹/₂ cup baked ham, julienne
    cut

¹/₃ cup fresh tomatoes,
    julienne cut
1 tablespoon chopped
    sweet pickle or pickle
    relish
Chives, finely chopped

Combine ingredients and chill. Do not add dressing until just before serving. Put on cold salad plates, sprinkle with chives. Tomato wedges and slices of hard-cooked egg may be used to garnish the salads. Serves 2.

*Dressing*
3 tablespoons mayonnaise
3 tablespoons olive oil
2 tablespoons vinegar
1 teaspoon Worcestershire
    sauce

1 teaspoon finely chopped
    chives
1 hard-cooked egg,
    chopped

Combine ingredients, mixing well.

# SALADS AND SALAD DRESSINGS

## TOWNHOUSE SALAD

3 cups cubed, cooked chicken
3 hard-cooked eggs, chopped
1 avocado, peeled, cubed and
   dipped in lemon juice
1 cup chopped cucumber
1 cup peeled, chopped
   tomato
2 cups croutons

1/2 cup crumbled blue
   cheese
6 slices crisply-cooked
   bacon, well-drained and
   crumbled
Iceberg lettuce
Bibb lettuce

Combine chicken, eggs, avocado, cucumber, tomato and dressing, mixing lightly. Chill thoroughly, about 2 hours. Just before serving, add croutons, blue cheese and bacon; toss lightly. Serve on a lettuce-lined plate, sprinkling and tucking Bibb lettuce leaves at random. Serves 4 to 6.

*Dressing*
1/2 cup Hellmann's
   mayonnaise
1/3 cup sour cream

1/4 teaspoon dried
   dill weed

Combine ingredients and mix until well blended.

*Note:* To make croutons, sauté bread cubes in 2 to 3 tablespoons corn oil until golden in color.

## TOSSED CHICKEN SALAD

1 1/2 cups chicken, cut into
   thin strips
3 cups shredded lettuce
1 cup thick mayonnaise
1 tablespoon tarragon vinegar
2 tablespoons chili sauce

1 tablespoon finely
   chopped green pepper
1 tablespoon finely
   chopped pimiento
6 ounces blue cheese,
   crumbled

Mix chicken and shredded lettuce. For dressing, combine the remaining ingredients. Place lettuce and chicken mixture on lettuce leaves and pour over the dressing. Garnish with wedges of hard-cooked eggs and black olives. Serves 4.

# SALADS AND SALAD DRESSINGS

## COLD CURRIED CHICKEN SALAD

1 16-ounce box regular rice
6-8 cups diced cooked
   chicken, or more
1 cup raw cauliflower
8-ounce bottle Creamy
   French Dressing
1 cup mayonnaise
1 tablespoon curry powder

½ teaspoon pepper
½ cup milk
1 cup green pepper
2 cups diced celery
1 cup diced red onion
1 head Romaine (garnish)
Salt to taste

Day before, cook rice and chicken. Early on serving day toss rice with cauliflower, and French dressing. Refrigerate. In a large bowl combine mayonnaise, curry, salt and pepper. Slowly stir in milk, add chicken and toss. Before serving add rice and cauliflower, green pepper, celery and onion. Serve with chopped peanuts, chutney, red currant jelly and flaked coconut. Serves 12 to 14.

## TUNA FISH AND EGG SALAD

3 hard-cooked eggs, chopped
2 ribs celery, finely chopped
½ cup mayonnaise
1 (6½-ounce) can tuna fish,
   drained and flaked

½ teaspoon grated onion
   (optional)
1 teaspoon lemon juice
   (optional)
Chopped pickle (optional)

Combine eggs, celery and mayonnaise; add tuna *last* which will keep the salad from becoming too oily. Add other desired ingredients; mix thoroughly. Chill.

# SALADS AND SALAD DRESSINGS

## COLD ROAST BEEF SALAD

1 1/2 pounds cold roast beef,
   julienne
12 small fresh mushrooms,
   sliced
12 cherry tomatoes, halved

1 (14-ounce) can artichoke
   hearts, drained and cut
   up
1 avocado, sliced

Toss ingredients together with dressing.

*Dressing*
1/2 cup olive oil or salad oil
1/4 cup red wine vinegar
2 teaspoons Dijon mustard
1/2 teaspoon sugar
Salt and pepper to taste

1 clove garlic, crushed
3 tablespoons blue cheese
2 tablespoons finely
   chopped parsley

Combine all ingredients, mixing well; chill.

## WEST INDIES CRAB SALAD

1 pound fresh lump crabmeat
1 medium onion, chopped
   fine
1/2 teaspoon salt
1/4 teaspoon freshly ground
   black pepper

4 ounces Wesson oil
3 ounces cider vinegar
4 ounces ice water

Place half of crabmeat in the bottom of a glass bowl; top with half of the onion. Repeat, making a second layer of crabmeat and onion. One ingredient at a time, pour over the oil, then the vinegar and, lastly, the ice water. Cover and keep refrigerated for 2 to 24 hours. Before serving, toss lightly (do not stir). Serve plain or on lettuce with fresh tomatoes and avocados. Serves 4.

# SALADS AND SALAD DRESSINGS

## SHRIMP SALAD

2 pounds cooked fresh shrimp
  (cook in crab boil)
2 medium onions, very thinly
  sliced
2 lemons, very thinly sliced
2 tablespoons capers with
  liquid
Dash Tabasco sauce
Dash Worcestershire sauce

⅔ cup oil
½ cup white tarragon
  vinegar
¼ cup finely chopped
  parsley
½ teaspoon salt
½ teaspoon freshly
  ground pepper

Using a glass bowl or crock, layer shrimp, onions, lemons, and capers. In a jar mix the oil, vinegar, Tabasco, Worcestershire sauce, parsley, salt and pepper. Shake well to mix. Pour over shrimp. Cover and chill at least 8 hours. Drain and serve. Serves 6 to 8.

## CHEESE RING

2 tablespoons unflavored
  gelatin
½ cup cold water
1 (10¾-ounce) can tomato
  soup
3 (3-ounce) packages cream
  cheese
1 cup mayonnaise

1½ cups chopped celery
½ cup chopped English
  walnuts
¼ cup chopped green
  olives
2 tablespoons chopped
  onion

Sprinkle gelatin on cold water to soften for 5 minutes. Warm tomato soup over low heat; add softened gelatin and cheese, stirring until blended. Cool; fold in remaining ingredients. Pour into a ring mold and chill until set.

*Filling:* Fill center of ring with a mixture of shrimp, cubes of avocado and mayonnaise seasoned with Worcestershire sauce. Serves 6 to 8.

# SALADS AND SALAD DRESSINGS

## MOLDED ASPARAGUS SALAD

3 (10-ounce) packages frozen
  asparagus or 2 pounds fresh
1 1/2 tablespoons unflavored
  gelatin
1/4 cup cold water
1 cup homemade mayonnaise
1 cup cream, whipped

1 teaspoon onion juice
1 teaspoon Worcestershire
  sauce
Salt and cayenne pepper
  to taste
1 (8-ounce) can fancy
  whole water chestnuts,
  drained and sliced

Butter large ring mold or two small ones. Set aside. Cook asparagus according to package directions; drain, reserving 1 cup of cooking water. Slice asparagus lengthwise. Sprinkle gelatin on cold water to soften; add to hot asparagus-water, stirring until dissolved. Chill until very thick. Combine mayonnaise and whipped cream; fold into gelatin mixture. Add onion juice, Worcestershire sauce, salt and cayenne pepper. Spoon one-third of the mixture into mold; put on one-half of the asparagus and one-half of the water chestnuts. Repeat to make second layer. Top with remaining one-third of mixture. Chill until firm; unmold. Serves 10 to 12.

## TANGY TOMATO ASPIC

4 envelopes unflavored gelatin
1 quart tomato juice
1 quart Mr. and Mrs. T.
  Bloody Mary Mix or
  Snap-E-Tom
4 leafy celery tops
1/2 medium onion
8 whole cloves

3 whole bay leaves
Juice of 1 lemon
1/2 teaspoon sugar
1 teaspoon salt
Tabasco sauce to taste
1/8 teaspoon ground black
  pepper

Soften gelatin in 1 cup cold tomato juice. Combine remaining ingredients and simmer for 1/2 hour; strain. Add softened gelatin and stir until thoroughly dissolved. Pour into 2 small, oiled molds or 1 large, oiled mold. Serves 18.

# SALADS AND SALAD DRESSINGS

## TOMATO ASPIC

3 envelopes unflavored gelatin
3½ cups tomato juice
½ cup lemon juice
2 tablespoons Worcestershire
   sauce
1 tablespoon sugar
Dash of Tabasco sauce
2 cups minced celery
1 medium green pepper,
   minced
1 cup sliced stuffed olives
1 small onion, grated

Sprinkle gelatin on 1 cup of the tomato juice to soften; place over low heat and stir until gelatin is dissolved. Remove from heat and stir in remaining 2½ cups tomato juice, lemon juice, Worcestershire sauce, sugar and Tabasco sauce. Chill mixture to the consistency of unbeaten egg whites; fold in remaining ingredients. Turn into a large ring mold and chill until firm. Unmold aspic onto a serving plate. The center of the ring may be filled with mayonnaise or marinated artichoke hearts. Serves 10.

*This recipe is from the Lexington caterer, Mary Ellen Hardin*

## SALMON MOUSSE

1 (16-ounce) can red sockeye
   salmon
1 tablespoon gelatin
1 (10½-ounce) can consommé
1 teaspoon Worcestershire
   sauce
1 small onion, grated
1 cup mayonnaise
1 tablespoon tarragon
   vinegar
Juice of 1 large lemon
Dash of soy sauce
Dash of Tabasco sauce
Salt and pepper to taste

Drain salmon and remove skin and bones. Dissolve gelatin in warmed consommé; add remaining ingredients and process in blender. Pour into a lightly greased 1½-quart mold or 10 to 12 individual molds.

# SALADS AND SALAD DRESSINGS

## TWO-LAYERED SHRIMP SALAD MOLD

*First layer*

1 (14-ounce) can artichoke
   hearts
4 cups Campbell's consommé
2 envelopes unflavored gelatin

Juice of 1 lemon
Worcestershire sauce
Garlic salt
Cayenne pepper

Halve artichoke hearts; arrange, uncut side down, in a 3-quart ring mold. Heat consommé; stir in gelatin until dissolved. Add lemon juice, Worcestershire sauce and seasoning; chill until beginning to set. Pour mixture over artichokes; chill until congealed.

*Second layer*

1 envelope unflavored gelatin
1/2 cup water
Juice of 1 lemon
1 tablespoon onion juice
Salt to taste
2 cups Campbell's consommé
1 1/2 cups mayonnaise
2 cups cooked shrimp,
   cut up

1 cup chopped celery
1 (3-ounce) bottle stuffed
   green olives, drained
   and sliced
4 hard-cooked eggs, finely
   chopped
2 pimientos, chopped
   very fine

Sprinkle gelatin on water to soften. Place over boiling water and stir until dissolved. Remove from heat; add lemon juice, onion juice and salt. Cool. Stir in mayonnaise; gradually add consommé, stirring until blended. Add remaining ingredients. Turn into mold on top of first layer and chill until firm. Unmold on lettuce and serve with extra mayonnaise.

## MOLDED CHICKEN AND CRANBERRY SALAD

*...a two-layered main dish salad with great eye appeal*

*First layer*

| | |
|---|---|
| 1 envelope unflavored gelatin | 1/2 cup orange juice |
| 1/4 cup cold water | 1/2 cup diced celery |
| 1 (16-ounce) can jellied cranberry sauce | 1/2 cup chopped walnuts |

Sprinkle gelatin on water to soften. Mash cranberry sauce and add orange juice and gelatin; place over low heat and stir until gelatin is dissolved. Remove from heat; chill to unbeaten egg white consistency. Fold in celery and walnuts; pour into an 8 1/2" square dish and chill until firm.

*Second layer*

| | |
|---|---|
| 1 envelope unflavored gelatin | 2 tablespoons chopped parsley |
| 1/4 cup cold water | |
| 1 cup hot chicken broth | 1 teaspoon lemon juice |
| 2/3 cup mayonnaise | Dash of pepper |
| 1/2 cup half-and-half | Dash of salt |
| 2 cups diced cooked chicken | |

Soften gelatin in water; stir in hot broth. Chill until partially set. Fold in remaining ingredients and pour on top of first layer. Chill until firm. To serve, cut into squares and place on lettuce leaves with a dab of homemade mayonnaise, if desired.

# SALADS AND SALAD DRESSINGS

## MOLDED GAZPACHO SALAD

2 packages gelatin
3 cups tomato juice (1/2 V-8)
1/4 cup wine vinegar
2 teaspoons salt
1/4 teaspoon pepper
Dash of Cayenne
2 large tomatoes chopped

1/2 cup finely chopped
  onion
3/4 cup finely chopped
  green pepper
3/4 cup finely chopped
  cucumber
1/4 cup chopped pimento

Soften gelatin in one cup of tomato juice. Heat until this simmers. Add the remaining juice, vinegar, salt, pepper, and cayenne. Chill until it begins to set. Stir in vegetables and pour into a greased, 6-cup ring mold. Serve with avocado dressing. See page 252.

## PLEASANT HILL MOLDED FRUIT SALAD

3 (3-ounce) packages lemon
  gelatin dessert
3 cups hot water
1 cup cold water
1 (8 3/4-ounce) can fruit
  cocktail

1 1/2 grapefruits, sliced and
  drained
2 oranges, sliced and
  drained
Melon balls in season
Berries or fruits of the
  season

Dissolve gelatin in hot water, then stir in cold water. Spoon a small amount of gelatin into a mold. Arrange some of the fruit decoratively in the bottom of the mold; place in refrigerator and let set. Gently add the rest of the fruit and pour in the remaining gelatin; chill until firm. Unmold on lettuce, decorate with parsley and serve with mayonnaise. For a special luncheon, serve with chicken salad and country ham biscuits.

*This is a Shakertown recipe.*

## WATERMELON BASKET

*...a colorful centerpiece for a brunch or picnic supper*

1 watermelon

*Suggested fruit:* melons, peaches, pineapple, grapes, berries, apples, bananas, oranges and grapefruit

Make a basket with a handle out of the watermelon. Placing the melon lengthwise, cut a basket handle from the top one-third. The remaining two-thirds of the melon becomes the basket after the pulp has been carefully scooped out. Save the good pieces for making watermelon balls. Cut "saw teeth" around the edge of the basket with a sharp knife. Refrigerate basket. When ready to use, fill basket with a variety of melon balls and cut-up fruits, well drained. Flowers may be tied to the handle for decoration.

## FROZEN FRUIT SALAD

1 tablespoon flour, sifted
1/4 cup sugar
1 teaspoon Dijon mustard
1/4 cup vinegar
1/2 teaspoon salt
1 pint whipping cream
1 pound seedless green grapes

1 (16-ounce) can pitted Royal Anne cherries, drained
1 (20-ounce) can pineapple chunks, drained
1/2 pound pecan halves

Combine flour, sugar, mustard, vinegar and salt in pan; bring to a boil, stirring constantly to make a smooth paste. Remove from heat; let cool. Whip cream well but not too stiff; stir into cool paste. Halve grapes, cherries and pineapple chunks; mix together with pecans. Fold in cream mixture. Place in individual molds, a single large mold or 2 ice trays. Cover with wax paper and freeze for at least 6 hours. Partially thaw before serving on Bibb lettuce with homemade mayonnaise. Serves 12.

*Note:* If used as a dessert, omit mayonnaise; garnish with mint leaves.

# SALADS AND SALAD DRESSINGS

## OLD FASHIONED FROZEN FRUIT SALAD

4 egg yolks
¼ cup sugar
¼ cup vinegar
1 (8-ounce) can crushed
    pineapple, drained

1 (6-ounce) jar red
    cherries, cut up
¼ pound pecans, broken
¼ pound marshmallows,
    cut into small pieces
1 pint whipping cream,
    whipped

Combine egg yolks, sugar and vinegar in the top of a large double boiler; stir over simmering water until thickened. Remove from heat; cool before adding pineapple, cherries, pecans and marshmallows. Fold in whipped cream; pour mixture into 8" square glass dish and freeze. Cut into squares and serve on Bibb lettuce.

## COOKED DRESSING FOR CHICKEN SALAD

½ cup sugar
2 tablespoons flour
1 tablespoon dry mustard
1 cup cream

8 egg yolks, slightly
    beaten
1 cup vinegar
1 scant tablespoon salt

In the top of a double boiler or in a saucepan, combine sugar, flour and dry mustard, blending well to smooth out lumps. Stir in cream; cook over medium heat, stirring constantly. Add egg yolks, vinegar and salt, continuing to stir until dressing is very thick. Pour warm dressing over cut-up chicken (½ cup is about the right amount for 1 pound of cut-up chicken). Let cool before adding other chicken salad ingredients. This dressing will keep 2 to 3 weeks if refrigerated. Makes 3 cups.

# SALADS AND SALAD DRESSINGS

## AVOCADO DRESSING

1 large avocado, mashed  
1/2 cup sour cream  
1/2 cup light cream  
2 tablespoons grated onion  
Tabasco to taste  

1 1/2 teaspoons salt  
1/8 teaspoon sugar  
1 clove garlic, crushed  
1 tablespoon lemon juice  

Blend and refrigerate several hours. Makes 8 servings.

## BLUE CHEESE DRESSING FOR A CROWD

1 quart Hellmann's  
   mayonnaise  
1/2 pint sour cream  
Juice of 3 1/2 lemons  
1 medium-sized onion, grated  

Garlic salt to taste  
3/4 pound blue cheese,  
   crumbled  
1 tablespoon chopped  
   parsley  

Place mayonnaise in large mixing bowl; add sour cream, lemon juice, onion and garlic salt, mixing well. Stir in blue cheese and parsley. Spoon into jars and store in refrigerator. This dressing will keep 3 weeks and may be used as a dip for fresh vegetables. Makes 2 quarts.

## BLUE CHEESE DRESSING

1 cup buttermilk  
4 ounces blue cheese  
1 pint mayonnaise  

1 teaspoon lemon juice  
2 or 3 cloves garlic  

Combine buttermilk and blue cheese; add mayonnaise and lemon juice. Beat with a wire whisk or electric hand mixer. Put garlic cloves on toothpicks; leave at least overnight in dressing. This salad dressing may be used also as a dip for raw vegetables. Makes 3 cups.

# SALADS AND SALAD DRESSINGS

## CREAMY SALAD DRESSING

1 egg
3 tablespoons sour cream
3 tablespoons olive oil
1 tablespoon red wine vinegar

1 teaspoon garlic salt
1/2 teaspoon coarsely
   ground fresh pepper

Beat all together with a wire whisk. Serve over a variety of torn lettuces. Croutons and freshly grated Parmesan cheese may be added.

## DILL DRESSING

3/4 cup salad oil
1/4 cup fresh lemon juice
1/2 teaspoon salt
1/2 teaspoon freshly ground
   black pepper

1/4 teaspoon dill weed
1 clove garlic
1/3 cup Hellmann's
   mayonnaise

Mix oil, lemon juice, salt, pepper and dill weed. Lightly pierce garlic clove several times with a toothpick; insert toothpick into clove and drop into dressing. Let stand for several hours. Remove and discard garlic clove; add mayonnaise and stir until thoroughly blended. Dill dressing may be used to marinate artichoke hearts, hearts of palm or other vegetables. Marinate at least 8 hours. Serve on Bibb lettuce with fresh tomato wedges. Makes 1 1/3 cups.

## EGG DRESSING FOR RAW SPINACH SALAD

3 hard-cooked eggs, grated
1 teaspoon prepared mustard
1 tablespoon prepared
   horseradish

1 to 2 teaspoons tarragon
   vinegar
Salt and pepper
Dash of Tabasco sauce
3/4 cup mayonnaise

Combine all ingredients, mixing thoroughly. Serve over spinach leaves. Makes 1 cup.

# SALADS AND SALAD DRESSINGS

## HERBED FRENCH DRESSING

1 1/2 cup safflower oil
1/2 cup lemon juice
1/4 cup cider vinegar
1 teaspoon kosher salt
1/2 teaspoon freshly ground
   pepper
1/2 teaspoon sugar

1 tablespoon minced
   onion
1 clove garlic, split
1 teaspoon oregano
1 teaspoon basil
1 teaspoon tarragon
1/2 teaspoon dry mustard

Combine all ingredients in the container of an electric blender; process until blended. Store in refrigerator; shake well before using.

## FRENCH DRESSING

2/3 cup olive oil
3 tablespoons tarragon
   vinegar
1 tablespoon fresh lemon
   juice
1 tablespoon water
1/4 teaspoon Worcestershire
   sauce

1/4 teaspoon Dijon
   mustard
3/4 teaspoon salt
1/2 teaspoon celery salt
1/8 teaspoon black pepper,
   freshly ground
2 dashes of cayenne
   pepper

Put all ingredients in a bottle or jar with tight-fitting lid; shake vigorously until blended. Keep refrigerated. Makes about 1 cup.

## CELERY SEED FRENCH DRESSING

1 1/2 cups vegetable oil
1 cup sugar
5 teaspoons salt
1 1/2 cups finely chopped
   yellow onion
1 3/4 cups catsup

1 1/2 cups cider vinegar
1 1/2 teaspoons dry
   mustard
1 1/2 teaspoons paprika
1 1/2 teaspoons celery seed
1 1/2 teaspoons chili
   powder

Combine the first 3 ingredients in a bowl; blend on low speed with an electric mixer. Add remaining ingredients, blending well. Makes 1 1/2 quarts.

# SALADS AND SALAD DRESSINGS

## FRUIT SALAD DRESSING

1/2 cup plus 2 tablespoons
  confectioners' sugar
1 teaspoon dry mustard
1 teaspoon salt
1 cup salad oil

1 small onion, finely
  grated
1/2 cup cider vinegar
1/4 teaspoon celery seed
1/2 to 1 teaspoon paprika

Combine first 5 ingredients in a glass bowl. Using a wooden spoon, stir out lumps; slowly add vinegar, celery seed and paprika, mixing thoroughly. Chill.

## HONEY FRUIT SALAD DRESSING

1 1/2 cups Hellmann's
  mayonnaise
1 cup honey
1/2 cup lemon juice

1/2 teaspoon salt
Dash of red pepper
4 ounces cream cheese,
  softened (optional)

Combine the first 5 ingredients, beating just until blended. Add cream cheese if a thicker consistency is desired.

## ITALIAN DRESSING

1/2 cup olive oil
2 tablespoons minced onion
1 tablespoon grated Parmesan
  cheese
2 teaspoons salt
3/4 teaspoon dry mustard
3/4 teaspoon Worcestershire
  sauce

3/4 teaspoon basil
3/4 teaspoon oregano
3/4 teaspoon sugar
3/4 teaspoon pepper
1/4 cup red wine vinegar
2 tablespoons lemon juice

Put all ingredients except vinegar and lemon juice into blender container; cover and blend for 30 seconds. Add remaining ingredients and blend for an additional 30 seconds.

# SALADS AND SALAD DRESSINGS

## MAYONNAISE

| | |
|---|---|
| 1/2 teaspoon dry mustard | 2 egg yolks |
| 1/2 teaspoon salt | 1 cup oil |
| 1/8 teaspoon cayenne pepper | 2 tablespoons fresh lemon juice |

Allow all ingredients to reach room temperature. Combine dry mustard, salt and cayenne pepper. In a large mixing bowl, beat egg yolks at medium-high speed of electric mixer until thickened and pale yellow; add mustard mixture. Slowly dribble in 1 tablespoon oil and beat until thoroughly blended. Beating constantly, continue to add oil, 1 tablespoon at a time, until 1/2 cup has been added. Dribble in lemon juice alternately with remaining oil until all has been used. Scrape mixer bowl frequently during entire procedure. Spoon mayonnaise into a jar with a tight-fitting lid; store in refrigerator. Makes about 1 1/4 cups.

*Note:* If oil is added too fast while making mayonnaise, it will separate. Should this occur, beat 1 egg yolk in another bowl and then slowly beat the curdled mayonnaise into it.

*Variation:* HORSERADISH MAYONNAISE
To 2 cups mayonnaise, add the grated rind of 1/2 lemon and salt to taste. Just before serving, stir in 1/4 cup freshly grated horseradish.

## BLENDER MAYONNAISE

| | |
|---|---|
| 1 egg | 1 tablespoon lemon juice |
| 1/4 teaspoon dry mustard | 1 cup Wesson oil |
| 1/2 to 3/4 teaspoon salt | |

Put egg in electric blender; whirl at high speed for 30 seconds. Do not turn blender off. Immediately add mustard, salt and lemon juice; blend for 20 seconds. While still on high speed, slowly pour in oil in a steady stream and process until thick. Makes 1 1/4 cups.

# SALADS AND SALAD DRESSINGS

## DRESSING FOR SWEET MOLDED SALADS

1/2 pint whipping cream,
   whipped
1/2 cup mayonnaise
   (homemade is best)

Finely-chopped pecans or
   walnuts

Fold whipped cream into mayonnaise, blending thoroughly. Serve on molded salads made with fresh fruits; garnish with nuts.

## MUSTARD SAUCE

1 quart Hellmann's
   mayonnaise
1/4 (6-ounce) bottle Escoffier
   Diable Sauce (no substitute)
1/2 (5-ounce) jar Mr. Mustard
   (no substitute)

1 tablespoon dry mustard
2 1/2 tablespoons
   Worcestershire sauce
Dash of Tabasco sauce
1 tablespoon tarragon
   (optional)

Combine ingredients in a large bowl; stir to mix, then use an electric mixer to blend well. Use as a dressing for salads and cold seafood and for chicken or turkey sandwiches.

## SHAKERTOWN COUNTRY DRESSING

1 teaspoon dry mustard
2 teaspoons sugar
1/4 teaspoon salt
2 tablespoons flour

1/2 cup cold water
2 egg yolks
1/4 cup vinegar
2 tablespoons butter

Dissolve mustard, sugar, salt and flour in water. Beat eggs and vinegar in the top of a double boiler; add dissolved ingredients. Cook and stir over boiling water until thick and smooth; add butter.

# SALADS AND SALAD DRESSINGS

## REMOULADE SAUCE

$^1/_2$ cup Creole mustard
$^1/_2$ cup chopped onion
$^3/_4$ cup oil
$^1/_4$ cup tarragon vinegar
2 teaspoons paprika
$^3/_4$ teaspoon cayenne pepper

2 teaspoons salt
2 medium cloves garlic,
   pressed
$^1/_2$ cup chopped green
   onions

Put ingredients, except green onions, into a blender container and mix for a few seconds. Stir in green onions. Store in a covered refrigerator bowl and chill well. Makes enough sauce to cover 4 to 5 pounds shrimp.

## POPPY SEED DRESSING

1$^1/_2$ cups sugar
2 teaspoons dry mustard
2 teaspoons salt
$^2/_3$ cup vinegar

2 cups salad oil
3 tablespoons chopped
   onion
3 tablespoons poppy seeds

Mix sugar, mustard and salt; add vinegar and stir until ingredients are dissolved. Add salad oil, onion and poppy seeds; whisk until thoroughly blended. Store in jar in refrigerator. Serve over assorted fruits. Makes 1 quart.

## ORANGE ROLLS

2 large oranges
1 cup sugar
2 1/2 teaspoons dry yeast or 1
   cake yeast
1/4 cup lukewarm water
1 cup milk

1/2 teaspoon salt
2 tablespoons melted
   shortening
3 1/2 to 4 cups flour
1/2 cup melted butter

Cut oranges in quarters and remove seeds, leaving peel intact. Put into the container of a blender or food processor and purée; add sugar, making a thick paste. Dissolve yeast in lukewarm water. Scald milk; allow to cool. Add yeast, salt, melted shortening and 3 tablespoons puréed orange. Stir in flour gradually, using enough to make a stiff dough. Cover and allow to rise in a warm place until doubled in bulk. Divide dough in 2 parts. Working with one-half at a time, roll out on a floured board until 1/4" thick. Brush with melted butter and spread with one-half of remaining puréed orange. Roll up dough and cut in 1" slices. Place in greased muffin tins or side-by-side in a greased 9" round cake pan; brush tops with butter and allow to rise again. Use remaining puréed orange on top of rolls; bake at 350° for 15 to 18 minutes.

## DILL BREAD

1 package dry yeast
1/4 cup warm water
1 cup small curd cottage
   cheese
2 tablespoons sugar
2 teaspoons grated onion
2 teaspoons Spice Islands
   dill weed

1 tablespoon melted
   butter
1/4 teaspoon soda
1 teaspoon salt
1 egg
2 1/4 cups flour

Soften yeast in water; set aside. Heat cheese to lukewarm; combine in a large bowl with sugar, onion, dill weed, butter, salt, soda, egg and yeast. Add flour to form soft dough, beating well. Cover, let rise until doubled. Beat down and place in a greased 1 1/2-quart casserole; let rise again until doubled. Bake at 350° for 40 minutes.

# BREADS

## CHEESE BREAD

1 1/2 cups milk
1/2 stick butter
1/3 cup sugar
1 tablespoon salt
1 1/2 cups grated extra sharp
  Cheddar cheese

2 eggs, well beaten
2 packages dry yeast plus
  1 teaspoon sugar,
  dissolved in 3/4 cup
  warm water (105° to
  115°)
6 cups all-purpose flour

Combine the first 4 ingredients and scald; remove from heat, add cheese and stir until melted. Cool to lukewarm; add eggs and yeast mixture. Beat in 3 cups of flour; allow mixture to rise in a warm place (85°) for 30 minutes. Beat in the remaining flour. Toss dough onto a lightly floured board; knead about 2 minutes until easily handled. Grease large ring molds or loaf pans with shortening (not butter). Roll or twist dough with hands and fill each mold or pan one-third full. Let rise in a warm place for 1 hour; bake at 350° for 30 minutes. Serves 30.

*This recipe is from Lexington caterer, Christine Gilmore*

## ICE BOX ROLLS

1/2 cup Crisco
6 tablespoons sugar
1/2 cup boiling water
1 package dry yeast dissolved
  in 1/2 cup warm water

1 egg, beaten
1/2 teaspoon salt
3 to 3 1/4 cups flour

Cream Crisco and sugar; add boiling water. Cool to lukewarm and add yeast, egg and salt. Stir in enough flour to make a soft dough. Cover and place in refrigerator overnight or until needed. Make rolls in desired shape; dip in melted butter. Place in a pan and let rise 1 to 2 hours. Bake at 400° for 15 minutes.

*Note:* 1 cake of yeast dissolved in 1/2 cup cold water may be substituted for dry yeast mixture.

## BROWN BREAD

2¼ cups graham flour
1 cup yellow cornmeal
1 heaping teaspoon baking
powder
1 teaspoon soda

1 teaspoon salt
1 cup milk
1 cup buttermilk
¼ cup brown sugar
¼ cup molasses

Combine dry ingredients, mixing well. Combine milk, buttermilk, brown sugar and molasses; stir into dry ingredients. Fill a well-greased 2-cup pudding mold no more than two-thirds full. Cover tightly and place on a trivet or rack in a large kettle; add enough boiling water to come half-way up the mold. Cover kettle closely; boil gently for 3 hours. Remove mold from water, uncover and set in a moderate oven for 15 minutes. Unmold.

*Note:* Batter may be steamed in tightly-covered loaf pans or in tin cans with tight-fitting lids, such as 1-pound baking powder cans or coffee cans.

*Filling*
2 oranges, quartered and
seeded
1 (8-ounce) package dates

1 (9-ounce) box raisins
1 cup pecans

Grind all ingredients and mix together (a food processor may be used). Spread filling generously on buttered slices of brown bread.

## BANANA - NUT BREAD

½ cup (1 stick) butter
1 cup sugar
1 cup mashed bananas
(approximately 2)
2 eggs, beaten
2 cups flour

1 teaspoon baking soda
½ teaspoon salt
2 teaspoons grated orange
rind
¾ cup chopped pecans

Cream butter; add sugar. Beat well. Add bananas and eggs. Mix. Sift flour, soda and salt together; stir into creamed mixture. Add orange rind and nuts. Bake in greased loaf pan at 350° for 1 hour.

# BREADS

## WHITE BREAD

6 tablespoons sugar
1 teaspoon salt
1/4 cup butter
1 1/2 cups milk, scalded

1 package dry yeast
  dissolved in 1/4 cup
  warm water
5 1/2 cups sifted flour
  (approximately)

Combine sugar, salt and butter in a large bowl; add scalded milk. Cool to lukewarm and add yeast. Add flour gradually, mixing well; knead dough until smooth. Cover and let rise in a warm place until doubled in bulk. Turn out on a floured board and knead lightly, using as little flour as possible. Divide dough into 2 equal portions and shape into loaves; place in well-greased loaf pans (8 1/2"x 4 1/2"). Brush tops with melted butter and let rise in a warm place until doubled in bulk. Bake at 375° for about 20 minutes. The bread freezes well.

## BUTTERSCOTCH BREAD

2 cups flour
1 1/4 teaspoons baking powder
3/4 teaspoon soda
1/4 teaspoon salt
1/2 cup chopped black walnuts

1 egg, beaten
1 cup brown sugar
1 tablespoon shortening,
  melted
1 cup buttermilk

Sift flour and measure; add baking powder, soda, salt and nuts. Combine egg, brown sugar, melted shortening and buttermilk; stir into flour mixture until moist (do not beat). Pour batter into a greased 9 1/2"x 5 1/2" loaf pan; bake at 350° for 45 minutes. Pour Sauce over hot bread before removing from pan.

*Sauce*

1/4 cup half-and-half
1/4 cup brown sugar

2 tablespoons butter
1 teaspoon vanilla

Combine ingredients and cook over medium heat until thickened.

## CRANBERRY-NUT BREAD

2 cups sifted flour, less
  1 tablespoon
1 cup sugar
1/2 teaspoon salt
1 1/2 teaspoons baking powder
1/2 teaspoon baking soda
2 eggs

Juice of 1 orange
2 tablespoons melted
  shortening
1 cup cranberries
1 cup chopped walnuts
1 tablespoon flour

Sift together the first 5 ingredients. Beat eggs and add juice and melted shortening. Combine with the dry ingredients; stir together until moist. Toss cranberries and walnuts in 1 tablespoon of flour; fold into batter. Spoon mixture into a greased and floured small loaf pan. Bake at 350° for 1 hour. Cool in pan for 10 minutes; remove from pan and cool on a wire rack.

## DATE NUT BREAD

1 cup chopped dates
1 tablespoon butter
1 cup boiling water
1 cup sugar
3/4 teaspoon salt

1 egg
2 cups flour
1 teaspoon baking soda
Pinch of cinnamon
1 cup chopped pecans

Add dates and butter to boiling water; let cool. Add remaining ingredients, mixing thoroughly. Grease and flour bottom and sides of a 9"x 5 1/2" loaf pan; pour in batter. Bake at 325° for 1 hour.

*Note:* This recipe will also make 3 or 4 miniature loaves.

# BREADS

## LEMON BREAD

1/3 cup shortening
1 1/3 cups sugar
2 eggs
1 1/2 cups sifted flour
1 1/2 teaspoons baking powder

1/4 teaspoon salt
1/2 cup milk
1/2 cup chopped nuts
Grated rind and juice of 1
lemon

Cream shortening and 1 cup sugar until fluffy. Add eggs, one at a time, beating well after each addition. Sift dry ingredients together and add alternately with milk to creamed mixture, beating well. Add nuts and lemon rind. Pour into a greased 8 1/2"x 4 1/2" loaf pan. Bake at 350° for 50 to 60 minutes. Blend remaining sugar and lemon juice; pour over bread as soon as it comes from oven.

## ZUCCHINI BREAD

2 1/2 cups sugar
2 cups finely-chopped
    zucchini, unpeeled
3 eggs , beaten
1 cup vegetable oil
3 cups all-purpose flour

1 1/2 teaspoons baking
    powder
1 teaspoon soda
1 teaspoon salt
2 teaspoons cinnamon
1 teaspoon vanilla extract
1 cup chopped nuts

Combine sugar, zucchini and eggs; add oil and beat. Blend in dry ingredients; stir in vanilla and nuts. Pour batter into 2 loaf pans or 3 mini-bread pans. Bake at 350° for 1 hour.

## SALLY LUNN

2 eggs
3/4 cups sugar
2 cups flour
2 teaspoons baking powder

1/8 teaspoon salt
1 teaspoon mace
1 cup milk
3 tablespoons melted butter

Beat eggs and add sugar gradually. Sift dry ingredients together and add alternately to eggs, along with milk. Add the melted butter and pour into greased 9"x 13" baking dish (or a tube cake pan). Bake at 400° for 25 to 35 minutes. Cut into serving pieces and pass with lots of butter.

## BEATEN BISCUITS

*...this is an old Kentucky specialty usually served with country ham*

7 cups soft wheat flour
3 tablespoons sugar
1 teaspoon salt

1 teaspoon baking powder
1 cup lard
1 1/3 cups skim milk

Combine flour, sugar, salt and baking powder; work in lard with clean hands. Add most of the milk to make a stiff dough; add the remaining milk as needed. Put dough in refrigerator for at least 2 hours to overnight. (Let dough warm about an hour if it has been cooled overnight.) Divide dough into fourths. Working with one-fourth at a time, cut into 1 1/2" cubes. Place in a food processor with steel blade; process for 2 minutes. On a floured board, roll out dough to 1/4" thickness; cut with a 2" biscuit cutter. Place biscuits on an ungreased cookie sheet; prick the top of each with a fork. Bake at 350° for 25 minutes. Makes 6 dozen.

# BREADS

## BAKING POWDER BISCUITS

2 cups flour
4 teaspoons baking powder
1 teaspoon salt

2 1/2 tablespoons
shortening
3/4 cup milk or water

Sift the dry ingredients together. Work shortening into the flour with a fork or tips of fingers. Make a well in the center; pour in the milk all at once. Stir well for 20 seconds until all the flour is moistened. Toss dough on a floured board at once and knead for 20 seconds. Pat or roll until 1/2" thick. Use as little flour as possible on the board when shaping the dough. Cut into rounds, place in pan and bake in very hot oven (450°) for 10 to 15 minutes. Makes 20 medium-sized biscuits.

## SAUSAGE COFFEE CAKE

1 pound bulk sausage
1/2 cup chopped onions
1/4 cup grated Parmesan
   cheese
1/2 cup grated Swiss cheese
1 egg, beaten
1/4 teaspoon Tabasco sauce
1 teaspoon salt

2 tablespoons chopped
   fresh parsley
2 cups biscuit mix
3/4 cup milk
1/4 cup mayonnaise
1 egg yolk
1 tablespoon water

Brown sausage and onions; drain. Add next 6 ingredients. Combine biscuit mix, milk and mayonnaise. Spread half of batter in a 9"x 9"x 2" greased pan. Pour in sausage mixture and cover with remaining batter. Mix egg yolk and water and brush on top. Bake at 400° for 25 to 30 minutes until cake leaves sides of pan. Cool 5 minutes before cutting into 3"squares.

*Note:* This recipe doubles easily in a 9"x 13" pan. It also freezes well.

## SHERRY COFFEE CAKE

1 yellow cake mix
1 ½ teaspoons cinnamon
⅓ cup sherry

½ cup brown sugar,
  firmly packed
½ cup chopped walnuts

Prepare cake batter according to directions on box, adding 1 teaspoon of cinnamon and substituting ⅓ cup sherry for ⅓ cup of the required water or milk. Pour batter into a greased 13"x 9" or 12"x 8" pan, according to directions of mix. Combine brown sugar, walnuts and remaining ½ teaspoon of cinnamon; sprinkle evenly on top of batter. Bake as directed; serve warm.

## CINNAMON BISCUIT RING

2 cans regrigerator biscuits
  (not flaky) containing 10
  biscuits each
½ cup melted butter

¾ cup sugar mixed with 1
  tablespoon cinnamon
¼ cup raisins
¼ cup chopped nuts

Dip each biscuit in melted butter, then in sugar-cinnamon mixture, covering all sides well. In an 8" or 9" pie pan, overlap biscuits, standing on end in a ring pattern. Place raisins and nuts between each biscuit. Bake at 375° for 20 to 30 minutes. Slide out of pan while warm. Biscuits will separate easily for serving. Makes 10 servings.

## CINNAMON COFFEE CAKE

2 cups brown sugar, packed
2 cups sifted flour
1 teaspoon cinnamon
1/2 cup melted butter

1 cup sour cream
1 teaspoon baking soda
1 egg

Combine brown sugar, flour and cinnamon, blending thoroughly; pour in butter and mix until crumbly. Reserve 1/2 cup of the mixture. Combine sour cream, baking soda and egg; add to brown sugar mixture, mixing well. Pour batter into a greased and floured 10"x 12" pan or two 8" pans; sprinkle with reserved crumbly mixture. Bake at 325° for 20 to 30 minutes. Serves 8 to 10.

## CREAM-STYLE CORN BREAD

2 tablespoons bacon grease
3 eggs, well beaten
1/2 cup vegetable oil
1 cup sour cream

1 (17-ounce) can
cream-style corn
1 cup self-rising cornmeal

Heat bacon grease in an iron skillet until very hot. Combine remaining ingredients and pour into hot skillet. Place in oven and bake at 350° for 20 to 30 minutes until set. Slice in wedges to serve. Serves 6.

## CORNMEAL MUFFINS

1 egg
1 cup buttermilk
1/2 teaspoon salt

1/2 teaspoon baking soda
3/4 cup cornmeal

Beat egg slightly; add buttermilk, salt and soda, mixing thoroughly. Stir in cornmeal and beat well. Preheat greased irons until hot enough to sizzle when batter is poured in. Fill irons one-half full and bake at 450° for about 10 to 12 minutes.

## HOT WATER CORN BREAD

1 cup white cornmeal
1/4 teaspoon salt
1 cup boiling water
(approximate)

2 tablespoons oil or bacon
grease
2 tablespoons milk

Combine cornmeal and salt in a small bowl; add a little boiling water, then add oil. Continue adding boiling water until the mixture reaches the consistency of a moist croquette; stir in milk. Heat a skillet containing 1/4" of oil. Drop the batter by spoonfuls into the hot skillet; smooth the top of the corn bread with the back of a spoon. Cook on medium heat until brown; turn over and cook the other side.

## CORN CAKES

3 1/2 cups cornmeal
1 tablespoon salt
2 teaspoons baking soda

2 eggs
1 quart buttermilk
1/2 cup melted shortening

Combine the first 3 ingredients. Combine eggs, buttermilk and shortening; slowly stir into dry ingredients. For each corn cake, pour about 1/4 cup batter onto a hot, lightly greased griddle. Turn when tops are covered with bubbles and edges are browned.

*This recipe is from Lexington caterer, Mary Ellen Hardin*

## HUSH PUPPIES

2 cups white cornmeal
2 teaspoons baking powder
1 teaspoon salt
2 tablespoons flour

1 egg, beaten
2 cups milk
1/3 cup minced onion

Sift together the first 4 ingredients; add egg, milk and onion, stirring well. Carefully drop batter by level tablespoons into deep hot oil (370°); cook only a few at a time, turning once. Fry 3 to 5 minutes until golden brown. Drain well on paper towels.

## CORN STICKS

1 cup plus 2 tablespoons
   cornmeal
Scant ½ cup all-purpose flour
1 tablespoon sugar
½ teaspoon baking powder
½ teaspoon soda
½ teaspoon salt
1 egg, beaten
1 cup buttermilk
2 tablespoons salad oil

Combine dry ingredients; add egg, buttermilk and oil, beating well. Grease corn-stick irons well; heat in oven until hot enough to sizzle. Remove from oven and fill about one-half full with batter. Bake at 450° for 10 to 15 minutes or until golden brown.

## JALAPEÑO CORN BREAD

1 cup yellow cornmeal
½ teaspoon soda
½ teaspoon salt
2 eggs
½ cup oil
1 cup sour cream
1 cup grated sharp
   Cheddar cheese
1 (17-ounce) can yellow
   cream-style corn
1 onion, chopped
2 to 5 Jalapeño peppers
1 clove garlic, minced

Combine all ingredients, mixing well. Pour into a greased 13"x 9" pan; bake at 400° for 20 to 30 minutes. Cut into 12 squares. This corn bread can be baked also in a 15"x 10" jellyroll pan and cut into small squares. Serves 12.

## SOUR CREAM MUFFINS

2 cups self-rising flour, sifted
1 cup (2 sticks) butter, melted
1 cup sour cream

Combine all ingredients, mixing thoroughly. Spoon into *ungreased* miniature muffin tins. Bake at 350° for 20 to 30 minutes. These muffins can be frozen. Makes 2 dozen.

## CORN BREAD

1 cup all-purpose flour
3 cups cornmeal
3/4 cup sugar
1 teaspoon baking powder

1 teaspoon salt
1/2 cup shortening or
 melted butter
3 cups buttermilk

Combine all ingredients and mix well. Spoon into a bundt pan and let stand for 10 minutes. Bake at 350° for 1 hour or until done. Cool 5 minutes before cutting.

## BLUEBERRY MUFFINS

2 cups all-purpose flour
2 teaspoons baking powder
1/2 teaspoon salt
1/2 cup butter or margarine,
 at room temperature
1 cup sugar
2 large eggs

1 teaspoon vanilla extract
1/2 cup milk
1 1/2 to 2 cups fresh or
 frozen blueberries,
 thawed and drained
1 tablespoon sugar mixed
 with 1/4 teaspoon
 ground nutmeg

Sift together flour, baking powder and salt. In a medium-sized bowl, cream shortening and sugar. Beat in the eggs thoroughly; add the vanilla. Stir in flour mixture about half at a time, alternating with milk, half at a time. Gently fold berries into batter. Spoon batter into greased muffin tins, filling three-fourths full. Sprinkle with nutmeg sugar. Bake at 375° for 25 minutes or until golden. Let muffins cool slightly before removing. Makes 1 1/2 dozen.

## BRAN MUFFINS

3 cups All-Bran cereal, divided
1 cup boiling water
1/2 cup vegetable oil
1 1/2 cups sugar
2 cups buttermilk

2 eggs, unbeaten
2 1/2 cups bread flour
2 1/2 teaspoons baking
   soda
1 teaspoon salt

Combine 1 cup All-Bran with boiling water and vegetable oil in a large bowl. Add remaining 2 cups All-Bran, sugar, buttermilk and eggs, mixing thoroughly. Sift flour, soda and salt together; add to cereal mixture. Spoon batter into muffin tins; bake at 400° for 15 to 20 minutes.
*Note:* Batter will keep for 3 weeks in refrigerator. To make tea cakes, bake in miniature muffin tins.

## RAISIN BRAN MUFFINS

*Step One*
2 cups All Bran cereal
1 cup white raisins

2 cups boiling water

Soak cereal and raisins in boiling water (raisins will swell a bit); cool.

*Step Two*
2 1/2 cups sugar
1 cup oil
4 eggs, beaten
4 cups All Bran cereal

5 cups sifted flour
1 1/2 teaspoons salt
5 teaspoons baking soda
1 quart buttermilk

Cream sugar with oil; add beaten eggs and cereal. Sift flour, salt and soda; add to creamed mixture alternately with buttermilk. Add ingredients from Step One, mixing thoroughly. Refrigerate but do not stir; use as needed. Grease muffin tins well or use paper cups in muffin tins, filling about one-half full. Bake in oven preheated to 400° for 15 minutes. Makes 6 dozen.

## DATE MUFFINS

1 teaspoon soda
1 cup hot water
1 cup chopped dates
1/2 cup vegetable shortening
  or butter

1 cup sugar
2 eggs
1 1/2 cups flour
Pinch of salt

Dissolve soda in the hot water. Pour over dates and set aside. Cream shortening with sugar; beat in eggs. Add flour and salt, mixing thoroughly; stir in date mixture. Grease muffin tins very well; pour in batter, filling no more than two-thirds full. Bake at 350° for 30 minutes.

*This is from Lexington caterer, Christine Gilmore*

## CINNAMON PUFFS

1/3 cup butter, softened
  (preferably unsalted)
1/2 cup sugar
1 egg
1 1/2 cups all-purpose flour

1 1/2 teaspoons baking
  powder
1/4 teaspoon salt
1/4 teaspoon nutmeg
1/2 cup milk

Place butter, sugar and egg in a food processor or blender and mix. In a bowl, sift together flour, baking powder, salt and nutmeg. Add dry ingredients and milk alternately to the batter. Fill greased miniature muffin tins two-thirds full. Bake at 350° for 20 to 25 minutes or until golden brown.

*Coating*
1/3 cup sugar
1 teaspoon cinnamon

1/4 cup butter, melted

Combine sugar and cinnamon. Roll hot muffins in melted butter, then in sugar-cinnamon mixture. Makes 2 dozen.

*Note:* These muffins can be frozen in aluminum foil. To serve, thaw in foil and heat at 350° for 10 to 15 minutes.

## ORANGE MUFFINS

1 cup (2 sticks) butter or
  margarine, softened
1 cup sugar
2 eggs, beaten
1 teaspoon soda
1 cup buttermilk

2 cups all-purpose flour,
  sifted
1/2 cup golden raisins
Grated rind and juice of 2
  oranges
1 cup brown sugar

Cream butter and sugar until light and fluffy. Add eggs, one at a time, beating well after each addition. Dissolve soda in buttermilk; add to creamed mixture alternately with flour, ending with flour. Stir in raisins and orange rind. Fill well- buttered muffin pans two-thirds full; bake at 375° for 25 minutes or until muffins test done. Meanwhile, mix brown sugar and orange juice; pour over muffins as soon as they come from the oven. Remove from pans immediately and place on a wire rack to drain. Makes 3 dozen.

## POPOVERS

1 cup milk
1 cup sifted all-purpose flour
1 tablespoon confectioners'
  sugar

1/2 teaspoon salt
4 eggs

Place milk in a large bowl; stir in flour with a wire whisk; add sugar and salt. Beat in eggs, one at a time, beating well after each addition.
Grease 6 ovenproof custard cups with salad oil; pour 1/3 cup batter into each. Bake at 400° for 20 minutes; reduce heat to 350° and bake an additional 10 minutes or until popovers are done. Serve hot with lots of butter.

## KENTUCKY SPOON BREAD

3 cups milk
1 1/4 cups white cornmeal
2 tablespoons butter, melted

3 eggs, well beaten
1 3/4 teaspoons baking
  powder
1 teaspoon salt

Bring milk to a rapid boil; add cornmeal, stirring until smooth and free from lumps. Continue to cook over low heat until mixture becomes very thick. Remove from heat and allow to cool and stiffen. Place cooked cornmeal in a large bowl; add butter, eggs, baking powder and salt. Beat with an electric mixer for 15 minutes. Pour into a greased casserole and bake at 375° for 30 minutes. Serve hot from the casserole.

## PANCAKES

2 eggs
3/4 cup whole milk
2 tablespoons melted butter
1 cup flour, sifted

1/2 teaspoon salt
2 tablespoons baking
  powder
2 tablespoons sugar

In a large mixing bowl, beat eggs; add milk and butter, blending well. Stir in flour, salt, baking powder and sugar until thoroughly mixed. For small pancakes, drop batter by tablespoon onto a lightly greased 425° griddle. Turn pancakes when bubbles appear on top; after turning, cook about 1 minute. Serve with melted butter and syrup.

*Note:* Whole wheat flour may be substituted. These pancakes are very light due to the large amount of baking powder.

## SOUR CREAM WAFFLES

1 cup flour
1 teaspoon baking powder
$^1/_2$ teaspoon baking soda
$^1/_2$ teaspoon salt

1 egg, separated
$^1/_2$ cup sweet milk
1 cup sour cream

Sift dry ingredients together. Beat egg yolk until light; add milk and sour cream. Combine the dry and liquid mixtures with a few swift strokes. Beat egg white until stiff but not dry; fold into the batter. Heat waffle iron to proper temperature. Cover the grid surface with batter until two-thirds full. Close lid and wait about 4 minutes. Waffle is ready when steam stops emerging.

*Note:* 1 cup buttermilk plus 1 tablespoon butter may be substituted for the sour cream.

## SMACK-YOUR-LIPS WAFFLES

2 cups sifted cake flour
$^1/_4$ teaspoon salt
4 teaspoons baking powder
$2^1/_2$ cups milk
2 egg yolks, beaten

2 egg whites, beaten until stiff
8 tablespoons butter, melted

Combine flour, salt and baking powder; add milk gradually, beating until smooth. Stir in egg yolks until well blended. Fold in egg whites, then melted butter and stir. Heat waffle iron. Cover grid surface about $^2/_3$ full; close lid and wait about 4 minutes. When waffle is ready, all steam will have stopped emerging. If lid is difficult to lift, wait another minute.

*Note:* Batter may be made in advance, omitting egg whites and butter, and refrigerated. Add the 2 ingredients when ready to cook waffles.

## SOUTHERN WAFFLES

1 cup flour
1 teaspoon baking powder
1 teaspoon salt
1 teaspoon sugar

Scant 1/2 teaspoon baking
   soda
1 cup buttermilk
1 egg, beaten
1/4 cup melted shortening

Mix and sift dry ingredients. Combine buttermilk, egg and shortening; add to dry ingredients, beating until smooth. Pour a spoonful of batter into each section of a hot waffle iron; bake until brown.

## LACY CORN CAKES

1 egg
1 cup buttermilk
1/2 teaspoon salt

1/2 teaspoon baking soda
3/4 cup cornmeal

Beat egg slightly; add buttermilk, salt and soda, mixing thoroughly. Stir in cornmeal and beat well. Drop batter from a tablespoon onto a preheated iron griddle, well greased with Crisco oil. When the top is full of tiny bubbles, the under side should be sufficiently brown. Turn and brown the other side.

## HERB BUTTER FOR FRENCH BREAD

4 tablespoons butter
1/4 teaspoon basil
1/4 teaspoon oregano

1/4 teaspoon thyme
1/4 teaspoon garlic powder
1 small loaf French bread

Melt butter in a saucepan and add herbs; simmer for 20 minutes. Spread between slices of French bread and heat in oven at 350.° This can also be spread on bread fingers. Bake at 200° for 30 minutes or until crisp. Makes 30 bread sticks.

## HERB BREAD STICKS

8 wiener buns
1/2 cup (1 stick) butter or margarine, softened
1 tablespoon rosemary, crumbled
1 tablespoon sesame seeds
1 heaping tablespoon grated Parmesan cheese

Split buns lengthwise; cut each half into 3 long "sticks." Spread a generous amount of butter or margarine on each piece. Combine rosemary, sesame seeds and Parmesan cheese; sprinkle on bread sticks. Bake at 250° for 30 minutes until crisp. Makes 4 dozen.

## BRAN ROLLS

1 cup solid vegetable shortening
3/4 cup sugar
1 1/2 teaspoons salt
1 cup All-Bran cereal
1 cup boiling water
2 eggs, beaten
2 packages dry yeast
1 cup lukewarm water
6 cups flour, sifted
Butter, melted

Combine the first 4 ingredients in a large mixing bowl; pour in boiling water, stirring until shortening is dissolved. Let cool; add eggs. Dissolve yeast in lukewarm water; add to mixture. Add flour 1 cup at a time, using a whisk or spoon for the first 4 cups. Use hands to mix in last 2 cups. Dough will not be stiff. Let dough rise in front of open door of 200-degree oven for 1 hour, covering dough with a warm, wet towel. Refrigerate dough overnight, covered. Punch down dough; roll out on a floured board to 1/3" thickness. Cut with a 2 1/2" cutter and fold over. Dip in melted butter; put in a 7"x 11" pan. Allow to rise 2 hours, covered with wax paper. Brush tops with butter and bake rolls at 400° for 10 to 12 minutes. Makes 5 to 6 dozen.

*Note:* These freeze well.

## CHOCOLATE ECLAIRS

*Cream Puffs*

½ cup (1 stick) butter          1 cup all-purpose flour
½ teaspoon salt                 4 eggs, unbeaten
1 cup water

Combine butter, salt and water in a heavy saucepan over medium heat; bring to a boil. When butter is melted, add flour all at once. Stir vigorously over very low heat until dough forms a smooth ball. Remove from heat and add eggs, one at a time, beating after each addition with electric mixer at medium speed. Continue beating until dough is no longer sticky, but quite glossy. Shape by dropping a spoonful onto a greased cookie sheet and elongating it with 2 spoons or by using a pastry tube. Bake cream puffs at 400° for 30 to 40 minutes; place on a wire rack to cool. Slit on one side and fill with Filling; pour Glaze on top. Refrigerate until serving time. Makes about 12.

*Filling*

1 (3¼-ounce) package vanilla      1½ cups milk
    pudding mix                   ½ cup heavy cream,
                                      whipped

Prepare pudding mix according to directions on package, using only 1½ cups milk. Cover pudding with wax paper and refrigerate; when well chilled, beat pudding and then fold in whipped cream.

*Glaze*

1 (6-ounce) package               2 tablespoons butter
    semi-sweet chocolate

Melt chocolate and butter in the top of a double boiler, stirring until well blended and smooth.

## CHOCOLATE TORTE

*Crust*

| | |
|---|---|
| 1 (12-ounce) box vanilla wafers, crushed | 1 ¼ sticks butter, melted |

Combine crushed vanilla wafers and melted butter, mixing thoroughly; press into bottom of a springform mold. Bake at 350° for 5 minutes.

*Filling*

| | |
|---|---|
| 1 (12-ounce) package semi-sweet chocolate chips | 1 ounce bitter chocolate (optional) |
| 4 tablespoons sugar | 8 eggs, separated |
| 6 tablespoons milk | 2 teaspoons vanilla extract |

Melt chocolate chips, sugar and milk (and bitter chocolate, if desired) over low heat, stirring until thoroughly blended. Remove from heat; beat in egg yolks and vanilla. Chill. Beat egg whites until stiff and fold into chocolate mixture. Pour into crust and chill overnight in refrigerator, or place in freezer for a few hours.

*Topping*

| | |
|---|---|
| 1 pint whipping cream | 1 tablespoon vanilla extract |
| 2 tablespoons confectioners' sugar | |

Whip cream with sugar and vanilla. (Make only one-half this amount if less topping is desired.) Spread over torte; chill several hours before cutting. Serves 12 or more.

## CHOCOLATE ICEBOX DESSERT

$^1/_2$ cup (1 stick) butter,
  softened
$^3/_4$ cup sugar
4 egg yolks
1 (1-ounce) square bitter
  chocolate, melted
1 teaspoon vanilla

$^3/_4$ cup pecans, coarsely
  chopped
8 double macaroons,
  crumbled
18 double ladyfingers
4 egg whites, beaten
1 pint whipping cream
3 tablespoons sugar

Cream butter and sugar together; add egg yolks one at a time, beating well after each addition. Stir in melted chocolate, vanilla, pecans, half of the macaroon crumbs and 2 crumbled ladyfingers. Fold in beaten egg whites. Pour mixture into a shallow bowl lined with 16 ladyfingers; sprinkle with remaining macaroon crumbs. Whip the cream with sugar; spread over all, leaving tips of ladyfingers exposed. Cover with wax paper and refrigerate overnight. Serves 8.

## CHOCOLATE DELIGHT

2 ounces semi-sweet
  chocolate
$^1/_2$ cup sugar
$^1/_4$ cup water
4 egg yolks, beaten
1 cup (2 sticks) butter
1 cup confectioners' sugar

4 egg whites, stiffly beaten
1 teaspoon vanilla extract
Ladyfingers
Whipped cream,
  sweetened
Peanut brittle, grated, or
  almond brickle chips

Melt the first 3 ingredients in a double boiler; add egg yolks, cooking until thick; cool. Cream butter, gradually adding sugar; add chocolate mixture, blending well. Fold in egg whites and vanilla. Line a large bowl with ladyfingers; pour in mixture. Chill. Top with whipped cream and grated peanut brittle or almond brickle chips. Serves 6 to 8.

# DESSERTS

## FABULOUS FUDGE NUT PUDDING

3 eggs
1 1/2 cups sugar
3/4 cup flour
3/4 cup butter, melted and
   cooled

1 cup chopped pecans
8 ounces semi-sweet
   chocolate, melted

Preheat oven to 350.° In a mixing bowl or saucepan, beat eggs, sugar and flour together until fluffy. Add butter and pecans and pour into a greased 8" square pan. Pour the melted chocolate over the batter and swirl through with a knife. Bake for about 30 minutes or until done.

## CHOCOLATE DESSERT ROLL

5 eggs, separated
1 cup superfine sugar
6 ounces sweet, dark
   chocolate, melted

3 tablespoons hot coffee
2 cups cream, whipped
Sweetened cocoa

Butter a 10"x 15" jellyroll pan; line with wax paper, then butter the paper. Beat egg yolks until light in color; add sugar and beat until fluffy. Stir in chocolate melted with coffee, then add stiffly beaten egg whites. Spread in pan and bake at 350° for 15 minutes; do not overbake. Cover cake with a damp towel until it cools, about 30 minutes. Loosen cake from pan and dust with cocoa; turn out onto wax paper and remove paper from bottom of cake. Spread with whipped cream and roll lengthwise to make a long, thin roll; dust top with cocoa. Slice and serve with a chocolate sauce. Serves 12.

## CHOCOLATE DESSERT CUPS

6 ounces semi-sweet
  chocolate
2 tablespoons butter
6 cupcake papers

Ice cream (any flavor)
Liqueur
Whipped cream
  (optional)

Melt chocolate and butter over boiling water; stir rapidly with an iced teaspoon. Ladle some chocolate into a cupcake paper cup that has been placed in a muffin tin. Swirl chocolate over bottom and sides to cover them completely with a layer of chocolate. Chill or freeze. When ready to use peel off paper and fill with ice cream. Top ice cream with a liqueur and garnish with whipped cream if desired. Serves 6.

## POTS DE CRÈME AU CHOCOLAT

13 ounces dark sweet
  chocolate
½ cup strong coffee
2 teaspoons brandy
6 egg yolks

6 egg whites, beaten until
  stiff
4 ounces blanched
  almonds, grated

Melt chocolate in double boiler with coffee, stirring until smooth. Remove from heat; stir in brandy. Add egg yolks, one at a time, mixing well after each addition. Fold in egg whites. Pour into pots de crème or custard cups; sprinkle with almonds. Chill at least 2 hours. Serves 8.

## PEACH ICE

12 fresh peaches, peeled
Juice of 7 oranges

Juice of 1 lemon
1¾ cups sugar

Force peaches through a ricer; add juices and sugar, mixing until sugar is dissolved. Freeze in a mold or in refrigerator trays.

# DESSERTS

## TANGERINE ICE

2 cups sugar
1 tablespoon grated tangerine
   rind
4 cups water

$^{1}/_{4}$ teaspoon salt
2 cups tangerine juice
$^{1}/_{4}$ cup lemon juice

Place sugar in a saucepan; add grated rind, water and salt. Boil for 5 minutes, stirring constantly, until sugar is dissolved. Add tangerine and lemon juices; freeze the mixture. Makes 1$^{1}/_{2}$ quarts.

## ORANGE ICE

1 teaspoon gelatin
1$^{1}/_{2}$ cups sugar
1 cup water

2 cups orange juice
3 tablespoons lemon juice

Sprinkle gelatin on 2 teaspoons water to soften. Boil sugar and water for 5 minutes; add softened gelatin, stirring until dissolved. Cool; stir in juices. Freeze in an ice cream freezer according to manufacturer's directions. (May also be made in the freezing compartment of a refrigerator.) Makes 1 quart.

## LEMON ICE

3 cups water
1$^{3}/_{4}$ cups sugar

1 tablespoon grated
   lemon rind
$^{3}/_{4}$ cup lemon juice

Bring water to a boil and stir in sugar until dissolved. Cool, then add lemon rind and juice. Freeze in a hand-cranked or electric ice cream freezer. Makes 3 pints.

## STRAWBERRY ICE

1⅓ cups sugar
1⅓ cups water

1 (16-ounce) package
    frozen unsweetened
    strawberries
1 to 2 tablespoons lemon
    juice

Boil sugar and water until sugar is dissolved. Chill. Purée strawberries in a blender container; add to sugar mixture. Add lemon juice to taste. Chill, then freeze in an ice cream freezer. Makes 1 quart.

## CHAMPAGNE SHERBET

2 cups water
2 cups sugar
¼ cup corn syrup
2 tablespoons grated lemon
    rind

¼ cup lemon juice
3 cups Brut champagne
4 egg whites
¼ cup confectioners'
    sugar

Boil water and sugar together until the sugar is dissolved. Add corn syrup and lemon rind and juice; cool. Stir in champagne; pour into refrigerator freezing trays and freeze until firm. Beat egg whites to soft peaks; gradually add confectioners' sugar, beating constantly until a soft meringue is formed. Turn frozen mixture into a chilled bowl; beat smooth. Stir in the meringue and return to freezer. Freeze until a spoonful mounds; beat again and refreeze. Serves 8 to 10.

*Note:* When making water ices, dissolve 3 large marshmallows in hot syrup and your ice will be smoother.

## RICH FRESH PEACH ICE CREAM

2 quarts half-and-half
10 egg yolks
4 whole eggs
3/4 cup sugar
1 cup dark brown sugar
1/2 teaspoon salt
2 tablespoons vanilla extract

1/2 teaspoon almond
  extract
2 quarts sliced soft fresh
  peaches
1 1/2 cups sugar
1 cup whipping cream

To make a custard, carefully scald the half-and-half. Beat egg yolks and whole eggs until fluffy. Add 3/4 cup sugar, brown sugar and salt; beat until smooth. Pour into scalded half-and-half, stirring constantly over *low* heat until mixture thickens enough to coat the spoon. Be very careful not to overcook, causing custard to curdle. Remove from heat; add flavorings. Chill overnight. Sprinkle the peach slices with 1 1/2 cups sugar; let stand, stirring occasionally, until sugar is dissolved. Pour custard into a 1 1/2- to 2-gallon ice cream freezer. It can come to within 2 inches of the top of container. Turn in the freezer until custard is thick. Remove the dasher and pour in the peaches. Return the dasher, add the cream and freeze until firm. Let stand 1 1/2 to 2 hours before serving. Makes 1 1/2 gallons.

## BANANA ICE CREAM

1 cup mashed bananas
1 cup orange juice
1/2 cup lemon juice

2 cups half-and-half
1 1/2 cups sugar
1/4 teaspoon salt

Combine all ingredients; mix well. Pour into refrigerator trays or freeze in an old-fashioned ice cream freezer. Serves 6.

## PECAN BALL

*This is a Bluegrass favorite*

| | |
|---|---|
| 1 pint vanilla ice cream | 1¼ cup pecans (plain or roasted), chopped |

Make 5 to 6 balls of ice cream and roll in chopped pecans to completely cover. Put each ball in wax paper, seal securely and freeze until ready to serve. Serve with hot fudge sauce or hot butterscotch sauce.

*Note:* To roast pecans, place on a cookie sheet in 350° oven for 15 minutes. Cool and chop.

## OVERBROOK VANILLA ICE CREAM

| | |
|---|---|
| 2 cups half-and-half | 1 teaspoon salt |
| 4 cups milk | 4 teaspoons vanilla |
| 12 egg yolks, beaten | 1 cup whipping cream (do |
| 2 cups sugar | not whip) |

In top of double boiler, scald half-and-half and milk. Beat egg yolks well; add sugar and salt and beat until well blended. Pour scalded half-and-half and milk over egg yolk mixture; return all to double boiler and cook, stirring constantly, until mixture coats a metal spoon. Cool. Put mixture into 1 gallon ice cream freezer; add whipping cream and vanilla. Freeze until firm. Makes 2½ quarts.

*Variation:* To make Burnt Almond Ice Cream use only 1⅔ cups sugar. Just before freezing the cream, add 6 or more tablespoons caramel syrup and 1 cup finely chopped toasted almonds.

*Caramel Syrup*

| | |
|---|---|
| ½ cup water | ½ cup sugar |

Mix water and sugar in a heavy skillet and cook the mixture until it makes a golden, thick syrup. Cool.

# DESSERTS

## GOLD BRICK SUNDAE

1 generous scoop vanilla ice
    cream
5 strawberries
2 tablespoons grated Heath
    Bars

2 tablespoons Magic Shell
    hardening chocolate
1 tablespoon Grand
    Marnier

Put ice cream in a brandy snifter or small bowl. Halve 4 strawberries; press around sides of ice cream. Sprinkle with Heath Bar crumbs and pour chocolate over top. Garnish with a whole strawberry; freeze. A half hour before serving, remove from freezer and put in refrigerator to soften. At serving time, pour on Grand Marnier. Serves 1.

## BAKED ALASKA

1 spongecake (recipe on
    page 318)
1 quart ice cream

6 egg whites
3/4 cup sugar
1/2 teaspoon vanilla
    extract

Make spongecake in shape desired: individual, oblong or round. Place ice cream on cake, leaving 1" of cake showing around the edge. Place in a freezer. Make meringue by beating egg whites until soft peaks form. Beat in sugar and vanilla gradually until mixture is very stiff; spread on top of ice cream, covering completely. Bake immediately in an oven preheated to 500° for 3 to 4 minutes (or return to freezer until ready to bake). Serve at once. Serves 12.

## MOCHA-MACAROON FREEZE

1 1/2 pounds almond
   macaroons
2 quarts mocha or coffee ice
   cream

2 pints whipping cream
3/4 to 1 cup dark rum

Cover the bottom and sides of a Revere-type bowl with macaroons which have been soaked in rum. Press them over inside of entire bowl within 1″ of the rim. Put 1 quart of ice cream in the bowl and cover with a layer of rum-soaked macaroons; add the remaining quart of ice cream on top. This can be made days ahead and kept in a freezer. When ready to serve, top with stiffly-whipped cream and crumbled macaroons. Mint leaves may be used as decoration.

## TANGERINE AND BURNT ALMOND BOMBE

Line a 1 1/2-quart melon mold with Tangerine Ice, page 284, making the ice 1 1/2 inches thick. Pack firmly, working quickly. Fill center with Burnt Almond Ice Cream, page 287, filling it level. Cover with wax paper; press lid on firmly. Place in freezer and allow to freeze solid. To serve, remove lid and paper; run a knife around edge of mold. Turn upside down on a well chilled platter. Place hot towels on top of mold to loosen bombe. Cut in thick slices to serve.

# DESSERTS

## PEACH FREEZE

2 cups coarsely crumbled
   almond macaroons
2 cups fresh peaches, peeled
   and mashed

1 cup sugar
1 cup cream
Peach brandy (optional)

Place 1 cup crumbled macaroons in the bottom of a square pan; set aside. Combine peaches and sugar. Whip cream until stiff, fold into peaches and spoon mixture over crumbled macaroons. Top with remaining cup of macaroons and freeze until solid. Cut in squares and serve plain or with a spoonful of peach brandy. Serves 12.

## FROZEN LEMON PUDDING

3 egg yolks, beaten
1/2 cup sugar
5 tablespoons fresh lemon
   juice
3 egg whites, beaten

1/2 pint heavy cream,
   whipped
3/4 cup vanilla wafers,
   crushed

Beat egg yolks, sugar and lemon juice; cook in top of double boiler, stirring constantly until thickened. Allow to cool before folding in whipped cream and beaten egg whites. The amount of lemon juice may be adjusted according to taste. Line a 3"x 10" dish or ice tray with wafer crumbs, reserving a small amount for garnish. Pour in lemon mixture and sprinkle top with crumbs. Freeze. Serves 6.

## CHOCOLATE MOUSSE

4 egg yolks
3/4 cup extra-fine granulated
  sugar
1/4 cup Grand Marnier
6 ounces semi-sweet
  chocolate
1/4 cup strong coffee
6 ounces (1 1/2 sticks) unsalted
  butter
3 to 4 tablespoons finely
  chopped glazed orange peel

4 egg whites
Pinch of salt
1 tablespoon granulated
  sugar
2 cups lightly-whipped
  cream
Semi-sweet chocolate or
  colored sugar

In a heatproof mixing bowl, beat egg yolks and sugar with a whisk or electric beater until thick and pale yellow; beat in Grand Marnier. Set mixing bowl in pan of barely simmering water; continue beating for 4 minutes or until mixture is foamy and hot. Then set bowl in pan of iced water and beat 4 minutes longer or until mixture is cool and has the consistency of mayonnaise. In the top of a double boiler over simmering water, melt chocolate with coffee, stirring constantly. Remove from heat and beat in the butter bit by bit. Chill. Beat chocolate mixture into egg yolk-sugar mixture; add orange peel and mix well. Beat egg whites and salt until soft peaks form; add 1 tablespoon sugar and continue beating until very stiff. Stir one-fourth of egg whites into chocolate mixture; gently fold in remaining egg whites. Pour into lightly-oiled 6-cup mold; cover with oiled wax paper; chill 8 hours. To unmold, run a sharp knife around sides and dip bottom of mold in hot water for a few seconds. Top with whipped cream and garnish with grated chocolate or colored sugar.

# DESSERTS

## BLENDER CHOCOLATE MOUSSE

2 whole eggs
2 tablespoons strong hot
    coffee
1 (6-ounce) package
    semi-sweet chocolate
    morsels

2 tablespoons Grand
    Marnier
3/4 cup scalded milk,
    half-and-half or cream

Put eggs into blender container; add coffee and blend. Add chocolate, Grand Marnier and milk; cover and process at high speed until mixture is smooth. Pour into pot de crème cups or shell sherbets. Cover and chill at least 3 hours. Serves 4-6.

## EGGNOG MOUSSE

2 envelopes unflavored gelatin
1 cup sugar
1 cup cold water
8 egg yolks

3/4 cup good Kentucky
    Bourbon
2 teaspoons vanilla
8 egg whites, stiffly beaten
Ground nutmeg or grated
    chocolate

Mix gelatin and sugar in the top of a double boiler; add cold water. Place over boiling water and stir until gelatin is thoroughly dissolved. Remove from heat. Beat egg yolks until light and fluffy; stir in Bourbon and vanilla. Pour in gelatin mixture and mix well. Chill until slightly thickened. Fold into egg whites; turn into a mold or bowl. Chill until firm. Unmold and garnish with nutmeg or chocolate. Serves 6 to 8.

## LEMON MOUSSE WITH FRESH RASPBERRY SAUCE

*Mousse*

| | |
|---|---|
| 1 envelope unflavored gelatin | 3 eggs, separated |
| 2 tablespoons white wine | ½ cup sugar |
| ⅓ cup fresh lemon juice | 1 cup heavy cream, |
| 1½ tablespoons grated lemon rind | whipped |

In a bowl, sprinkle gelatin over white wine to soften. Add lemon juice and rind and stir over simmering water until gelatin is dissolved. In another bowl, beat egg yolks with 3 tablespoons sugar until mixture ribbons. Slowly add gelatin mixture and stir. In another bowl, beat egg whites until foamy; add remaining sugar and beat till meringue holds soft peaks. Add whipped cream to egg yolk mixture and fold in one-half meringue. Add cream mixture to remaining meringue and fold together. Chill mousse 2 hours.

*Sauce*

| | |
|---|---|
| 1 (10-ounce) package frozen (or 1 cup fresh) raspberries, thawed and drained | 2 to 3 tablespoons sugar |
| | 1 tablespoon lemon juice |
| | 1 tablespoon Grand Marnier |

In blender or food processor, combine raspberries, sugar, lemon juice and liqueur. Purée. Strain through very fine sieve to remove seeds. Add more flavoring if needed. Serve over mousse or on bottom of plate and put spoonful of mousse in middle of sauce. Garnish with mint sprig. Serves 8 to 10.

# DESSERTS

## APRICOT SOUFFLÉ

1 cup dried apricots
½ cup sugar
Juice of ½ lemon

8 egg whites, at room
  temperature
Whipped cream

Stew apricots according to directions on package; add sugar and lemon juice. Place mixture in blender container; process to a medium-thin consistency. Beat egg whites until stiff; fold in apricot mixture. Pour into a 2-quart soufflé dish which has been buttered and sugared. Bake at 400° for 18 to 20 minutes. Serve with whipped cream. Serves 6.

## AMARETTO MOUSSE

4 tablespoons (½ stick) sweet
  butter
5 eggs
1 cup granulated sugar
1½ teaspoons unflavored
  gelatin

¾ cup amaretti (tiny
  macaroons), crushed
1½ tablespoons Amaretto
  liqueur
1½ cups heavy cream,
  chilled

Melt butter in top of double boiler over simmering water. Beat eggs with sugar and gelatin; add to melted butter and cook, stirring constantly until thickened, 6 to 8 minutes. Remove from heat. Add ½ cup of the crushed amaretti and the Amaretto, blending well. Cool, then refrigerate until mixture just begins to set. Whip cream to soft peaks; gently fold into Amaretto mixture. Spoon into 8 to 10 serving glasses or a serving bowl. Chill until set, about 4 hours. Just before serving, sprinkle with reserved crushed amaretti. Serves 10.

## WHITE CHOCOLATE SOUFFLÉ

2 tablespoons butter
1½ tablespoons flour
½ cup milk, scalded
2 squares white chocolate
1 tablespoon sugar

½ teaspoon vanilla
  extract
5 egg yolks, well beaten
3 tablespoons sugar
6 egg whites
1 tablespoon sugar

Melt butter, add flour and stir until it starts to turn golden; set aside. Scald milk; add chocolate and sugar and stir until melted. Add to sauce, stirring constantly. Continue to cook 5 minutes after it thickens. Add vanilla and set aside. Beat egg yolks with 3 tablespoons sugar; mix with batter. Beat egg whites until stiff, adding 1 tablespoon sugar during the last minutes of beating. Fold thoroughly and carefully into the mixture one-fourth of the beaten egg whites; add the remaining egg whites, cutting them in lightly but completely by raising and folding the mixture over and over. Pour the batter into a buttered and lightly sugared soufflé dish and bake in a hot oven (400°) for 20 minutes or in a moderate oven (350°) for 35 to 45 minutes. Serve at once with Grand Marnier Sauce (page 306).

## ENGLISH CUSTARD

6 egg yolks
½ cup sugar

¼ vanilla bean
2½ cups whole milk

Using a wire whisk, beat egg yolks and sugar until smooth and sugar is dissolved. Scrape seeds from vanilla bean into milk and bring to a boil. Slowly pour milk into egg mixture while stirring. Cook over medium heat, stirring constantly, until custard thickens and coats a metal spoon. Never allow it to boil. Remove from heat; strain through a fine sieve and cool. Serve chilled.

# DESSERTS

## CRÈME BRULÉ

3 cups whipping cream
6 tablespoons sugar
6 egg yolks, beaten

2 teaspoons vanilla
½ cup brown sugar

Heat cream in double boiler; stir in sugar. Beat egg yolks until light; gradually pour hot cream over yolks; stir in vanilla. Strain mixture into baking dish. Place dish in a pan containing one inch of water. Bake at 350° in preheated oven until firm (it is done when an inserted knife comes out clean). Chill thoroughly. Before serving cover surface with brown sugar and place under broiler until sugar is melted and browned.

## BAKED BLUEBERRIES

8 tablespoons sugar, divided
1 tablespoon flour
3 teaspoons grated lemon
  rind, divided
1 quart blueberries, washed
1 egg

6 macaroons, finely
  crumbled
2 tablespoons vanilla
  wafer crumbs
Whipped cream

Combine 3 tablespoons sugar, flour and 2 teaspoons grated lemon rind; toss with blueberries. Place in a greased baking dish. Lightly beat egg; stir in 5 tablespoons sugar, 1 teaspoon rind, macaroon crumbs and vanilla wafer crumbs. Spread mixture over blueberries. Bake at 350° for 30 minutes or until crust forms. Serve warm with whipped cream.

## EASY BAKED CUSTARD

2 cups milk                     1 teaspoon vanilla
2 eggs                          Dash of nutmeg
1/3 cup sugar

Place ingredients in a one-quart measuring cup or in the container of an electric blender. Mix until just blended. Pour into 4 custard cups; set in a pan of cold water. Cover with a tight-fitting lid. Bring water to a hard boil; turn off heat and leave covered for 45 minutes. Serves 4.

*Variation:* A teaspoon of fruit preserves may be placed in the bottom of each cup before filling with custard.

## FRESH BERRIES WITH ORANGE CREAM

1 pint strawberries, washed     1 tablespoon sugar
   and hulled

Cut berries in half lengthwise or leave whole; sprinkle with sugar.

*Topping*
1/2 cup sugar                   1/2 cup orange juice
2 teaspoons grated orange       1 cup heavy cream,
   rind                            whipped

Combine sugar, orange rind and juice in small pan. Bring to boil, stirring only until sugar dissolves; simmer 10 minutes. Remove from heat and *cool completely.* Gently fold whipped cream into orange syrup. Serve over berries. Serves 4.

*Variation:* Substitute fresh raspberries and use lemon juice and rind.

## ELEGANT GRAPES

2 pounds seedless white
   grapes
1 cup sour cream
1 tablespoon brown sugar

2 tablespoons of your
   favorite liqueur

Wash grapes and remove stems. Mix sour cream, brown sugar and liqueur; pour over grapes. Chill for at least 1 hour before serving in individual dessert dishes. Serves 8.

## SCHAUM TORTE

6 egg whites
2 cups sugar
1 teaspoon white vinegar

1 teaspoon vanilla extract
   *or* seeds scraped from a
   1" vanilla bean pod
Raspberries and tangerine
   sections
Candied ginger, chopped

Beat egg whites until dry; add sugar slowly, beating until dissolved. Add vinegar and vanilla extract or seeds. Spoon into a springform pan which has been greased with vegetable oil. Bake at 300° for 1 to 1¼ hours. Set aside and cool in pan. Do not be disturbed when torte falls. Remove from pan and place on a large platter; let set overnight. At serving time, smother torte with fruit and ginger. Cover with Custard Sauce. Serves 8.

*Note:* Other combinations of fruit may be used.

*Custard Sauce*
3 or 4 egg yolks
½ cup sugar
⅛ teaspoon salt
2 cups milk

1 teaspoon vanilla extract
   *or* seeds scraped from a
   1" vanilla bean pod

Beat egg yolks; add sugar and salt. In a double boiler, scald milk; stir in egg mixture and vanilla. Cook over a small amount of simmering water, stirring constantly until thick enough to coat the spoon rather heavily. Remove from heat; chill before serving.

## STRAWBERRIES WHITE HOUSE

1 egg white
1/8 teaspoon cream of tartar
1/4 cup sugar
1/2 cup whipping cream, whipped
1/2 teaspoon vanilla extract
1 quart fresh strawberries, hulled

6 tablespoons wild strawberry preserves
3 tablespoons Kirschwasser
3 tablespoons Grand Marnier
Additional whipped cream for garnish

Beat egg white with cream of tartar until frothy. Gradually add sugar while beating until the mixture stands in firm peaks. Fold in the whipped cream and vanilla extract; spread mixture over the bottom and sides of a fairly shallow serving dish. Arrange the strawberries on the meringue, stem side down. Combine strawberry preserves, Kirschwasser and Grand Marnier; spoon over the berries. Serve with additional whipped cream. Serves 8.

## STRAWBERRIES SABAYON

2 pints fresh strawberries, washed and hulled

Place in container; cover and refrigerate until time to serve. Divide strawberries among 6 dessert plates; spoon Sauce over top. Serves 6.

*Sabayon Sauce*
4 egg yolks
2 tablespoons sugar

1/4 cup Grand Marnier
1/2 cup heavy cream, whipped

Place egg yolks in top of a double boiler; beat with a wire whisk until thickened. Gradually add sugar, beating until fluffy and light. Do not let water boil; keep it simmering. *Slowly* add Grand Marnier; continue cooking and beating until mixture mounds, about 5 to 6 minutes. Remove from heat; set in a pan of ice water (more ice than water). Beat until cool; gently fold in whipped cream. Refrigerate, covered, for 2 hours. Sauce may be made up to 8 hours ahead. Stir gently to mix well before using.

# DESSERTS

## PECAN TORTE

3 egg whites
1 cup sugar
8 soda crackers, rolled into
   fine crumbs
1/2 teaspoon salt

1 teaspoon vanilla extract
1 cup finely chopped
   pecans
1 cup cream, whipped

Beat egg whites until stiff, gradually adding sugar; fold in remaining ingredients. Pour mixture into a greased pie pan; bake at 350° for 40 to 45 minutes. Refrigerate. Serve cold, garnished with whipped cream.

## STRAWBERRY FLUFF

6 egg whites (at room
   temperature)
2 teaspoons vanilla extract
1/2 teaspoon cream of tartar

2 cups sugar
1 pint whipping cream
2 quarts fresh strawberries

Combine egg whites, vanilla and cream of tartar; beat until frothy. Gradually add sugar, 1 tablespoon at a time, beating until stiff peaks form. Drop meringue by one-third cupsful, touching each other, around the edge of a 10" pie plate, forming a ring. Bake at 225° for 1 hour. Turn off oven; cool in oven 1 hour. Carefully remove meringue to serving dish. Beat whipping cream until soft peaks form; mix with 1 quart of strawberries. Place mixture in center of meringue; place remaining strawberries around the outside of meringue. Serve with Sherry Custard Sauce.

*Sherry Custard Sauce*
2 cups milk
6 egg yolks
1/4 cup sugar
1/8 teaspoon salt

1 cup whipping cream
3 tablespoons sherry
1/2 teaspoon vanilla

Scald milk in double boiler. Beat egg yolks, sugar and salt together. Gradually pour mixture into milk stirring constantly until it thickens. Whip cream and fold into egg sauce. Add sherry and vanilla. Chill.

## PECAN ROLL

| | |
|---|---|
| 7 eggs, separated | Confectioners' sugar |
| ¾ cup sugar | 1 cup whipping cream |
| 1½ cups ground pecans | 1 teaspoon vanilla |
| 1 teaspoon baking powder | |

Brush 10"x 15" jellyroll pan with oil; line with wax paper and oil the paper. With an electric beater or heavy whisk, beat egg yolks with sugar until mixture is pale in color and thick enough to fall in "ribbons" when beater is lifted. Stir in ground pecans and baking powder. Beat egg whites until stiff; fold into egg yolk mixture. Spread batter in the prepared pan; bake at 350° for 15 to 20 minutes or until golden. Cool cake in pan; cover with damp towel and chill. Dust with sifted confectioners' sugar; turn out on a board covered with two overlapping sheets of wax paper. Carefully strip paper from bottom of cake. Whip cream until almost stiff; add vanilla and ¼ cup confectioners' sugar. Beat until cream holds a peak; spread over cake. Roll up cake, using wax paper as an aid, and slide onto flat serving platter. Sprinkle the roll with more sifted confectioners' sugar. Serve plain or with chocolate sauce.

## MERINGUE KISSES

| | |
|---|---|
| 4 egg whites, at room temperature | Pinch of salt |
| 1⅓ cups sugar | ½ teaspoon vanilla or almond extract |

Beat egg whites until frothy; gradually add sugar and salt, beating until very stiff and not grainy. Add flavoring. Shape into 4" to 5" circles with back of spoon. Bake on oiled paper at 250° for about 1 hour.

## ALMOND ROCA SUPREME

6 egg whites, at room
  temperature
1 cup sugar
1 teaspoon vinegar
Pinch of salt

1 pound almond roca,
  ground, or almond
  brickle chips
1½ pints whipping
  cream, stiffly beaten

Beat egg whites, sugar, vinegar and salt until very stiff. Cut 3 rounds of brown paper the size of a pie pan. Place papers on cookie sheets; cover with meringue. Bake at 225° for 1 hour on the bottom oven rack. Remove, peel off paper and allow to cool. Fold almond roca into whipped cream; spread one-fourth over a meringue which has been placed on a serving plate. Top with second meringue and spread with another one-fourth of filling. Cover with third meringue and ice top and sides of stack with remaining filling. Refrigerate overnight. Cut into wedges to serve.

## ALMOND PUDDING

18 ladyfingers, split
1 cup unsalted butter
2 cups confectioners' sugar
6 egg yolks, beaten
1 cup chopped almonds,
  slightly toasted

1½ teaspoons almond
  extract
6 egg whites, stiffly beaten
12 macaroons, crumbled
Whipped cream

Line a spring mold with ladyfingers; set aside. Cream butter until light; gradually add sugar and beat in egg yolks. Stir in almonds and almond extract; fold in egg whites. Spread a thin layer of mixture in prepared mold; add a layer of macaroons. Continue layering process, ending with creamed mixture. Let stand 24 hours in refrigerator. Remove from mold; serve with whipped cream.

## LEMON ANGEL PIE

*Meringue Shell*

| | |
|---|---|
| 4 egg whites | Dash of salt |
| ½ teaspoon cream of tartar | 1 cup sugar |

Beat egg whites until foamy; add cream of tartar and salt. Beat until stiff while adding sugar, 2 tablespoons at a time. Meringue should form shiny, stiff peaks. Spread into a buttered 9″ pan, pushing up high on sides to resemble a pie shell; bake at 300° for 40 minutes.

*Filling*

| | |
|---|---|
| 4 egg yolks | ¼ cup lemon juice |
| ½ cup sugar | 1 cup whipping cream, |
| Grated rind of 2 lemons | whipped |

Beat egg yolks and sugar; stir in lemon rind and juice. Cook in the top of a double boiler until thick, stirring constantly. Remove from heat and cool thoroughly. Fold in whipped cream and pour into cooled meringue shell. Refrigerate for several hours before serving. Serves 6 to 8.

## AMARETTO ANGEL CAKE

| | |
|---|---|
| 1 angel food cake | 1 pint strawberry ice |
| ½ cup Amaretto liqueur | cream |
| 1 pint pistachio ice cream | 2 cups heavy cream |

Using a serrated knife, cut the cake to have three layers. Sprinkle each layer with 2 tablespoons of Amaretto. Place the first layer on a serving platter; put cut slices of pistachio ice cream on this bottom layer. Put second layer of cake on top of pistachio ice cream. Top second layer of cake with slices of strawberry ice cream. Put third layer of cake on top. Whip cream until thick and blend in the remaining Amaretto. Frost cake all over with whipped cream. Freeze cake until ready to serve. Remove from freezer to refrigerator 30 minutes before cutting. Serves 16.

## ANGEL FOOD DESSERT WITH CARAMEL SAUCE

1 angel food cake
1 1/2 envelopes unflavored
   gelatin
1 1/2 cups milk, divided
3 egg yolks, beaten

1/8 teaspoon salt
1 cup sugar
2 egg whites, stiffly beaten
1 cup whipping cream,
   whipped

Break prepared angel food cake into pieces in a large dish. Stir gelatin into 1/2 cup cold milk. Combine remaining milk with egg yolks, salt and sugar, beating well; cook until mixture thickens and coats metal spoon. Remove from heat and stir in softened gelatin. Chill until cool but not set. Combine beaten egg whites and whipped cream; fold into gelatin mixture. Pour over cake; chill until firm. Serve with warm Caramel Sauce. Serves 8.

*Caramel Sauce*
1 cup brown sugar
6 tablespoons butter

1/2 cup light cream

Combine and cook over low heat, stirring constantly, until sugar dissolves; boil for 3 minutes longer.

## CRÈME FRAICHE

2 cups heavy cream

5 teaspoons buttermilk

Combine cream and buttermilk in a screwtop jar; shake for 1 minute, then let stand at room temperature for 24 hours. When cream thickens, refrigerate at least 24 hours. It keeps well for 2 to 4 weeks.

*Note:* Crème fraiche is used in French cooking. Sour cream may curdle in hot sauce; crème fraiche will not. It can be whipped, but do not overwhip as it will turn to butter. It is a delicious accompaniment to baked apples, poached pears and all berries, and can be used as a garnish for cold poached vegetables.

## WOODFORD PUDDING

4 egg yolks
1 cup sugar
3/4 cup (1 1/2 sticks) butter,
  softened
1 teaspoon soda

3/4 cup buttermilk
1 cup blackberry jam
2 1/2 cups flour
1 teaspoon ground
  allspice
1/2 teaspoon ground
  nutmeg

Beat eggs with 1/4 cup sugar. Cream remaining sugar with butter. Dissolve soda in 2 tablespoons buttermilk; add to creamed mixture. Stir in egg yolk mixture, remaining buttermilk and jam. Sift flour with spices and add to batter. Place in a greased and floured 4"x 10 1/2" loaf pan or an 8" square cake pan. Bake at 325° for 40 minutes. Pudding may be topped with Meringue or Bourbon Sauce.

*Meringue*
4 egg whites
1 cup sugar

1/4 teaspoon cream of
  tartar
3/1 teaspoon vanilla
  extract

Beat egg whites until almost stiff; gradually add sugar and cream of tartar, beating until glossy-stiff. Stir in vanilla; pile Meringue on pudding and bake 15 minutes longer at 325.°

*Note:* If the pudding is to be kept for several days, do not add Meringue.

*Bourbon Sauce*
1/2 cup (1 stick) butter
1 cup sugar
4 egg yolks, beaten

Pinch of salt
1 cup cream, heated
1/2 cup Bourbon

In the top of a double boiler, cream butter and sugar; beat in egg yolks and salt. Slowly add hot cream and stir until thickened, then add Bourbon. Serve warm. This sauce is good on any dessert pudding.

## GRAND MARNIER SAUCE

1 cup rich milk
Vanilla bean
4 egg yolks
1/2 cup sugar

3/4 cup heavy cream
Pinch of salt
4 tablespoons Grand
Marnier

Scald milk with a piece of vanilla bean that has been split open. Beat egg yolks and gradually add to milk, beating constantly; add sugar. Blend in cream and salt; cook in the top of a double boiler until sauce coats a metal spoon. Remove from heat and allow to cool slightly; stir in Grand Marnier. Serve hot or cold.

## BUTTERSCOTCH SAUCE

1 1/2 cups light brown sugar,
   firmly packed
1/3 cup butter

3/4 cup light corn syrup
1/8 teaspoon salt
1 cup half-and-half

Combine sugar, butter, corn syrup and salt; heat to boiling, stirring until sugar is completely dissolved. Add half-and-half very slowly, stirring constantly. Cook until sauce thickens or until it reaches 228.° Serve warm over ice cream, gingerbread or cake. Makes 2 cups.

## GRAND CHOCOLATE SAUCE

2 ounces semi-sweet
   chocolate
1/4 cup butter (no substitute)
3/4 cup sugar
Pinch of salt

1/4 cup cocoa
1/2 cup half-and-half
1 teaspoon vanilla or
   almond extract

Melt chocolate with butter in a saucepan over low heat. Mix sugar, salt and cocoa, smoothing out lumps; add to chocolate mixture. Slowly pour in half-and-half; cook, stirring constantly, until sugar is dissolved. Remove from heat; add flavoring. Serve warm over ice cream or cake. Makes 1 1/2 cups.

# CAKES

## CHOCOLATE KAHLUA CAKE

1 box chocolate cake mix
1/2 cup oil
1 small box instant chocolate
   pudding

4 eggs
3/4 cup strong coffee
3/4 cup Kahlua and crème
   de cacao, mixed

Combine all cake ingredients at medium speed until well blended. Pour into greased and floured 9"x 13" pan; bake at 350° for 40 to 45 minutes. Cool in pan. Mix glaze ingredients together. Poke holes in cooled cake and glaze. For a different cake, substitute white or yellow cake mix with instant vanilla pudding. Bake in three 8" or 9" layers at 350° for 30 to 40 minutes. Frost with whipped cream topping.

*Glaze*
1 cup powdered sugar
2 tablespoons strong coffee

2 tablespoons Kahlua
2 tablespoons crème de
   cacao

## COCONUT MIST CAKE

1 cup (2 sticks) butter or
   shortening
3 1/2 cups confectioners' sugar,
   sifted
4 eggs, separated
3 cups flour
1/4 teaspoon salt

2 teaspoons baking
   powder
1 cup milk
1 teaspoon lemon extract
1 teaspoon vanilla
1 cup coconut

Cream shortening, gradually add sugar and cream until fluffy; add egg yolks; beat well. Sift dry ingredients; add to creamed mixture alternately with milk, flavorings and coconut. Beat egg whites until stiff, fold into mixture quickly and thoroughly. Put in 3 greased 9" loaf pans; bake at 375° for 20 to 30 minutes. Frost with coconut or plain white frosting.

## CHOCOLATE MINT SQUARES

| | |
|---|---|
| ½ cup (1 stick) butter, softened | ½ teaspoon salt |
| 1 cup sugar | 1 (16-ounce) can chocolate syrup |
| 4 eggs | 1 teaspoon vanilla extract |
| 1 cup all-purpose flour | |

Cream butter; gradually add sugar, beating until light and fluffy. Add eggs, one at a time, beating well after each addition. Combine flour and salt; add to the creamed mixture alternately with chocolate syrup, beginning and ending with flour mixture. Pour batter into greased and floured 13"x 9"x 2" baking pan; bake at 350° for 25 to 28 minutes. Cool completely. (Cake will shrink from sides of pan).

*Frosting*

| | |
|---|---|
| ¼ cup butter, softened | 2 tablespoons crème de menthe |
| 2 cups sifted confectioners' sugar | |

Cream butter; gradually add sugar and crème de menthe, mixing well. Spread evenly over cake; chill about 1 hour.

*Chocolate glaze*

| | |
|---|---|
| 1 (6-ounce) package semi-sweet chocolate bits | ¼ cup butter |

Combine chocolate bits and butter in the top of a double boiler; bring water to a boil. Reduce heat to low; stir until chocolate melts. Spread over frosted cake; chill for at least 1 hour before cutting.

## WHITE CHOCOLATE CAKE

1 cup pecans
2½ cups cake flour
1 teaspoon baking powder
1 cup (2 sticks) butter
2 cups sugar
4 eggs, separated

¼ pound white
  chocolate, softened
  over hot water
1 cup buttermilk
1 cup canned shredded
  coconut
1 teaspoon vanilla extract

Toast pecans in oven at 350° for 5 minutes; chop and set aside. Sift flour and baking powder together. Cream butter with sugar until fluffy; add egg yolks and chocolate and beat vigorously. Add sifted dry ingredients and buttermilk alternately in small amounts, beating well after each addition. Stir in pecans, coconut and vanilla. Fold in stiffly-beaten egg whites. Pour into a greased and floured tube pan; bake at 350° for 45 to 60 minutes. When cool, spread top and sides with Brownstone Icing.

*Brownstone Icing*
1 (5⅓-ounce) can
  evaporated milk
2 cups sugar
1 cup (2 sticks) butter

1 tablespoon light corn
  syrup
1 teaspoon vanilla

Combine first four ingredients and boil over low heat, stirring constantly. Do not allow to scorch. Cool; add vanilla and beat until creamy.

# CAKES

## CREAM CHEESE CAKE

*Crust*

3/4 pound graham crackers,   1 teaspoon cinnamon
   rolled into crumbs      1/2 cup (1 stick) butter,
1/2 cup sugar              melted

Mix crumbs, sugar and cinnamon in bottom of 9" round springform pan; add butter, mixing thoroughly. Press firmly against bottom and sides of pan; chill well.

*Filling*

3 (8-ounce) packages cream   1 cup sugar
   cheese, softened        1 teaspoon vanilla
4 eggs

Beat cheese with rotary beater until creamy. Beat eggs; add sugar and vanilla, mixing well. Add to cheese and continue beating until light. Pour into crust and bake at 375° for 25 minutes. Remove from oven and cool.

*Topping*

1 cup sour cream        1/2 teaspoon vanilla
2 tablespoons sugar

Mix ingredients; spread on top of cooled cake. Return to oven; bake at 475° for 5 minutes. Cool, then refrigerate for 24 hours before serving. Serves 12.

## CHOCOLATE CINNAMON FUDGE CAKE

2 cups flour
2 cups sugar
¹/₂ cup shortening
¹/₂ cup margarine
¹/₄ cup cocoa
1 cup water

1 teaspoon vanilla
1 teaspoon cinnamon
1 teaspoon soda
¹/₂ cup buttermilk
2 eggs

Place flour and sugar in a large bowl and mix well. Combine shortening, margarine, cocoa and water and bring to a rapid boil. Remove from heat and pour over flour-sugar mixture. Add vanilla, cinnamon, soda, buttermilk and eggs; beat well. Bake in a greased 9"x 12" pan at 350° for 30 to 35 minutes. While cake is still hot, poke holes in it and frost.

*Frosting*
¹/₄ cup cocoa
¹/₄ cup plus 2 tablespoons
   milk
¹/₂ cup margarine
1 pound confectioners' sugar

1 teaspoon vanilla
1 cup nuts or 1 cup
   coconut

Combine cocoa, milk and margarine in a saucepan; bring to boil, stirring constantly. Remove from heat; add sugar and beat until blended. Stir in vanilla and nuts or coconut. Spread on hot cake.

# CAKES

## PECAN CAKE

1 cup (2 sticks) butter,
    softened
1 pound light brown sugar
6 eggs, well beaten
3 1/2 cups flour
1 teaspoon baking powder
1/3 teaspoon salt
1/2 cup Bourbon whiskey

1 tablespoon nutmeg
1 pound broken pecans
1/2 pound white raisins,
    cut
1/2 pound dates, cut
1/2 pound candied
    cherries, cut (optional)

Cream butter and sugar; add well-beaten eggs. Sift flour before measuring; sift again; reserve 1/2 cup flour for nuts and fruit; to the rest of the flour add baking powder and salt; sift again. Soak nutmeg in whiskey at least 10 minutes; add alternately with flour mixture to creamed mixture. Flour nuts, raisins, dates and cherries well so they do not stick together; fold into batter. Pour batter into a large tube pan which has been greased and lined with greased brown paper. (Or use 4 small loaf pans greased and lined with greased brown paper.) Allow batter to settle in pan about 10 minutes; decorate the top with pecans and cherries (optional). Bake at 325° for 2 1/2 to 3 hours if a tube pan is used; 1 1/2 to 2 hours if loaf pans are used. If top seems to brown too quickly or tend to crack, cover lightly with heavy brown paper or light foil. Let cake remain in pan 30 minutes before removing it. Peel off brown paper; when cool, wrap in plastic wrap and aluminum foil. If it is to be stored a long time, cover top with a piece of cheesecloth which has been soaked in whiskey.

## SOUR CREAM POUND CAKE

2³/₄ cups sugar
1 cup butter or margarine,
  softened
6 eggs
3 cups sifted all-purpose flour
¹/₂ teaspoon salt

¹/₄ teaspoon baking soda
1 cup dairy sour cream
¹/₂ teaspoon lemon extract
¹/₂ teaspoon orange
  extract
¹/₂ teaspoon vanilla
  extract

Combine sugar and butter; beat until light and fluffy. Add eggs, one at a time, beating well after each addition. Sift together flour, salt and soda; add to creamed mixture alternately with sour cream, beating after each addition. Add flavorings and beat well. Pour into a greased and floured 10" tube pan. Bake at 350° for 65 to 70 minutes or until cake tests as done. Cool 15 minutes; remove from pan. When cool, frost or sprinkle with powdered sugar, if desired.

## BROWN SUGAR POUND CAKE

3 cups flour
¹/₂ teaspoon salt
¹/₂ teaspoon baking powder
1 cup (2 sticks) butter
  (no substitute)
¹/₂ cup Crisco shortening
1 cup dark brown sugar,
  packed

2 cups white sugar
5 eggs
1 scant cup milk
1 tablespoon almond
  extract
1 tablespoon vanilla
  extract
2 cups chopped pecans

Sift flour, salt and baking powder together; set aside. Cream butter and Crisco shortening thoroughly; slowly add sugars, beating until fluffy. Add eggs, one at a time, beating well after each addition. Combine milk and flavorings; add to egg mixture, alternating with flour mixture. Fold in pecans. Pour batter into a greased and floured tube pan; bake at 300° for 2 hours.

*Note:* Batter may be divided and baked in 2 loaf pans.

# CAKES

## LEMON NUT CAKE

1 pound butter
2 cups sugar, sifted
6 egg yolks, beaten
3 cups cake flour
4 ounces candied pineapple,
   chopped

12 ounces candied
   cherries
5 cups whole pecans
   (1 1/2 pounds)
2 ounces lemon extract
6 egg whites

In a large mixing bowl cream butter and sugar; add egg yolks; add cake flour. Lightly flour fruit and pecans and add to mixture; add lemon extract. Beat egg whites until stiff and fold in. Line 2 big loaf pans or 4 or 5 small ones with foil. Put batter into pans and bake at 300° for 1 hour. When done lift loaves from pans and wrap. This keeps them moist for a long time. They are good for Christmas gifts.

## PINEAPPLE-BANANA CAKE

3 cups flour
2 cups sugar
1 teaspoon salt
1 teaspoon cinnamon
1 teaspoon baking soda
3 whole eggs
1 1/2 cups cooking oil

2 cups thinly-sliced ripe
   bananas
1 ( 8 1/4-ounce) can
   crushed pineapple,
   including juice
1 cup chopped pecans
1 teaspoon vanilla extract

Sift together into a large bowl the flour, sugar, salt, cinnamon and soda. In a small bowl, break eggs and beat lightly with a fork. *Do not use mixer.* Make a well in dry ingredients; pour in the eggs, oil, bananas, pineapple, pecans and vanilla. Stir by hand with a spoon just until blended; do not overbeat. Bake in a greased and floured tube or bundt pan at 325° for 50 to 60 minutes, then at 350° for an additional 10 minutes. *Do not open oven while cake is baking.* Leftover cake should be refrigerated. Pineapple-banana cake freezes well.

## FRESH APPLE CAKE

1 1/2 cups Wesson oil
2 cups sugar
2 eggs
3 cups flour
1 1/2 teaspoons soda
1 teaspoon salt
1 teaspoon cinnamon
1 teaspoon nutmeg

1 teaspoon ground cloves
1 teaspoon vanilla
4 large Winesap or
  Jonathan apples, peeled
  and chopped
1 cup pecans, chopped
1/2 (6-ounce) package
  dates, chopped

Mix oil and sugar; beat in eggs. Add remaining ingredients, mixing thoroughly. Pour into a tube pan or bundt pan that has been well greased with butter. Bake at 325° for 1 1/2 hours. For cupcakes, spoon batter into tins; bake at 325° for 30 minutes.

## HOLIDAY CAKE AND SAUCE

1/4 cup (1/2 stick) butter
1 cup sugar
1 egg
1 cup flour
2 teaspoons baking powder
1 teaspoon soda

1 teaspoon cinnamon
1/4 teaspoon salt
2 cups apples, very thinly
  sliced
1/2 cup raisins
1 cup chopped pecans

Cream butter and sugar; add egg and beat well. Sift dry ingredients together; gradually stir into creamed mixture. Fold in apples, raisins and pecans. Pour batter into a greased and floured 13"x 9"x 2" pan and bake at 350° for 40 minutes. Serve with Brown Sugar Sauce. Serves 12.

*Brown Sugar Sauce*
1 cup brown sugar
1/4 cup cream

2 tablespoons light corn
  syrup
2 tablespoons butter

Combine all ingredients and bring to a boil; transfer to the top of a double boiler to keep warm until ready to serve.

# CAKES

## GINGER CAKE

2 1/2 cups sifted flour
1 1/2 teaspoons soda
1/2 teaspoon salt
1/2 cup butter
1/2 cup sugar
1 egg
1 teaspoon cinnamon

1 teaspoon ginger
1/2 teaspoon ground
  cloves
1/4 teaspoon allspice
1/4 cup rum
1 cup molasses
1 cup hot water

Sift flour, soda and salt together. Cream butter with sugar until fluffy; add egg and beat well. Put spices in rum and let set for a few minutes; stir into creamed mixture. Combine molasses and water; add alternately with sifted dry ingredients, beating thoroughly after each addition. Pour batter into greased and floured 9" square pan; bake at 350° for 50 minutes or until done. Serve with Rum Sauce. Serves 10 to 12.

## RUM SAUCE

1 cup (2 sticks) butter
2 1/4 cups sugar

1 cup whipping cream
1/4 cup Myers dark rum

Combine butter, sugar and cream in the top of a double boiler. Stir until sugar is dissolved, keeping sides of pan free of crystals. Add rum. Serve hot.

## SPICE CAKE

1 1/2 cups flour
1/2 teaspoon soda
1/2 teaspoon cloves
1 teaspoon cinnamon
1 cup (2 sticks) butter

1 cup sugar
2 eggs, beaten
1/2 cup buttermilk
1/2 cup chopped nuts
1/4 cup raisins

Sift flour, soda, cloves and cinnamon together. Cream butter and add sugar gradually, beating until fluffy. Add eggs and beat until blended. Alternately add flour mixture and buttermilk, mixing thoroughly. Fold in nuts and raisins. Bake in a greased and floured 8" square pan at 350° for 20 minutes or until it tests done with a straw. Frost with caramel icing, if desired.

## JAM CAKE

1 cup butter
2 cups sugar
5 eggs, beaten
1 teaspoon soda
1 cup buttermilk
2 tablespoons rum
3 cups cake flour
1/4 teaspoon salt

1/2 teaspoon cinnamon
1 1/2 teaspoons cloves
1 1/2 teaspoons allspice
1 cup blackberry jam,
  with seeds
1 cup chopped nuts
1 cup cut raisins

Cream butter and sugar until light. Add eggs, one at a time beating after each addition. Dissolve soda in buttermilk; add rum and stir gradually into butter and sugar mixture. Sift dry ingredients together three times. Stir into mixture, adding jam, nuts and raisins last. Bake in 3 greased and floured 9" cake pans at 325° for 40 minutes.
Serve with brown sugar frosting.

## EASY BROWN SUGAR FROSTING

1/4 cup (1/2 stick) butter
2 tablespoons Crisco
1 cup brown sugar, packed
1/4 cup milk

1 1/2 cups sifted
  confectioners' sugar
1/2 teaspoon vanilla
  extract

Put butter, Crisco and brown sugar in a saucepan; bring to a boil over low heat, stirring constantly. Slowly pour in milk; boil 2 minutes. Cool. Add confectioners' sugar and vanilla; beat until creamy and smooth.

# CAKES

## LADYFINGER CAKE

*... very light and delicious (don't let the Crisco fool you)*

| | |
|---|---|
| 1 cup Crisco shortening | ¹/₄ teaspoon salt |
| 2 cups sugar | 1 tablespoon vanilla |
| 6 eggs | extract |
| 2 cups sifted cake flour | |

Cream shortening and sugar with an electric mixer, beating until light and fluffy. Add 4 eggs, one at a time, mixing well after each addition. Gradually stir in 1 cup flour; add salt and remaining eggs. Stir in the second cup of flour; add vanilla and beat batter until smooth. Bake in a greased and floured 9" tube pan at 350° for 50 to 60 minutes.

## SPONGE CAKE

*...perfect for Baked Alaska*

| | |
|---|---|
| 3 eggs, separated | Pinch of cream of tartar |
| ¹/₂ cup sugar | ²/₃ cup cake flour |
| 1¹/₂ teaspoons vanilla extract | ¹/₄ cup melted butter |

Beat egg yolks until pale yellow; gradually add sugar and beat 5 minutes. Stir in vanilla. Beat egg whites until soft peaks form; add cream of tartar and beat until stiff but not dry. Gently fold one-fourth of egg whites into yolk mixture, then fold in one-third of flour. Continue to add egg whites and flour alternately, being careful not to lose the air in the egg whites. Finally, fold in melted butter. Pour batter into greased and floured 13"x 9"x 2" pan; bake at 350° for 18 to 20 minutes.

## LADYFINGERS

3 egg whites
1/3 cup confectioners' sugar
2 egg yolks

1/4 teaspoon vanilla
  extract
1/3 cup sifted cake flour
1/8 teaspoon salt

Beat egg whites until stiff but not dry; gradually beat in sugar. Beat egg yolks until thick; add vanilla. Gently fold in beaten whites; fold in flour and salt. Shape batter into fingers on a baking sheet covered with ungreased heavy paper. Sprinkle with additional confectioners' sugar; bake at 350° for 12 minutes.

## ANGEL FOOD CAKE

1 cup sifted cake flour
1 cup egg whites
1/4 teaspoon salt
1 teaspoon cream of tartar

1 1/4 cups sugar
3/4 teaspoon vanilla
  extract
1/4 teaspoon almond
  extract

Sift flour once; measure and sift three more times. Beat egg whites and salt together and, when foamy, add cream of tartar and continue beating until eggs are stiff enough to stand in peaks but not dry. Fold in sugar, two tablespoons at a time. Fold in flavoring. Sift a small amount of flour over mixture and fold in with a rubber spatula. Continue until all flour has been used. Turn mixture into an ungreased tube cake pan and bake at 325° for 30 minutes. Remove from oven and invert pan for 1 hour. Remove and serve.

*Filling*
1 cup sugar
1/4 cup flour
2 eggs

1 cup cream
2 tablespoons whiskey
1 cup chopped pecans

Combine first 4 ingredients in the top of a double boiler; cook over hot water, stirring constantly, until thickened. Add whiskey just before removing from heat. Let cool; stir in pecans. Slice an angel food cake in half crosswise; spread filling between halves.

# CAKES

## ALMOND CAKE WITH RASPBERRY SAUCE

*...has the consistency of cheese cake*

3/4 cup sugar
1/2 cup unsalted butter,
   at room temperature
8 ounces almond paste
3 eggs
1 tablespoon Kirsch or Triple
   Sec

1/4 teaspoon almond
   extract
1/4 cup all-purpose flour
1/3 teaspoon baking
   powder
Confectioners' sugar

Combine sugar, butter and almond paste, blending well; beat in eggs, liqueur and almond extract. Gently blend in flour and baking powder just until mixed. Do not overbeat! Pour batter into a buttered and floured 8" round pan. Bake at 350° for 40 to 50 minutes or until tester comes out clean. Invert on a cake plate and sprinkle with confectioners' sugar.

*Sauce*

1 pint fresh, or 1 (12-ounce)
   package frozen, red
   raspberries

2 tablespoons sugar (or
   less) to taste

Combine ingredients in a blender container and purée. Press through a sieve to remove seeds. Serve over thin slices of cake. Serves 10 to 12.

## ALMOND COOKIES

1 cup (2 sticks) butter,
   softened
1/2 cup sugar
2/3 cup finely ground
   blanched almonds

1 1/2 cups flour
Confectioners' sugar

Cream butter and sugar; add almonds and flour, mixing thoroughly. Chill dough at least 4 hours. Roll into small balls; press flat with a smooth-bottomed glass slightly buttered and dipped in sugar. Bake at 350° until light brown edges appear. Remove to paper towels and dust with sifted confectioners' sugar. Makes 3 dozen.

## ALMOND MACAROONS

1 (8-ounce) can almond paste
1 cup sugar
3 egg whites
1/2 teaspoon almond
extract

Cut up almond paste into small pieces; add sugar and egg whites. Beat with electric mixer until smooth, with no lumps remaining; add almond extract. Drop by teaspoonsful onto cookie sheet lined with brown paper; bake at 325° for 30 minutes. Lift brown paper to cooling rack and cool cookies completely before removing paper. These macaroons freeze well. Makes 2 1/2 dozen.

## CRANBERRY WALNUT COOKIES

3 1/4 cups all-purpose flour
1 teaspoon baking powder
1/4 teaspoon baking soda
1 teaspoon salt
1 1/4 cups butter or margarine,
softened
2/3 cup white sugar
1 cup brown sugar
2 eggs
1 1/2 teaspoons vanilla
extract or almond
extract
1 cup chopped walnuts
2 cups fresh cranberries,
finely chopped

Sift together the first 4 ingredients; set aside. Cream butter; gradually add sugars, beating until fluffy. Add eggs and flavoring, beating 1 minute on high speed. Turn to low speed; add flour mixture and walnuts, blending well. Work in cranberries (with hands, if necessary). Shape dough into 3 rolls, 2" in diameter; wrap in wax paper and refrigerate until firm. Slice 1/4" thick; place on an ungreased cookie sheet. Bake at 375° for 10 to 12 minutes.

# COOKIES

## BUTTER THINS

*... a good Christmas Cookie*

14 tablespoons (1 ¾ sticks)
  butter, softened
¾ cup plus 2 tablespoons
  sugar

2 egg yolks, well beaten
2 scant cups flour
Seedless red currant or
  red raspberry jam

Cream butter and sugar; beat in egg yolks and flour. Chill dough for several hours. Shape dough into 1" balls; press the handle of a wooden spoon into each and add a small amount of jam. Place on an ungreased cookie sheet and bake at 375° for 8 to 10 minutes or until edges are brown. Watch carefully to prevent burning. Butter Thins freeze beautifully.

## BANANA OATMEAL COOKIES

¾ cup butter or margarine,
  softened
1 cup brown sugar, packed
1 egg
½ cup mashed ripe bananas
1 teaspoon vanilla extract

1 cup flour
1 teaspoon salt
½ teaspoon baking soda
3 cups uncooked oats
  (regular)
½ cup raisins
½ cup chopped pecans

In a large bowl, whip butter until creamy; add sugar, beating until fluffy. Add egg, banana and vanilla; mix thoroughly. Sift together flour, salt and baking soda; blend into creamed mixture. Stir in oats, raisins and pecans. Drop by heaping teaspoonsful onto greased cookie sheet. Bake at 375° for 15 to 20 minutes. Makes 5 to 6 dozen.

## CHRISTMAS COOKIES

2¹/₂ cups flour
¹/₂ teaspoon baking soda
¹/₂ teaspoon salt
1 egg, slightly beaten
2 tablespoons white vinegar

1¹/₂ teaspoons grated
  lemon rind
1 teaspoon vanilla extract
1 cup butter
1 cup sugar
Red and green decorating
  sugars

Sift flour with soda and salt. Combine egg, vinegar, lemon rind and vanilla. Cream butter and add sugar gradually, beating well. Add dry ingredients and egg mixture alternately, a little at a time, blending well after each addition. Drop dough by teaspoonsful onto an ungreased cookie sheet; flatten each, using a measuring cup greased on the bottom and dipped in flour. Sprinkle with decorating sugars. Bake at 400° for 10 to 12 minutes. Makes about 80.

## CHEESE-MARMALADE COOKIES

¹/₂ cup (1 stick) butter,
  softened
1 (5-ounce) jar Old English
  cheese spread

1 cup flour
1 (12-ounce) jar orange
  marmalade

Combine butter and cheese spread; add flour gradually, blending well. Chill the dough until firm; roll it into a thin sheet. Using a water glass, cut out circles. Place 1 rounded teaspoon of marmalade in center; fold over to half-moon shape and crimp edges. Chill well before cooking. Bake 10 minutes in a preheated 300° oven. Makes about 2¹/₂ dozen.

## COCONUT PUFFS

| | |
|---|---|
| 1 cup sugar | 2 cups dry shredded |
| 1 tablespoon corn starch | coconut |
| 3 egg whites, beaten stiff | 1 teaspoon vanilla |

Mix sugar and cornstarch. Add gradually to egg whites, beating constantly. Cook in double boiler until thick around edges. Remove from heat. Add coconut and vanilla. Drop by small spoonfuls on oiled pan. Bake at 300° until delicately brown. Remove from pan while hot. Makes 30 1½" puffs or 60 ¾" puffs.

## ICE CREAM WAFERS

| | |
|---|---|
| ½ cup (1 stick) butter or | 1 egg |
| margarine, softened | ½ teaspoon vanilla |
| ½ cup sugar | ¾ cup flour, sifted |

Blend butter and sugar until creamy; beat in egg and vanilla. Stir in flour gradually. Drop by small teaspoonsful onto a greased cookie sheet (not too close together as cookies will spread). Bake at 350° for 10 to 12 minutes. Remove from cookie sheet immediately.

*Note.* Chopped nuts, raisins or chocolate bits may be added to dough before baking; or each cookie may be topped with a nut.

## FRUIT ROCKS

*...delicious Christmas cookies*

10 tablespoons butter
10 tablespoons sugar
3 eggs
1/2 tablespoon light corn
   syrup
1/4 teaspoon ground cloves
1/4 teaspoon cinnamon
1/4 teaspoon ground allspice
1/4 cup sherry or Bourbon

1 1/2 cups flour
2 pounds pecans
1/2 pound candied
   cherries, pieces halved
1/2 pound candied
   pineapple, diced
1/4 pound candied citron,
   diced

Cream butter; gradually add sugar, eggs, syrup, spices and sherry, mixing well. Blend in flour; add nuts and fruits. Drop spoonsful of batter onto a greased cookie sheet. Bake at 300° for 20 to 25 minutes. Makes 6 1/2 dozen.

## GRAHAM CRACKER COOKIES

1 stick butter
1 stick margarine
1 1/4 cups brown sugar

1 cup chopped nuts
44 graham cracker squares

Combine butter, margarine and brown sugar in a saucepan. Bring to a boil; cook while stirring until sugar is dissolved and mixture is blended. Remove pan from heat; stir in nuts. Cover a jelly roll pan with aluminum foil; coat with vegetable cooking spray or lightly grease with vegetable oil. Lay graham crackers on foil; pour hot mixture over all. Bake at 350° for 10 minutes.

# COOKIES

## LACE COOKIES

| | |
|---|---|
| ¼ cup butter, softened | 1 teaspoon baking powder |
| 2 cups light brown sugar | ½ cup flour |
| 2 eggs | ½ pound pecans or |
| 1 teaspoon vanilla | English walnuts, broken |

Cream butter and sugar; add eggs and vanilla, beating well. Combine baking powder, flour and nuts; add to creamed mixture, blending well. Drop half teaspoonsful of dough 3" apart onto greased and lightly-floured cookie sheets. Bake at 350° for 5 minutes, watching carefully to prevent burning. Remove from oven; cool for 1 minute before removing from cookie sheet. Makes 5 dozen.

## OATMEAL LACE COOKIES

| | |
|---|---|
| 2½ cups regular oats | ½ cup melted butter |
| 1 cup brown sugar, packed | 1 egg, beaten |
| 2 teaspoons baking powder | |

Combine oats, brown sugar and baking powder; pour in melted butter and mix thoroughly. Beat in egg. Drop by teaspoonsful onto a greased cookie sheet. Bake at 350° for 8 to 10 minutes or just until edges start to brown. Allow cookies to cool 1 to 2 minutes before removing from cookie sheet.

## TRAVIS HOUSE COOKIES

| | |
|---|---|
| 1 egg white | ⅛ teaspoon salt |
| 1 cup brown sugar | 1 teaspoon vanilla |
| 1 tablespoon flour | 1 cup pecans, chopped |

Beat egg white until very stiff; add brown sugar gradually, beating constantly. Fold in flour, salt and vanilla. Drop by teaspoonsful onto cookie sheet; bake at 325° until cookies begin to brown, about 10 minutes. Makes about 1 dozen.

## LEMON WAFERS

1 cup butter, softened
1 cup sugar
1 teaspoon grated lemon rind
2 tablespoons fresh lemon
   juice

1 egg
2½ cups flour
¼ teaspoon salt
¼ teaspoon soda

Cream butter and sugar and add lemon rind and lemon juice. Add egg and beat well. Combine the flour, salt and soda and gradually blend into butter and sugar mixture. Make 2 logs of dough 1½" in diameter. Refrigerate until firm. Preheat oven to 400.° Cut logs into thin slices and place on greased cookie sheet. Lower heat 350° and bake for 5 minutes. Makes 3 dozen.

## MOLASSES COOKIES

¾ cup plus 1 tablespoon
   unsalted butter, melted
1 cup granulated sugar
¼ cup dark molasses
1 egg, lightly beaten
1¾ cups unbleached
   all-purpose flour

1 teaspoon ground
   cinnamon
½ teaspoon ground
   cloves
½ teaspoon ground
   ginger
½ teaspoon salt
½ teaspoon baking soda

Combine melted butter, sugar, molasses and egg, mixing thoroughly. Sift flour with spices, salt and baking soda; add to sugar mixture, blending well. Cover a baking sheet with foil. Drop batter by teaspoonsful onto foil, leaving 3" between them. Bake at 350° for 8 to 10 minutes or until cookies start to darken. Remove from oven while still soft; let cool on foil. Makes 4 dozen.

## PECAN CHEWIES

½ cup (1 stick) butter,
  softened
1¼ cups brown sugar, packed
1 egg
1¼ cups all-purpose flour

¼ teaspoon baking soda
⅛ teaspoon salt
½ cup chopped pecans
  (or more, if desired)

Combine butter and brown sugar; cream until light and fluffy. Add egg and beat well. Sift dry ingredients together; stir into creamed mixture. Fold in pecans. Drop the batter from a teaspoon, about 2″ apart, onto a greased cookie sheet. Bake at 350° for about 8 minutes or until done. Makes 3 dozen.

## PECAN COOKIES SUPREME

1 cup (2 sticks) margarine,
  softened (do not use butter)
1 cup brown sugar
½ cup white sugar
1 egg, separated

1½ teaspoons vanilla
  extract
2 cups flour
1 teaspoon salt
2 teaspoons cinnamon
1½ cups chopped pecans

Cream margarine with sugars; add egg yolk and vanilla, mixing until smooth. Sift dry ingredients together and add to creamed mixture; mix thoroughly. Press dough into a greased 15″x 10″ jellyroll pan. Pour the unbeaten egg white in a corner of the pan; tilt pan in all directions until egg white has coated all of the dough. Pour off excess egg. Lightly press pecans into dough. Bake at 300° for 30 minutes. Cookies must be cut in pan while still warm.

## POTATO CHIP COOKIES

1 pound butter
1 cup sugar
3½ cups all-purpose flour,
   unsifted

1 cup crushed *unsalted*
   potato chips
2 teaspoons vanilla
Confectioners' sugar

Cream butter; add sugar and continue to beat until light. Add flour, potato chips and vanilla, mixing well. Shape into small balls; place on a greased cookie sheet and flatten with the bottom of a small glass. Bake at 350° for 15 minutes or less. *Do not overcook.* Remove from cookie sheet and sprinkle with confectioners' sugar. Makes 6 dozen.

## TEA CAKES

½ cup (1 stick) butter
1 cup sugar
1 large egg
1 tablespoon cream or milk

1 teaspoon vanilla extract
   or lemon extract
1½ cups all-purpose flour
1 teaspoon baking powder
¼ teaspoon salt

Cream butter and sugar; beat in egg, cream and flavoring. Sift dry ingredients together and add to creamed mixture. Shape dough into a roll 1½" in diameter; wrap in foil and refrigerate. Cut dough in ⅛" slices; sprinkle with sugar and top with a raisin. Place on a chilled, lightly buttered baking sheet. Bake at 325° for about 5 minutes or until brown. Remove quickly from sheet.

## SCOTCH SHORTBREAD

1 cup (2 sticks) sweet butter, softened (no substitute)

1/2 cup confectioners' sugar

2 cups sifted all-purpose flour

Cream butter; gradually beat in sugar until smooth. Gradually work in flour, mixing thoroughly. Shape dough into two balls; place on an ungreased cookie sheet; flatten to ³/₄" thickness and 7" diameter. Pinch edges all around and prick all over with a fork. Refrigerate at least 30 minutes. Bake at 375° for 5 minutes; reduce heat to 300° and bake 35 to 40 minutes or just until pale golden. Makes 2 rounds.

*Note:* For smaller cookies to use as individual strawberry shortcakes, divide dough into 10 balls. Place on cookie sheet and flatten. Bake at 350° for 10 minutes or until pale golden.

## FROSTED BROWNIES

1/2 cup (1 stick) butter or margarine, softened

1 cup sugar

4 eggs, well beaten

1 (16-ounce) can Hershey chocolate syrup

1 cup all-purpose flour

1/2 cup chopped pecans

Cream butter and sugar; add eggs and chocolate syrup. Stir in flour and add nuts. (All may be done in a food processor, except flour and nuts.) Pour batter into a 11"x 16"x 2" pan. Bake at 350° for 25 minutes. Let cool, then frost.

*Frosting*

1¹/₃ cups sugar

1/3 cup milk

1/2 cup (1 stick) butter

1 (6-ounce) package Nestlé chocolate chips

Combine and boil *exactly 1 minute;* remove from heat and add chocolate chips. Beat until chocolate is melted and mixture starts to stiffen. Do not over-mix. Spread evenly over cake. When completely cooled, cut into squares.

## WALNUT SQUARES

*Crust*

| | |
|---|---|
| ¹/₂ cup (1 stick) butter | 2 tablespoons |
| 1 cup flour | confectioners' sugar |

Cream butter, flour and sugar until blended. Press into the bottom of an 8"x 12" pan and bake at 350° for 15 to 20 minutes.

*Filling*

| | |
|---|---|
| 1¹/₂ cups brown sugar | 2 eggs |
| 2 tablespoons flour | 2 teaspoons cocoa |
| ¹/₂ teaspoon salt | ¹/₂ cup coconut |
| 1 teaspoon vanilla extract | 1 cup chopped walnuts |

Combine all ingredients, mixing thoroughly. Spread over crust; bake an additional 15 to 20 minutes. Cool completely.

*Frosting*

| | |
|---|---|
| ¹/₄ cup (¹/₂ stick) butter | ¹/₂ teaspoon vanilla |
| 1¹/₂ cups powdered sugar | extract |
| 2 tablespoons strong coffee | |

Combine ingredients; spread to cover. Cut into 2" squares. Makes 2 dozen.

## BROWNIES

| | |
|---|---|
| ¹/₂ cup (1 stick) butter, softened | 1 teaspoon vanilla extract |
| 1 cup sugar | ¹/₂ cup sifted all-purpose flour |
| 2 squares unsweetened chocolate, melted | ¹/₈ teaspoon salt |
| 2 eggs, beaten | ¹/₂ to ³/₄ cup chopped pecans or walnuts |

Cream butter and sugar; stir in melted chocolate. Beat in eggs and vanilla; fold in flour and salt. Stir in nuts. Spread in an 8"x 8"x 2" greased baking pan. Bake at 350° for 20 to 25 minutes. Cool in pan on a wire rack. When cool, cut into squares. Makes 16 (2") squares.

# COOKIES

## LEMON BARS

*Crust*

2 cups flour
1 cup margarine

½ cup confectioners'
   sugar

Combine ingredients, mixing thoroughly; press dough in the bottom of a greased 13"x 9" pan. Bake at 300° for 30 minutes or until lightly browned.

*Filling*

4 eggs, beaten
2 cups sugar
½ cup fresh lemon juice,
   unstrained

¼ cup flour
1 teaspoon baking powder
Dash of salt
Confectioners' sugar

Combine eggs, sugar and lemon juice; add flour, baking powder and salt, beating until fluffy. Spread evenly over baked crust. Bake at 300° for 30 to 40 minutes. Cut into 3"x 1"bars while still warm and dust with confectioners' sugar. Makes 3 dozen.

## COCONUT CREAM PIE

1 cup sugar
¼ teaspoon salt
½ cup flour
3 cups half-and-half
3 egg yolks, beaten
2 tablespoons butter

1¼ teaspoons vanilla
   extract
½ cup grated coconut
½ pint whipping cream,
   whipped
¼ cup coconut, toasted
1 baked 9" pastry shell

Combine sugar, salt and flour in a heavy saucepan. Stir in half-and-half and beaten egg yolks. Cook slowly until the custard thickens and will coat a metal spoon. Remove from heat immediately and stir in butter, then allow to cool. When cool, add vanilla and coconut. Pour into pastry shell and top with whipped cream and toasted coconut.

## THE VERY BEST CHESS PIE

½ cup (1 stick) butter, melted  1½ teaspoons vinegar
1½ cups sugar  1 teaspoon vanilla extract
1 tablespoon flour  1 unbaked 9" pastry shell
3 eggs

Combine all ingredients, mixing until well blended. Pour into pastry shell and bake at 350° for 35 minutes. Serves 6.

## CHESS TARTS

½ cup (1 stick) butter, melted  1 teaspoon vinegar
1½ cups sugar  1 teaspoon vanilla extract
3 eggs, beaten  8 pastry tart shells,
1 teaspoon cornmeal  unbaked

Combine butter, sugar and eggs; beat until blended. Add remaining ingredients; mix thoroughly. Pour into tart shells; bake at 375° for 30 minutes.

## CHOCOLATE CHESS PIE

¼ cup butter  Pinch of salt
1½ ounces unsweetened  ½ cup milk
   chocolate  2 eggs
1½ cups sugar  1 teaspoon vanilla extract
1 tablespoon flour  1 unbaked 9" pastry shell

Melt butter and chocolate; pour into a mixing bowl. Add sugar, flour, salt, milk, eggs and vanilla; beat with electric mixer for 6 minutes. Pour filling into pastry shell; bake at 350° for 40 minutes.

## BLACK BOTTOM PIE

20 gingersnap cookies
5 tablespoons butter, melted
1 tablespoon gelatin
1/4 cup cold water
2 cups half-and-half
1/2 cup sugar
4 teaspoons cornstarch
4 egg yolks, beaten
2 ounces bitter chocolate,
 melted

1 teaspoon vanilla extract
3 egg whites
1/4 teaspoon cream of
 tartar
1/2 cup sugar
2 tablespoons dark rum
1 cup whipping cream
3 tablespoons
 confectioners' sugar
Shaved semi-sweet
 chocolate

Roll or grind gingersnaps until fine. Mix with butter and press into a 9" pie pan. Bake at 325° for 10 minutes. Soak gelatin in water. Scald half-and-half; add sugar mixed with cornstarch. Whisk in egg yolks and cook, stirring constantly, until the custard coats a spoon heavily. Remove from heat and take out 1 cup custard; add melted chocolate and beat until well blended and cool. Stir in vanilla; pour into prepared gingersnap crust and chill. While remaining custard is hot, add the soaked gelatin. Cool but do not allow to set up. Make a meringue of the egg whites, cream of tartar and 1/2 cup sugar. Fold into the custard; add rum. Pour on top of the chocolate layer; chill until firm. Whip cream stiff with confectioners' sugar; spread on top of rum custard. Garnish with shaved chocolate.

## CHOCOLATE VELVET PIE

*Crust*
1 (7-ounce) box vanilla wafers
2 tablespoons extra fine sugar
6 tablespoons butter, melted

Grind vanilla wafers fine. Combine with sugar and butter; press into bottom and sides of a 9" pie pan. Bake at 350° for 7 to 10 minutes until slightly brown. Chill thoroughly, preferably in freezer.

*Filling*
3/4 cup (1 1/2 sticks) butter, softened
1 cup plus 2 tablespoons extra fine sugar
2 squares unsweetened chocolate, melted
2 teaspoons Grand Marnier or vanilla extract
3 large eggs (not extra large)
1 pint heavy cream
Shaved chocolate for decoration

Cream butter and sugar; add chocolate and Grand Marnier or vanilla. Beat in eggs, one at a time, until very smooth. Pour into pie shell. Whip cream; spread on top or use pastry tube to decorate. Sprinkle with shaved chocolate; chill thoroughly.

## KENTUCKY CHOCOLATE PIE

1 cup sugar
6 tablespoons flour
2 eggs
1/2 cup margarine, melted
1 cup pecans, chopped
6 ounces semi-sweet chocolate chips
1 1/2 teaspoon vanilla
1 unbaked 9" pastry shell
1 cup cream, whipped

Combine sugar and flour; add remaining ingredients, except cream, and pour into unbaked pie shell. Bake at 325° for 50 to 60 minutes. Serve with whipped cream.

## CHOCOLATE MERINGUE PIE

2½ cups milk
3 ounces unsweetened
  chocolate
6 tablespoons flour
1¼ cups sugar
¼ teaspoon salt

5 egg yolks, beaten
2 tablespoons butter
1 teaspoon vanilla extract
1 baked pastry shell
1 cup whipping cream,
  whipped (optional)

Scald milk with chocolate and beat until smooth. Mix flour, sugar and salt and sift together; add chocolate mixture, blending well. Beat in egg yolks; cook until mixture is thickened, stirring constantly. Remove from heat and stir in butter. Allow filling to cool; add vanilla. Pour into baked pastry shell; cover with whipped cream or meringue. Serves 6 to 8.

*Meringue*
5 egg whites
Pinch of cream of tartar

½ cup sugar

Beat whites with cream of tartar until peaks form. Gradually add sugar, a small amount at a time, and continue beating until stiff. Pile on cooled pie and bake at 325° until golden.

## CHOCOLATE CARAMELS

2 cups sugar
1½ cups light corn syrup
½ cup (1 stick) butter
3 to 3½ ounces unsweetened
  chocolate

1 cup half-and-half
1 cup whipping cream
1 teaspoon vanilla extract

Combine sugar, syrup, butter, chocolate and half-and-half; cook, stirring frequently, to 220° on candy thermometer. Slowly add whipping cream and cook to 236° or 238°. Remove from heat, add vanilla and pour into a buttered pan. When cool, cut into squares.

## PUMPKIN PIE

2 cups pumpkin
1 1/2 cups brown sugar
5 eggs, beaten
1 cup heavy cream
1/2 cup (1 stick) butter, melted
1/4 cup dark molasses
3 tablespoons Bourbon

1 teaspoon vanilla extract
3 teaspoons cinnamon
2 teaspoons nutmeg
2 teaspoons allspice
1/2 teaspoon ginger
1/2 teaspoon salt
1 unbaked 9" pastry shell

Combine ingredients, mixing thoroughly. Pour into pastry shell and bake at 400° for 1 hour or until a knife inserted into center of filling comes out clean.

## PEACH COBBLER

*...a delightful two-layer, deep-dish pie*

About 8 cups sliced fresh
    peaches
2 cups sugar
3 tablespoons all-purpose
    flour
1/2 teaspoon ground nutmeg

1 teaspoon almond extract
1/3 cup melted butter or
    margarine
Pastry for a double-crust
    8" pie

Combine peaches, sugar, flour and nutmeg; set aside until syrup forms. Bring peaches to a boil; reduce heat to low and cook 10 minutes or until tender. Remove from heat and blend in almond extract and butter. Lightly butter a 2-quart shallow, oblong casserole. Roll out one-half of pastry to 1/8" thickness on a lightly floured board; cut to fit casserole. Spoon one-half of peaches into casserole and top with cut pastry. Bake at 475° for 12 minutes or until golden brown. Spoon remaining peaches over baked pastry. Roll out remaining pastry and cut into 1/2" strips; arrange in lattice design over peaches. Return casserole to oven for 10 to 15 minutes or until lightly browned. Serves 8 to 10.

# PIES

## GRAHAM CRACKER PIE

| | |
|---|---|
| 1 cup graham cracker crumbs | 1 cup sugar |
| 1/2 cup pecans, chopped | 1 teaspoon vanilla |
| 1/2 cup flaked coconut | 1/4 teaspoon salt |
| 4 egg whites | Whipped cream |

Place a package of graham crackers in food processor bowl and process until fine. Put pecans in processor bowl and chop lightly. Combine cracker crumbs, pecans and flaked coconut; set aside. Beat egg whites until stiff but not dry; add salt and sugar gradually; add vanilla; stir in graham cracker crumbs, pecans and coconut. Put mixture in a greased 9"x 9"x 1 3/4" cake pan or a 9" pie pan. Bake at 350° for 30 minutes. Serve warm or cold with whipped cream flavored with vanilla or whiskey. Serves 6 to 8.

## VERY LEMONY MERINGUE PIE

| | |
|---|---|
| 1 3/4 cups sugar | 1/2 cup lemon juice, |
| 7 tablespoons cornstarch | unstrained |
| 1/4 teaspoon salt | Grated rind of 2 lemons |
| 2 cups water | 1 baked 9" pastry shell |
| 5 egg yolks, beaten | |

Sift sugar, cornstarch and salt into a saucepan; gradually stir in water. Cook over medium heat, stirring constantly, until mixture comes to a boil. Continue to stir while boiling for one minute. Remove pan from heat; pour part of hot mixture slowly onto egg yolks, beating constantly. Pour back into remaining hot mixture, mixing well. Continue to cook and stir while bringing to a boil. Boil for one minute, stirring constantly. Remove from heat and add lemon juice and rind. Pour into pastry shell, top with meringue and bake at 400° for 8 to 10 minutes.

*Meringue*
| | |
|---|---|
| 5 egg whites | 1/2 cup sugar |
| 1/4 teaspoon salt | |

Beat egg whites with salt until frothy. Add sugar gradually. Beat until stiff. Spread completely over hot filling, sealing to edge of crust; swirl into peaks.

## MINCEMEAT PIE

1 (28-ounce) jar Borden's
    Mincemeat
1 large apple, peeled and
    diced

1/4 cup brandy
1/4 cup sugar
1 unbaked pastry shell

Mix contents of jar with apple, brandy and sugar. Pour into pie shell and bake at 400° for 20 to 30 minutes.

## STRAWBERRY TARTS

2 cups strawberries
1 cup sugar
1 cup water

2 tablespoons corn starch
5 tablespoons strawberry
    jello

Cook sugar, corn starch and water until thick and clear. Add jello and pour over strawberries. Spoon into cooked tarts. Serve cold.

## SHAKERTOWN TART SHELLS

1 cup flour
1/2 teaspoon salt

1/3 cup plus 1 tablespoon
    shortening
2 tablespoons water

Mix flour and salt; cut shortening into flour until very small balls form. Sprinkle in water, a little at a time, while mixing lightly with a fork until flour is moistened; mix into a ball that cleans the bowl. Do not overwork. Roll out on a floured board; cut in circles to cover small tart molds. Pierce with a fork and trim. Cover with another mold and bake at 475° for 6 to 8 minutes. Remove top mold and brown tart shells slightly; browning takes about 2 minutes. Makes 1 dozen. Tart shells may be filled with fresh fruits of the season: peaches, strawberries, blackberries or raspberries. Top with whipped cream.

# PIES

## PECAN PIES IN MINIATURE

*Pastry Shells*
1 (3-ounce) package cream
  cheese, softened

$^1/_2$ cup (1 stick) butter,
  softened
1 cup all-purpose flour,
  sifted

Combine cream cheese and butter; cream until smooth. Add flour, mixing well. Refrigerate dough 1 hour; then shape into 24 (1") balls. Place balls in miniature muffin tins; press dough against bottom and sides, shaping into shells.

*Filling*
$^3/_4$ cup dark brown sugar,
  firmly packed
1 egg, slightly beaten
1 tablespoon butter, melted

$^1/_2$ teaspoon vanilla
  extract
$^1/_4$ teaspoon salt
$^1/_2$ cup broken pecan
  pieces

Combine brown sugar, egg, butter, vanilla and salt; mix well. Spoon into pastry shells. Top each with 1 teaspoon of pecan pieces, pressing them into filling. Bake at 350° for 25 minutes. Serve plain or with a spoonful of sweetened whipped cream. Makes 2 dozen.

## CANARY COTTAGE PECAN PIE

3 eggs
1 cup white sugar
1 $^1/_4$ cups light corn syrup
$^1/_4$ teaspoon salt

1 teaspoon vanilla extract
2 cups chopped pecans
1 unbaked 9" pastry shell

Beat eggs until light; add sugar gradually. Add syrup and vanilla; beat until blended. Fold in pecans. Pour into pie shell; bake at 375° for 15 minutes. Reduce oven temperature to 325°; bake 30 minutes longer or until outer edge of filling is set. Filling will completely set when cooled. May be served with a dollop of whipped cream or vanilla ice cream.

## MAZARENE TARTS

| | |
|---|---|
| 6 tablespoons butter, frozen | ⅛ teaspoon salt |
| 1 cup all-purpose flour | 1 egg yolk |
| 2 tablespoons sugar | 1 tablespoon cold water |

Using a food processor, with metal blade in place, arrange butter by tablespoons around bottom of container. Combine flour, sugar and salt and sift over butter. Process, turning machine rapidly on and off, for about 5 seconds or until mixture resembles coarse meal. Add egg yolk and water; process until dough forms a ball. Roll out dough ⅛" thick on a lightly floured surface. Cut in rounds large enough to cover inverted miniature tart or muffin pans. Prick all over with a fork; chill. Bake at 325° for 15 to 20 minutes. Cool before filling.

*Filling*

| | |
|---|---|
| 1 cup pineapple or apricot preserve | 1 tablespoon rum |
| | Confectioners' sugar |

Mix preserves and rum; spoon into cooled pastry shells. Sprinkle with confectioners' sugar before serving.

## BOURBON BALLS

¼ cup (½ stick) butter,
softened
2 pounds confectioners' sugar,
sifted
⅔ cup Bourbon

1 cup chopped pecans
4 ounces semi-sweet
chocolate, cut in fine
pieces
1 (1″) square of paraffin

Cream butter with 1 pound of sugar; blend Bourbon with 1 pound of sugar. Combine the sugar mixtures and pecans, mixing thoroughly. Refrigerate until chilled; shape into small balls. Melt chocolate and paraffin together in the top of a small double boiler over hot, not boiling, water. Working rapidly, dip balls one at a time in the chocolate; place on wax paper to dry.

## KENTUCKY CREAM CANDY

3 cups sugar
1 cup cream

½ cup water
Pinch of soda

Combine ingredients in a heavy, greased saucepan; stir until boiling. Cook, covered, about 3 minutes until sides of pan are washed free of crystals. Uncover and cook, without stirring, to the hard-ball stage, 262.° Remove from heat and pour onto a buttered marble slab or platter; let cool enough to handle easily. Pull for about 15 minutes; cut into pieces with well-buttered scissors. Wrap candies in foil and store in a closed tin.

## DATE ROLL

3 cups sugar
1½ cups milk

1 pound unsugared dates,
pitted and chopped
2 cups pecans

Mix sugar and milk, cook until it makes a soft ball in cold water (234° to 240°). Add dates; boil 5 minutes, stirring constantly. Take off stove and beat until thick; add pecans. Turn out onto a damp cloth and roll up. Chill; slice when firm.

## BUCKEYES

2½ cups confectioners' sugar
½ cup (1 stick) butter or
   margarine, softened
½ cup plus 2 tablespoons
   creamy peanut butter

½ teaspoon vanilla
   extract
⅛ cake paraffin
6 ounces semi-sweet
   chocolate bits

Combine confectioners' sugar, butter or margarine, and peanut butter, blending thoroughly. Roll into small balls and freeze on wax paper. Melt paraffin over boiling water, then add chocolate bits; stir until thoroughly melted and mixed. Insert a toothpick into each ball, dip two-thirds deep into the warm chocolate and set on wax paper to cool. Makes 4 dozen.

## CARAMELS

4 cups white sugar
1½ cups light corn syrup

1 quart whipping cream

Using a 5-quart saucepan, heat sugar and syrup in 1½ cups of cream, stirring until well dissolved. Cook on medium-low heat to 230°; slowly pour in 1½ cups of cream and again cook to 230.° Add the final cup of cream and cook to 240.° Do not stir when mixture is boiling. The cooking time is about 2 hours. Remove from heat; pour at once into a buttered jelly roll pan. When cool, cut into pieces and wrap each one in wax paper.

## CHOCOLATE FUDGE

2 cups sugar
¾ cup milk
2 ounces unsweetened
   chocolate

2 tablespoons light corn
   syrup
2 tablespoons butter
1 teaspoon vanilla extract

Combine the first 4 ingredients in a heavy saucepan; heat until chocolate melts, stirring gently. Bring mixture to a boil. Cook over moderate heat, without stirring, to the soft-ball stage, 234.° Remove candy from heat; add butter and let stand until cool. Add vanilla; beat with a wooden spoon until fudge begins to lose its sheen. Pour into a buttered pan and mark into squares.

# CANDY

## DIVINITY CANDY

| | |
|---|---|
| ¹/₂ cup light corn syrup | 3 cups sugar |
| ¹/₂ cup water | 3 egg whites, at room temperature |

Bring syrup and water to a boil in a heavy saucepan; add sugar, stirring to dissolve. When boiling, cover pan and cook about 3 minutes until steam has washed down crystals on sides of pan. Remove lid and cook over moderate heat, without stirring, to the hard -ball stage, 254.° While syrup is cooking, beat egg whites in a large bowl, just until they hold their shape. When syrup is ready, pour over egg whites in a steady thin stream, whipping slowly at the same time. Toward the end, add the syrup more quickly and whip faster. Do *not* scrape pan. Beat until candy will hold its shape when dropped from a spoon. Using 2 teaspoons, form small round pieces on wax paper. Makes 1¹/₂ pounds. Half may be tinted with red coloring to a delicate pink and topped with a pecan half. The remaining white divinity may be topped with half a cherry.

*Note:* Choose a dry day to make divinity.

## SUGARED PECANS

| | |
|---|---|
| 2¹/₂ cups pecan halves | 1 teaspoon salt |
| 1 cup sugar | 1 teaspoon ground cinnamon |
| ¹/₂ cup water | 1¹/₂ teaspoons vanilla |

Place pecan halves on a cookie sheet; bake at 325° for fifteen minutes. Cook sugar, water, salt and cinnamon without stirring to soft ball stage. Remove from heat, add vanilla and stir until creamy. Stir in pecans and pour onto a buttered platter. Separate with a fork while cooling. Store in tin boxes.

## SWEET RED PEPPER HASH

*...really picks up a chicken sandwich*

| | |
|---|---|
| 12 sweet red peppers | 3 1/2 cups sugar |
| 2 cups vinegar | |

Grind peppers; add vinegar and sugar. Cook 1 1/2 hours until thickened. Put in sterilized jars. Makes 4 1/2 pints.

## SPANISH MUSTARD PICKLE

| | |
|---|---|
| 12 ripe cucumbers, peeled and seeded | 1 1/2 quarts baby ears of corn |
| 12 large white onions | 1 quart pickling onions |
| 4 ribs celery | 2 fresh, hot red pepper pods |
| 2 white cabbages | 1 cup pickling salt |
| 1 large head cauliflower | |

Cut cucumbers, onions and celery into small pieces. Finely shred cabbage and divide cauliflower into small florets. Break corn in half, if nice; cut pickling onions in half, if too big. Salt vegetables in layers and let stand for 6 hours. Allow to drain overnight in a cheesecloth bag. Put in a kettle with the following:

| | |
|---|---|
| 2 tablespoons celery seed | 3 pounds light brown sugar |
| 2 tablespoons turmeric | |
| 2 tablespoons white mustard seed | 1/4 cup flour |
| 1/4 pound (or more) Coleman's mustard | Vinegar |

Cover well with vinegar and bring to a boil; boil until vegetables are tender-crisp. Remove hot red pepper pods. Pack hot vegetables into hot pint jars. Cover with boiling liquid to 1/2" from top of jar. Cut red peppers into pieces and add one piece to each jar.

# PICKLES AND RELISHES

## WATERMELON RIND PICKLE

Rind of 1 watermelon
7 cups sugar
2 cups vinegar
1/2 teaspoon oil of clove

1/2 teaspoon oil of
  cinnamon
1 lemon, sliced thin

Pick the thickest rind you can find. Trim green skin and pink fruit from rind and cut in pieces of desired size. Cover with lime water, made by using 1 tablespoon slaked lime to 1 quart water. Let stand overnight. Drain, rinse and cover with cold water; cook until tender but not soft. Drain. Combine sugar, vinegar, oils and lemon slices; heat to boiling. Pour syrup over rind and let stand overnight. Drain off the syrup, heat and pour over rind. On third day, heat rind in the syrup until transparent. Pack in hot jars, adding some of the lemon slices to each one. Cover with boiling syrup, leaving 1/2" headspace.

## BREAD AND BUTTER PICKLES

16 cups small firm cucumbers
2 green peppers, seeded
8 small white onions
1 quart crushed ice
1/2 cup salt
3 cups vinegar

5 cups sugar
1 1/2 teaspoons turmeric
1/2 teaspoon ground
  cloves
2 teaspoons mustard seed
1 teaspoon celery seed

Slice cucumbers, green peppers and onions very thin; place in layers in a crock with salt. Cover with ice and place a weighted lid over crock. Refrigerate for 3 hours or longer. Drain. Make a syrup of vinegar, sugar, turmeric, cloves, mustard seed and celery seed. Add to vegetables. Heat slowly with very little stirring. Scald; *do not boil.* Place in sterilized jars and seal them at once. Makes 9 pints.

# PICKLES AND RELISHES

## MIXED PICKLE

1 quart sliced, small (4"), firm
   cucumbers
1 quart whole (2") cucumbers
2 quarts cauliflower florets
1 quart small ears of corn
   (canned may be used)

1 quart small (pearl)
   pickling onions
1 quart cut celery (small
   pieces)
1 red bell pepper, slivered

Cover prepared vegetables with a brine made from 1 gallon water, 1 cup pickling salt and 1 tablespoon alum. Let stand 24 hours; drain. Prepare pickling syrup as follows:

2 quarts white vinegar
6 cups light brown sugar
2 sticks cinnamon, broken
1 heaping teaspoon ground
   allspice
1 1/2 teaspoons ground ginger
1/2 teaspoon ground cloves
1 1/4 ounces dry mustard

1/2 cup flour
3 tablespoons celery seed
2 small red pepper pods,
   finely cut
3 1/2 tablespoons white
   mustard seed
Turmeric (to color)

Combine ingredients and pour over drained vegetables. Scald for a few minutes, but do not boil. Pack in hot jars. Makes 13 pints.

## EASY REFRIGERATOR PICKLES

6 cups thinly sliced
   cucumbers
2 cups thinly sliced onions
1 1/2 cups sugar
1 1/2 cups vinegar
1/2 teaspoon salt

1/2 teaspoon mustard seed
1/2 teaspoon celery seed
1/2 teaspoon ground
   turmeric

In a glass or crockery bowl, alternately layer the sliced cucumbers and onions. Combine all remaining ingredients in a medium saucepan. Bring to a boil, stirring just until sugar is dissolved. Pour vinegar mixture over sliced vegetables; cool slightly. Cover tightly and refrigerate pickles for 24 hours before serving. They may be stored up to 1 month.

# PICKLES AND RELISHES

## GREEN TOMATO PICKLES

7 pounds small green
  tomatoes, *very* thinly sliced
2 cups pickling lime dissolved
  in 2 gallons cold water
2 quarts vinegar
8 cups (4 pounds) sugar

1 tablespoon pickling salt
1 tablespoon cinnamon
1 tablespoon ground
  cloves
1 tablespoon mixed
  pickling spice

Cover sliced tomatoes with lime solution; allow to soak for 24 hours. Drain and rinse well several times; cover with cold water and soak for 3 hours. Drain well. Combine remaining ingredients and boil for 5 minutes; pour over tomatoes and let stand overnight. Boil slowly, uncovered, for 35 minutes. Ladle tomatoes into hot, sterilized jars; cover with syrup to within 1/2" of top of jar.

*Note:* Pickling (hydrated) lime is available at groceries and hardware stores.

*Variation:* To make cucumber pickle, omit sliced tomatoes and substitute 7 pounds of large cucumbers, peeled, seeded and sliced crosswise to 1/2" thickness. Cook slowly for 35 to 50 minutes or until transparent.

## ZUCCHINI PICKLE

2 pounds small zucchini
1/2 pound onions
1/4 cup salt
2 cups sugar
2 cups vinegar

1 teaspoon celery seed
1 teaspoon turmeric
1/2 teaspoon prepared
  mustard
2 teaspoons mustard seed

Cut zucchini and onions very thin. Cover with water; add salt and let stand in refrigerator for 2 hours. Bring sugar, vinegar, celery seed, turmeric, mustard and mustard seed to a boil. Pour over drained vegetables. Let stand for 2 hours. Bring mixture to a boil, then simmer 5 minutes. Pack hot, sterilized jars. Fill to within 1/2" of top, making sure vinegar solution covers vegetables. Cap each jar at once. Makes 2 quarts.

## PICKLED PEACHES

1 1/2 pints vinegar
6 cups sugar
1/2 ounce whole cloves

1/4 ounce cinnamon sticks
7 pounds peaches
    (preferably clingstone),
    peeled

Combine the first 4 ingredients and boil hard until mixture thickens to a sticky syrup (about 30 minutes). Drop in peaches and boil until they can be easily pierced with a fork (10 to 15 minutes). Pack peaches in hot sterile jars and cover with boiling syrup, leaving 1/2" headspace. Seal while hot. Store jars in a cool, dark place.

## CHUTNEY

3 large onions, diced
8 ounces Cantonese candied
    ginger, diced
1 pound light brown sugar
1 lime, diced
2 1/2 cups vinegar
Juice from 2 (15-ounce) cans
    crushed pineapple
2 tablespoons salt
1/2 teaspoon chili powder
1/2 teaspoon nutmeg
1/4 teaspoon cayenne pepper

1 teaspoon garlic powder
2 tablespoons whole
    mustard seed
2 tablespoons curry
    powder
1 under-ripe cantaloupe,
    cut in chunks
1 pound dates, sliced
2 cups crushed pineapple
1 (3 1/3-ounce) can flaked
    coconut
1 pound seeded raisins

Bring first 13 ingredients to a boil; lower heat and simmer 1 hour. Add remaining ingredients, stirring thoroughly. Increase heat slightly; cook without stirring until mixture reaches the boiling point. Pour into sterilized jars and seal.

# PICKLES AND RELISHES

## BORDEAUX SAUCE

1 quart cider vinegar
2 cups sugar
1/2 cup flour
2 tablespoons turmeric
2 quarts chopped cabbage
1 quart chopped green
    tomatoes

2 bunches celery,
    chopped
6 cucumbers, chopped
5 large onions, chopped
2 green peppers, chopped
2 red peppers, chopped
1 tablespoon celery seed
1 tablespoon mustard seed

Combine vinegar, sugar and flour and cook until as thick as batter; add turmeric. Pour over chopped vegetables and boil for 20 minutes, stirring to prevent scorching. Remove from heat; add celery seed and mustard seed. Pour into sterilized jars and seal.

## CHOW-CHOW RELISH

2 quarts (4 to 5 pounds) green
    tomatoes, chopped
2 quarts (1 large head)
    cabbage, chopped
2 quarts (4 to 5 pounds)
    onions, chopped
5 green bell peppers
3 red bell peppers

3/4 cup salt
3 pounds sugar
2 quarts vinegar, divided
1 cup flour
1 (1 1/2-ounce) can dry
    mustard
2 tablespoons turmeric
2 tablespoons celery seed

Combine first 6 ingredients and let stand several hours. Drain in cloth bag overnight. Add sugar and 1 quart of vinegar. Bring to a boil; simmer 15 minutes. Set aside overnight. The next day, combine flour, mustard and 1 quart vinegar. Cook in a double boiler until thick; add turmeric and celery seed. Add to vegetable mixture and cook for 15 minutes over low heat, stirring to prevent sticking. Put in sterilized jars and seal, or process as you would for other pickles. Makes 10 to 12 pints.

# INDEX

# INDEX

# INDEX

# INDEX

# INDEX

# INDEX

# INDEX

# INDEX

# INDEX

# INDEX

# INDEX

## BLUEGRASS WINNERS

The Garden Club of Lexington, Inc.
P.O. Box 22091
Lexington, KY 40522

Please send _____ copies of **Bluegrass Winners** at $16.50 plus $2.00 each for postage and handling. Kentucky residents add 83¢ per book for 5% sales tax. Gift wrap 75¢ each. Enclosed is my check or money order for $_____.

Name_____

Address_____

City_____ State_____ Zip_____

All proceeds from sale of **Bluegrass Winners** benefit the community through projects of The Garden Club of Lexington, Inc.

---------------------------------------------------------------------

## BLUEGRASS WINNERS

The Garden Club of Lexington, Inc.
P.O. Box 22091
Lexington, KY 40522

Please send _____ copies of **Bluegrass Winners** at $16.50 plus $2.00 each for postage and handling. Kentucky residents add 83¢ per book for 5% sales tax. Gift wrap 75¢ each. Enclosed is my check or money order for $_____.

Name_____

Address_____

City_____ State_____ Zip_____

All proceeds from sale of **Bluegrass Winners** benefit the community through projects of The Garden Club of Lexington, Inc.

---------------------------------------------------------------------

## BLUEGRASS WINNERS

The Garden Club of Lexington, Inc.
P.O. Box 22091
Lexington, KY 40522

Please send _____ copies of **Bluegrass Winners** at $16.50 plus $2.00 each for postage and handling. Kentucky residents add 83¢ per book for 5% sales tax. Gift wrap 75¢ each. Enclosed is my check or money order for $_____.

Name_____

Address_____

City_____ State_____ Zip_____

All proceeds from sale of **Bluegrass Winners** benefit the community through projects of The Garden Club of Lexington, Inc.